Vital Signs

D1500793

Vital Signs

A Complete Guide to the Crop Circle Mystery
and Why It Is NOT a Hoax

ANDY THOMAS

Frog, Ltd.
Berkeley, California

For Kaye and Jordan

Published by Frog, Ltd.

Frog, Ltd. books are distributed by
North Atlantic Books
P.O. Box 12327
Berkeley, California 94712

Cover and book design by Paula Morrison

Printed in Singapore

First published in 1998 by S B Publications, 19 Grove Road, Seaford, East Sussex, BN25 1TP, UK

North Atlantic Books' publications are available through most bookstores. For further information, call 800-337-2665 or visit our website at www.northatlanticbooks.com.

Substantial discounts on bulk quantities are available to corporations, professional associations, and other organizations. For details and discount information, contact our special sales department.

Library of Congress Cataloging-in-Publication Data

Thomas, Andy, 1965–
    Vital signs : a complete guide to the crop circle mystery and why it is not a hoax / by Andy Thomas.
        p. cm.
    Includes index.
    ISBN 1-58394-069-3
    1. Crop circles. 2. Curiosities and wonders. I. Title.
    AG243 .T398 2002
    001.94—dc21
                                    2002013277

Front Cover: Close-up of the center of the staggering crop formation at Milk Hill, Wiltshire, August 12, 2001. Photo: Werner Anderhub.

Back Cover: *Above:* Inside the Avebury "web," Wiltshire, August 11–12, 1994. Photo: Steve Alexander. *Below:* The "web" as seen next to the henged embankments of Avebury village. Photo: Andrew King.

Title Page: A military plane flies over the "galaxy" at West Stowell, Wiltshire, July 23, 1994. Photo: Andy Thomas.

1 2 3 4 5 6 7 8 9 / 07 06 05 04 03 02

Contents

Acknowledgments

Huge thanks to everyone who has assisted in the creation of this book, giving their time to locate or donate photographs, impart advice, technical assistance or information, with particular gratitude to those who offered their hospitality and made me welcome in their homes:

(Alphabetically) Steve Alexander, Marcus Allen, Werner Anderhub, Rod Bearcloud, Francine Blake, Robert Boerman, Rick Branston, Derek Carvell, Tony Caldicott (R.I.P.), Anthony Cheke, Andrew Collins, Karen Douglas, Michael Glickman, Jay Goldner, Christine Green, Michael Green, Eltjo Haselhoff, Ofmil C Haynes Jr, Michael Hesemann, Hans Hesselink, John Holloway, John Holman, Joop van Houdt, Michael Hubbard, ilyes, Bert Janssen, Jeremy Kay, Andrew King, Ulrich Kox, Frank Laumen, John Martineau, Dr. Terence Meaden, Denise Miller, Andreas Müller, Patricia Murray, Nick Nicholson, Martin Noakes, Janet Ossebaard, Debbie Pardoe, Jason Porthouse, David Russell, Ron Russell, Karen Ryan, Wolfgang Schindler, Wolfgang Schöppe, Danny Sotham, Jack Sullivan, Nancy Talbott, Suzanne Taylor, Nigel Tomsett, Grant Wakefield, Richard Wintle.

Not forgetting gratitude for all the work carried out by hundreds of people who have been involved in active crop circle research over the years, without whom this book would not exist.

Greetings also to all the many friends and relatives who have given their help and moral support or shown interest beyond the call of duty!

Very special thanks to the following:

The music of Anthony Phillips for keeping me sane during the preparation of the revised edition (check out *www.anthonyphillips.co.uk.*)

Steve Benz for opening the doors, Lindsay Woods and all at SB Publications.

Allan Brown for design consultancy.

Barry Reynolds, Andreas Müller, Michael Glickman and Karen Douglas for factual checking and suggestions.

Mike Leigh for his kind Foreword.

Kaye Thomas for proof-reading, patience, moral support and for putting up with me since that fateful honeymoon.

Foreword

In my 1993 film *Naked,* Johnny, my garrulous, frustrated anti-hero, is obsessed with the impending millennial apocalypse. "The end of the world is nigh, Bri," he informs Brian, the lonely security guard, "The game is up." His head buzzes with ideas and references. He quotes *Revelation,* he predicts a catastrophe due on August 18, 1999, when the planets would line up in the formation of a cross, and he suggests mankind's eventual evolution "into a species of pure thought ... well beyond our comprehension. Into a universal consciousness."

Nearly ten years on, and into the Third Millennium, the world hasn't ended—yet. But an inescapable sense of apocalyptic doom does increasingly pervade our times, witness September 11th, 2001.

And yet, throughout this decaying decade, one remarkable positive element in our world has been quietly growing and developing in the most exciting and extraordinary ways—the crop circles.

What would Johnny have made of these phenomena? I'm sure he would have found them deeply inspiring. They might even have rendered him speechless! I'm almost glad I didn't know much about the circles when I made *Naked,* or I'd have had to yield to the temptation to take Johnny out of the urban claustrophobia of the film and let him loose in the countryside. But the image of him in the middle of a formation is compelling, and he certainly ought to have mentioned crop circles.

I have come to the circles relatively recently, via my old and close friend Michael Glickman, who is much referred to in this book. For me, it was immediately and ineluctably clear that these beautiful and joyous creations not only transcend our ordinary understanding of the material world, but confront our sense of the spiritual, too. To learn about the formations is remarkable enough, but to see and enter and savor them is truly awesome.

And in this excellent book, which Michael calls "the best overview of the subject, and the nearest we have to a standard reference text," Andy Thomas takes us systematically through the most impressively comprehensive range of aspects of this vast and important subject.

In his direct, conversational, and sometimes delightfully ironic style, he discusses the circles for what they are, for what they seem to be, and for what they might be. He gives us a copiously illustrated history, and he explores possible meanings of the circles on many levels, including the philosophical, when he ponders the notion of a universal intelligence.

He also introduces us to the weird and wonderful world of the croppies themselves—a microcosm of the sanity and madness of real life!—and he deals, fairly but firmly, with the hoaxers and their preposterous claims. For me, he might actually be too fair on these people, and maybe he affords them too much space, since cynicism and dishonesty deserve only very short shrift. But that is Andy's strength: he is nothing if not balanced.

I love the fact that the author of this book is a musician who discovered crop circles only by accident during his honeymoon in Wiltshire in the early 1990's.... Or was it an accident? Might it have been something else?

Either way, poised as we are on the brink of ever more mind-blowing formations and hidden messages, it is a blessing that we have a guide as inspired as Andy Thomas.

MIKE LEIGH
London, April 2002

The Vale of Pewsey, Wiltshire, the beautiful setting for many major crop circles over the years.
Photo: Andy Thomas

Introduction

A humid August evening in the heart of London. A small crowd gathers around the doorway of a basement hall at Neal's Yard, the city's "New Age" center. Incense floats on the air, mingled with fumes from the capital's ceaseless traffic. On the door a humble photocopy advertises a "Review of the Year" for those mysterious and beautiful symbols found etched into fields each summer. I, like some of those around me, am a relative wide-eyed newcomer to the crop circles, with just two seasons under my belt. The excitement is tangible. Impressive views of 1992's unique patterns are promised, on slides and videos. After a long wait, we allow ourselves to be ushered into a small lecture room in the depths of the building. Here, magic will be spilled out onto the blank screen hanging before us and strange and fascinating tales surrounding the latest impressive designs will be told....

An hour later and my blood pressure is rising. The room is like a sauna and everyone is sweating profusely, tension growing. But it's not just the heat. So far, the promised views of crop formations have eluded. Instead, we have been treated to a long video about a recent circle-hoaxing competition, interviews with people claiming to have made this or that pattern on other occasions and precious little else. No sweeping aerial shots of huge glyphs carved into golden meadows, no intriguing anecdotes or insights into the nature of the true phenomenon. Some of the audience are growing restless. When does the real show begin? Where is the other side of the story? Astonishingly, the screen falls into darkness and the lights come on. The speaker, who just a year previously had been so enthusiastic, shuffles on and sheepishly sums up his view of the 1992 crop circles. They're all man-made hoaxes, he has concluded, apart from the odd natural "vortex circle." No evidence is shown for this, apart from the weak testimony we've just seen. I begin to twitch with anger. I can see from some of the faces in the crowd that I'm not alone. But the speaker also has supporters in the room, apparently hardened skeptics. They rally round when dissenting voices begin to challenge. How can he really believe the total-hoax scenario in the face of all the contrary evidence? For every cutting enquiry he has an answer. But they don't convince. Not me, anyway. My stomach muscles knot tighter. It's not just that I disagree with his view, but this is not what was promised. I have expensively dragged my wife Kaye across south-east England to share what I thought was going to be an enlightening experience. Now I am embarrassed and fuming.

The final straw breaks when our tormentor is asked to explain the floating white lights videoed in and around formations over the years. These have been "explained" to him, he responds. They are dandelion seeds, backlit by the sun, blowing in the breeze. The skeptics clap, but hoots of derision come from others. Suddenly I find myself rising from the bench as my rational self gives way — or takes over? The room, almost as one, turns to look at me and I let rip, chiding the speaker for having wasted our time and money to come up with nothing better than this kind of stupidity. Some laugh at my outburst, but there's also a ripple of applause. I can stay in the room no longer. Taking Kaye by the hand, red-faced at her partner's unexpected intervention, I cross to the exit, the sounds of the crowd mixed with the thud of my heart pounding furiously. In the warm air of the city and the dull reek of the underground system, my rage knows no bounds as we head home....

Looking back, I realize these were the first words I ever publicly spoke at a major circle gathering. Something important snapped within me and there was no turning back. It was a crucial development in my fascination with the crop circles, when an interest became a passion. My first, transformational, experience of them was in the summer of 1991 while honeymooning in Wiltshire (as told in the book *Quest For Contact*), but it was this which provided the pivotal moment. Together with the previous autumn's "Doug and Dave" hoax stories which had plastered the media, it dawned on me with a skewed but justified logic which history vindicates, that if so many were willing to go to such extreme lengths to debunk, there must be something really important going on. The speaker's blind insistence that the circles were nothing more than mischievous landscape art, in the absence of any clear evidence, convinced me even more that here was an unexplained mystery which deserved much closer attention. It's nice to know from a description of the same incident from the speaker's point of view, in a skeptical book he published later, that the event stuck in his mind too, even if I am portrayed as an object of ridicule. The resulting passion has led me to pursue my convictions through public presentations, within the pages of journals, the *www.swirled-news.com* website, my other books and this volume which attempts to pull together all the myriad aspects of an extraordinary phenomenon. Many, equally touched, have pursued the truth in their own ways.

Is the book you now hold in your hands, then, a rant against crop circle debunkers and a hymn to blind faith in other-worldly origins for the symbols? Not quite. Although I do not accept the view that the circles are nothing more than human art and present a substantial case here as to why, my vocation has always been to bring to people's attention a marvel which I and a sizeable body of others feel is of tremendous potential significance *whatever is creating it*. Perhaps it's the remarkable effect it has on people, not the source, that counts and it shouldn't be fought over. This is an aspect too casily ignored and one which is explored in this book's conclusion. But the crop circles *may* be hugely important in the wider scheme of things, and their origins *might* matter. They have been unfairly lambasted to the point where those who could find their lives enhanced by them are being falsely repelled and kept from the knowledge of their real scale, history and nature by a skeptical stigma which has been allowed to grow without sensible grounds. The evidence and statistics point to something much deeper occurring than just mundane art terrorism and it's time to stand up and say so. The continual propaganda of unproven hoax claims and highly-publicized ambitious but flawed man-made circle-making demonstrations created in unrealistic conditions demand this attempt to set the record straight and give people an opportunity to have all sides of the phenomenon presented and discussed before them so they can come to their own conclusions. There have clearly been a notable number of man-made formations over the years, but the majority of events remain unexplained. True understanding of what is going on has been smothered and trivialized by years of unfounded cynicism, opinionated loudmouths, media indifference and sheer ignorance on the part of the public through no fault of its own. This negativity has infiltrated many lines of communication and too many articles and interviews have been contributed by fourth-hand information peddlers and debunkers masquerading as authorities.

While specifically reclaiming it from the clutches of hoax theorists, this book does not provide a solution to the mystery—no-one yet knows the answer, whatever they may claim. But I hope it reaches a little nearer than other forums to identifying some of the jigsaw pieces that initially seem to fit, in attempts to explain the circles' source, while acknowledging the dilemmas and illogicalities which simultaneously emerge. The following examination should at least focus the debate more clearly and encourage further contemplation which may eventually take us a few steps closer to some kind of comprehension. Along the way many underexposed crop circle truths are illuminated, but a few unhelpful circular myths which have arisen from sensationalism and over-generalization are also challenged and one or two aspects which have gained exaggerated importance over time are put into softer focus and a less personality-based perspective. As these pages record, the research arena, investigative and speculative, has not been an unblemished bed of roses.

So what does the subtitle *A Complete Guide to the Crop Circle Mystery* mean in this context? Despite other tomes on the subject, there have been few which sum up in one volume everything someone new to the circles needs to know to make a valued assessment. The aim of this work is to fulfill this function while also acting as a good summation for those already entranced. It is, however, intended as more than just a dry factual run through and is a wide look at the entire *phenomenon* in the truest sense of the word. Thus, over five chapters, the necessarily technical nature of the opening section, which explores the patterns themselves and how they appear to be constructed, gives way to revealing the extraordinary stories and bizarre theories surrounding them. Along the line insights are given into the enormous impact they have had on individuals and the research community, and how they have been treated by skeptics, believers and the media alike.

In these ways, this guide is "complete." To be truly complete, of course, it would have to be the thickness of a telephone directory. Within this format it's impossible to cover in fine detail all the observational data which has been amassed over the years and notes throughout the book and an extensive guide to other works on the subject (Appendix A, where full publication details are given) clearly signpost other sources which people may like to access. I have thus deliberately avoided including too much mechanical information of measurements and the suchlike and have restricted the scope of the book, with a few notable exceptions, to cover the English crop circles which, in general, are the most impressive and of which I have most personal experience. England remains the main center of activity, although it is by now a truly global phenomenon.

Though intended as derogatory, the award given in 1997 to the study of crop circles as the "Novel British Pseudo-science most likely to endure" by *The Skeptic* magazine is testament to the resilience of the evidence for something real and important in the face of endless attack and cynicism which has failed to stop the circles taking their place in popular culture. In the same season, the *Collins Dictionary* introduced a new feature, *Words That Define the 20th Century,* in which a year is summed up by a single reference. 1926 is given to "Television," for instance, whereas 1965 is "Mini-skirt." 1990 is summed up by two words—"Crop Circle." The year the patterns burst into the public eye in a big way has clearly stuck in the national consciousness. Their images are regularly used in advertising to sell cars, TV channels and records without anyone flinching. Crop formations have become almost as much a part of English seasonal life as motorway queues and strawberries at Wimbledon and are becoming increasingly familiar in the international scenery. Yet the facts point to a cause far beyond the mundane explanations routinely offered by the closed-minded, the implications of which may be shocking to those who have never looked beyond the patterns' superficial attractiveness. The hitherto underestimated impact of the crop symbols which emerges from this book reveals that, whatever is responsible for them, in their own modest way they are acting as catalysts for world change whether anyone likes it or not.

Crop circles are importantly rare examples of paranormal phenomena which can be experienced by everyone and don't rely on people being in the right place at the right time to witness them. Unlike, say, UFOs, evidence for the existence of which often relies on second-hand accounts or blurry images, crop formations can be visited by all, touched, examined, seen. Ironically, instead of making things easier in assessing their authenticity, if anything this has deepened controversy. But nothing lasts forever and even the circles remain little more than a few weeks before the harvesters move in. Recording the designs with detailed surveys and photographs is all that preserves something of their presence for posterity. As active survey teams are increasingly thin on the ground, it's photography which plays the biggest part in this preservation.

If nothing else, this book provides a feast for the eyes with a series of spectacular pictures taken by a variety of talented photographers who have played an important role in bringing these strange and breathtaking patterns to people's attention. A network of enthusiasts out searching and keeping their ears to the ground ensure that few get missed nowadays and planes are regularly hired to obtain stunning aerial views to complement intriguing photographic evidence from internal surveys.

These visuals in themselves prove one thing: that whatever the arguments and discussions which may forever surround their appearance, the crop circles are unspeakably beautiful and often stir unexpected emotions within people who never thought that a few swirled areas of flattened plants could touch the heart so deeply.

This revised edition substantially updates the circular history in Chapter 2 (which originally ended in 1997) and adds another four years' worth of ever-more amazing images from the fields. Elsewhere, there have been modifications and updates to accommodate this ever-evolving and consistently absorbing mystery.

ANDY THOMAS

Note on Photographs, Dates and Place Names
While photographs of some formations are interspersed with the main text which refers to them, the more prominent ones are included in the color section and can be found there (page numbers for these are signposted in the text). The majority of crop patterns mentioned are illustrated somewhere, with a few exceptions here and there. Most photographs are accompanied by place and date information. The dates refer, for the most part, to the day, month and year the formation appeared (not when the photo was taken, which may have been days or weeks after). Data in this area can vary from being highly accurate to somewhat approximate. Where the latter, the most likely date is used or the day of the month is omitted. Place names are given as the nearest town or village (unless another obvious landmark is more appropriate, ie. Barbury Castle—a hill-fort), but these can be contentious, especially where formations fall exactly between two locations. Where this occurs, I have generally given the more commonly accepted association. These criteria are also applied within the text.

Stems flow inside the formation at Cissbury Ring, West Sussex, July 15, 1995. Photo: Andy Thomas

1. NEWS OF THE SWIRLED

Crop circles are the striking patterns which mysteriously appear each summer flattened into fields, their origin and purpose unknown. Starting largely with simple circles and sporadic appearances over the centuries, their geographical distribution and design complexity suddenly began to develop and evolve in the last decades of the 20th century. Before delving into the heady realms of the history, potential meaning and cultural impact of the formations, we need to start with the basics and document the regularly observed features which define them. Where and when do they appear? What is actually found inside? How do they appear to be constructed?

What's in a Name?

When whoever it was first coined the term "crop circle," they couldn't have known just how widespread this christening would spread nor ultimately how little justice it would do to what these little swirls would turn into. Nevertheless, the name stuck and its continuing presence in our language is just about mitigated by the fact that even the highly complex designs of later years still utilize the circle as their basic component. Happily, its antiquated alternative, "corn circle," is gradually falling into disuse as people finally realize that these mysterious depressions appear in many diverse types of crops. Other titles, switched around at random to give textual variety (as they are in this book) range from "crop formations" to "patterns," "glyphs" and even "agriglyphs." The more symbolic designs are often referred to as "pictograms." But "crop circle" has lodged in the public consciousness and will forever be the overriding description for the markings which appear each summer mostly in fields of sown plants.

Names for individual designs tend to adhere to the place and the year, ie. "Barbury Castle 1991," unless a shape is so specific it can be referred to directly, such as "The Mandelbrot Set" (also 1991). Certain genres can also suggest acceptably obvious descriptions, such as "asteroids" and "galaxies" (Chapter 2). However, there has been an increasing trend of individuals fixing their own sometimes bizarre and more personalized labels to some formations which somehow manage to stick, like "God's Telephone" or "The Kebab," much to the irritation of others who feel their true meanings, if any, could be compromised by such flippancy.

Oval swirl at Sompting, West Sussex, July 14, 1994. Photo: Andy Thomas

Times and Crops

Most formations appear overnight. Fields untouched in the last glow of dusk generally reveal their new emblems in the first light of the following dawn. This factor has been used for and against the theory that people are responsible for making them. On one hand, the cover of night would be ideal to hide man-made activity, but on the other it would make a difficult task even harder in pitch darkness. These arguments are in any case deflated by a number of well-documented daylight appearances, most notably at Stonehenge in 1996 (see Chapter 2). While many designs are viewable from roads and residential areas, a significant quota graces isolated land, visible only from the air.

Although there are occasional reports of winter formations in wild growth or out-of-season crops,[1] the majority of circles appear from the late months of spring, usually around April, onwards through until late summer, August or September, for the obvious reason that this is when the fields of England, at least, are filled with stems high enough to be neatly etched into. This suspicious predilection for a mature medium to work in is in itself one reason some believe the designs are intelligently premeditated, although it is possible a natural force which could produce such effects (see Chapter 4 for discussions on all these possibilities) may be enhanced by sunshine and warmer climates and attracted to certain types of organic matter. Databases from the mid to late 1990s reveal mid-July as the peak period of circle appearances and, oddly, the early hours of Mondays and Wednesdays as favorite days for the circles.

Remains of a pictogram at Patcham, East Sussex, August 1992, showing how some patterns survive the harvest. Photo: Andy Thomas

The creations end their life when the combine harvesters move in, but sometimes remain visible for a while if the blades can't reach low enough to lift all the flattened crop. Later, a ghost image will often reappear in green where fallen seedheads begin to sprout. Ploughing is the ultimate death knell, but even then a shadow of the former visitation is sometimes visible the following season—new stems are sometimes stunted or elongated in growth on these areas for reasons which are still not clear.

Some formations have been known to cross field boundaries, like this ring encompassing an entire T-Junction at East Kennett, Wiltshire, July 11, 1993. Photo: Andrew King

Any crop seems to be a potential target for the phenomenon. Wheat and barley are still the most prolific types grown in England and thus make up the canvas for the bulk of formations, but designs have also appeared in many others, including oilseed rape (canola), rye, oats, flax, peas and sweetcorn maize (this one particularly in the USA—impressive, given how thick and high the stems are). Even waterlogged Japanese rice-paddies have been visited. Rape formations are often the first to arrive each year, as this tall distinctive plant with the bright yellow flowers matures very early in the season. On rare occasions, undergrowth, wild grass and even garden lawns have played host to patterns.

Designs tend to be confined to one field, but there have been examples which have crossed boundaries into other crops, superimposed over two or even three fields as with the ring which encompassed an entire T-junction at East Kennett, Wiltshire in 1993.

Other Mediums

There have also been reports of geometrical patterns inexplicably appearing in mediums like sand, soil and snow. It is hard to know whether or not these are the same phenomenon at work although some of the shapes have certainly been reminiscent of crop glyphs. In 1994, for instance, residents near a frozen river in Boston, Massachusetts, reportedly awoke one morning to find pictogram shapes on the water, created by large sections of ice having been completely removed. The surface was too thin to walk on and a layer of snow would have betrayed any footprints had anyone tried anyway. In 1990, also in the US, Mickey Basin, a dry lake-bed in Oregon, found itself host to a huge Hindu symbol known as a sriyantra, etched into the soil with 3-inch furrows. The total length of the lines was around thirteen miles.[2] In 1998, a perfect *two-mile*-long aboriginal figure was discovered at Marree, Australia, ploughed into the Adelaide desert. Other ground markings are regularly found around the world which may connect with the crop circles, although things like the large cylindrical holes in Switzerland, 30 feet deep with smooth sides and no traces of soil removal, seem less related. For the purposes of this book, we'll stick to markings in growing crops as our focus.

Swirls and Lays

What, then, constitutes a crop circle? To begin with, as the next chapter reveals, the majority of patterns to appear were indeed simple circles before their extraordinary evolution began. The manner in which the crop is swirled around to create the effect is worthy of a whole study in itself and was explored in early books on the phenomenon in detail

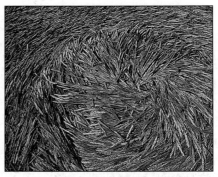

Four circle centers showing the variety of extraordinary and beautiful effects found inside some crop glyphs. Clockwise, from top left: 1. The "charm bracelet," Silbury Hill, Wiltshire, August 16, 1992. (Photo: Grant Wakefield) 2. Patcham, East Sussex, June 29, 1992. 3. Patcham, East Sussex, June 24, 1992. 4. Milk Hill, Wiltshire, August 8, 1997. (Photos: Andy Thomas)

A "crop triangle" at Reigate Hill, Surrey, June 27, 1993, just off the M25 motorway. Photo: Andrew King

Squaring the circle.... The farmer himself inexplicably tramped out the edges of this single circle to make a square at Clatford, Wiltshire, July 1993. Photo: Andy Thomas

before the debate over origins and meaning took over.[3] It is easy to imagine, for those who have never witnessed the beauty of the circles' construction at first hand, that formations are simply a mess of crushed stalks inside. In fact, one of the very reasons many believe something special is occurring is the often intricate and visually striking way the stems are laid without much apparent damage to the plants. This aspect is seldom reported by the media. What you find *inside* circles can sometimes be as impressive as the whole pattern witnessed from a distance.

The circular components of any design are usually swirled clockwise or counterclockwise from a center point outward. However, the logical path of this swirl doesn't always follow a tight spiral, but often flows widely outward, sometimes in a distinct S-shape, in such a manner as to suggest that the entire circle must have gone down as one almost instantly, instead of a flattening force going round and round out from the center, as the floor lays of *known* man-made formations have a tendency to do (particularly noticeable in the one made for NBC US television in 1998). The position of the centers themselves are often marked either by a bare area of soil or a clear "hole" in the middle of a vortex of stems (although there have been a variety of imaginative variations) and are usually significantly offset from the *mathematical* center, sometimes by several feet. Some circles have even been known to have two or more physical centers. However, there have also been cases where crop has been

splayed radially as if something has burst outward, with no discernible spiral. The edges of circles can vary, some being clear-cut and sharply defined, others jagged and fuzzy.

Different shapes have more interesting lays depending on their configurations, but nearly all adhere to the basic outward swirl. A number of triangles have appeared over the years, for instance, but these are essentially circles with extended bulges where stems flow outward to create the points, sometimes bending round on themselves back into the circular area. Rectangular pathways which connect various parts of a design are largely laid straight in one direction, spilling out over or into the shapes they adjoin, although a long path at Denton, East Sussex in 1995 was a rarity in having a center two-thirds of the way up its length where the crop suddenly changed direction. At the end of the day, if the circle-making force (whatever it is) needs to create a certain shape, it usually finds a way. The only truly flattened *square* to appear (otherwise, there have largely been *outlines* of squares) was in actuality a single circle at Clatford, Wiltshire in 1993 which the farmer himself chose to convert by squaring off the edges with his feet!

The finesse with which these lays are effected is sometimes astonishing. A number of formations have been observed where *individual* stems have been drawn into the outer edges of circles from *behind* standing unaffected crop, which clearly excludes the notion of physical implements being applied.[4]

Edge of a dumbbell at Newhaven, East Sussex, July 20, 1997, showing stems swept into the lay of the circle from behind standing, unaffected plants. Photo: Andy Thomas

Strange "lodging" at Winterbourne Monkton, Wiltshire, July 1991. Though a path crosses the field, which might affect the way the wind moves, one half has been devastated while the other remains untouched. Some believe such odd effects are not the result of straightforward elemental forces. Photo: Andy Thomas

On the ground, as with the Silbury Hill "Koch Snowflake" of 1997 (pages 67 and 120), it is sometimes impossible to see the logic of the lay with some of the more elaborate patterns. Plants seem to flow in many different directions, swirling here, going straight there. Elevation often provides the answer; aerial views reveal the true genius of the complexity, resolving apparent randomness into shimmering geometric patterns within the flattened crop itself.

Lodging Questions

Some areas of laid plants are not conventional designs and can result from bird and animal activity, over-fertilization and wind damage, but question marks remain over what other extensive patches of this alleged "lodging" really are. Whole fields can be devastated by apparent wind effects, sometimes in direct connection with turbulent weather but not always. On these less easily explained occasions, it has been observed that the qualities of the downed crop are remarkably similar to the floor lays and swirls of circles and have even been found to have "proper" circular shapes within them. The biophysicist W C Levengood (see this chapter) has examined samples from such strange lodging and discovered very similar effects within the plants to those taken from glyphs. He calls such areas "non-geometric crop formations" and believes they are created by the same forces which make specific patterns, but which have discharged unstably in an unformed and chaotic state.

More unusual "lodging" which may be related to circle-making forces, West Stowell, Wiltshire, date unknown. Photo: Andrew King

Crushing Remarks

It has become an oft-quoted myth that there is *never* any damage to laid crop in formations, but this is born of a general truth; that the plants aren't generally crushed or broken, but bent over neatly at the base of the stem. Mostly, they are not chaffed or marked with any evidence of mechanical flattening, yet the simple act of walking around new patterns will often leave obvious impairment in young green plants. Thicker crops like oilseed rape are particularly vulnerable to physical crushing and bruising when stepped on and snap easily, yet many stems in these formations are often curved neatly at 90-degree angles without any cracking.

There is a danger of over-generalizing, however. The truth is, a certain amount of plant breakage *is* sometimes found in formations which are widely accepted by non-skeptics as being "genuine," ie. not man-made. Perhaps even

forces beyond our comprehension are capable of making mistakes.

But largely, the stems remain undamaged and most, if given the chance, will continue to ripen normally as the weeks go on. Young crop, especially, will often begin to stand up again only days after being affected, and early season patterns can be virtually invisible within a week or so. Sightseers often put paid to the chances of recovery, though. No plant can contend with being trampled by several hundred pairs of feet for long.

Crop Selective

One fascinating feature of circle lays is that the flattening force sometimes appears to distinguish between separate species when performing its task. Stray seeds from neighboring fields often blow into another (say barley into wheat). Where these sprouted immigrants lie in the path of a formation it has been noted on several occasions that they can be left untouched, standing upright where the rest of the stalks around them have been laid. This single-stem-standing effect has been noted many times, but the fact that it seems to choose the foreign component in the

Some circles suggest fairly violent forces being applied in the laying process. These stems at Mannings Heath, West Sussex, July 31, 1996, have been ripped up at the roots with soil still attached. Photo: Andy Thomas

Left: In amongst the circle-flattened crop, single standing stems can remain entirely unaffected, as here at West Overton, Wiltshire, July 28, 1994. Photo: Andy Thomas

Right: Crop swirls around a stone in the lay of a dumbbell pattern, Roundway, Wiltshire, July 16, 1996. A little eddy in the flow was clearly created by the obstacle as the circle-laying process met it. Photo: Andy Thomas

crop so often is mystifying. This effect was particularly conspicuous in the Cley Hill, Wiltshire hexagon of 1997 (page 64) where thistles growing through wheat were left completely untouched by whatever had knocked all the stems down surrounding them.

Layers and Lines

Besides any lack of apparent damage to the crop itself, one of the most telling pointers that many designs are not simply splurged out by feet, planks or garden rollers is the extraordinary quality of layering. What may at first glance look like one flattened swathe of stems is sometimes, when lifted, a mask for *another level* going in quite another direction underneath. This is not a uniform effect and pseudo-layering can very occasionally be produced simply by tight swirling, but it very often occurs in straighter areas which are less easily explained. Sometimes the lower layer can simply be a narrow underlying path, but circles have been observed which have had extensive multi-level flows going in many different directions across a wide area. The "galaxy" formation at West Stowell, Wiltshire in 1994 was a prime example of this (pages 52 and 113). This layering has never been replicated by man-made techniques.

Underlying paths, however, are a subject of some contention. There is evidence to suggest that what may be thin construction lines, or "tracer paths," are put down as an integral part of some of the most complicated designs before

Lifting the top layer of flattened crop can often reveal other layers flowing in quite different directions. Exton, Hampshire, August 4, 1992. Photo: Grant Wakefield

the remaining crop is laid over them. (By observing the layers and overlaps of the floor patterns it is fairly easy to assess the sequence in which parts of the formation went down; sometimes it's clear that several bits must have gone down *simultaneously*.) A good demonstration of this can be seen in the aerial shots of the Stonehenge fractal of 1996 (page 116), where a visible arcing line has clearly been created first and used as the backbone for the circles which make up the pattern. The 1991 "whale" at Lockeridge, Wiltshire was also found to have been initially laid out with a series of complex paths. Cynics point to this quality as a clear sign of human planning, but a convincing counter argument is provided by the strange logic of the way in which these paths themselves have been placed, as with the "whale," which would sometimes actually make things *harder* to construct around them with standard human methods.[5] There seems no reason to think that some kind of higher intelligence would be so perfect that it wouldn't need to sketch in guidelines first. Their place in the "natural force" debate is more uncertain.

The Role of Tramlines

Another controversial feature of the phenomenon is the role apparently played by the tractor "tramlines" which cross the majority of English fields, used by farmers to spray the crops throughout the season. Although many circles have been found which have sat neatly between these lines with no visible signs of human entry (and indeed in fields which have had no lines at all), the early pictograms in particular often seemed to hug the tramlines as guides through their central axis. Yet as soon as skeptics began to loudly point this out, a whole spate of formations occurred which *didn't* seem to utilize the lines in this way. As ever, the crop circles seem to delight in confounding any expectations of them. Nevertheless, in the years since, a number of patterns have clearly seemed to use the tractor marks as an integral part of their design. Why should this be?

Perhaps, as speculated above, even higher powers need something to use as guidelines, and tramlines act as a ready-made grid on which to draw. Alternatively, the effect known as "gap-seeking," which has been noted on several occasions, may hold the key. In many formations where tramlines cross parts of the design, it can be seen that the laid crop momentarily appears to divert into the gap before correcting itself, almost as if a force has suddenly been sucked into a vacuum created by an absence of stems. Circles placed on these areas can be severely disrupted. In the man-made hypothesis, there is no reason why this should occur. Perhaps this tendency for the thin empty spaces created by the tramlines to tug the laying process may also act as an attractor for entire designs, thus hugging them to the point where the lines become their central spines.

The tractor "tramlines" which cross most major English fields can affect the way crop circles form in a curious process known as "gap-seeking." This tramline is viewed from the edge of a tiny ringed circle at Sompting, West Sussex, June 6, 1994. Photo: Andy Thomas

Where tractor lines cross circle lays, inexplicable standing curtains of crop are sometimes left, as here at Bishops Cannings, Wiltshire, July 13, 1997. Photo: Andy Thomas

There's often something about the tramlines which the crop circles certainly seem to respond to, to the point where their outlines are clearly marked out over *laid* crop, thin standing curtains of untouched stems either side of the tractor marks, leaving their trajectories clearly signposted. Again, there seems no logical reason why the crop shouldn't just uniformly sweep down to cover the gaps, as is generally the case.

The Role of Grapeshot

One baffling aspect of the phenomenon is the presence of "grapeshot," tiny circles of varying sizes which often accompany major designs, at times no more than a foot across. They can sometimes go unnoticed until aerial surveillance reveals them, in-between tramlines, untouched and unvisited. Some are clearly integral features, but others are randomly scattered across the field or even superimposed over whole patterns. This apparent randomness was truer of earlier events and grapeshot have become less common and taken on a more controlled role as years have passed. Sometimes they arrive simultaneously with their parent formation, but frequently materialize in the days and weeks after. A number of pictograms, conversely, have begun as simple grapeshot and suddenly expanded.

Some formations are accompanied by tiny circles known as "grapeshot," but others consist of nothing *but* grapeshot, as with this late 1980s formation, location unknown. Photo: Michael & Christine Green

It has been speculated that these circular pepperings are the equivalent of an artist daubing a brush at the edge of a canvas, like little energy discharges wiping off excess "paint." Otherwise, they may indicate some kind of unstable element in the circle-making process, which was gradually reigned in as the phenomenon improved its abilities or the creative force became stronger. Some clusters of grapeshot, which can be ringed, are more reminiscent of "signatures" which recur in several designs, as with the very similar motifs accompanying the Alton Barnes, Stanton St Bernard and East Kennett pictograms of 1990 (page 104).

Defining the Hand that Lays …

The overwhelming urge to discover the mechanics of *how* the crop is laid down has led researcher Michael Glickman, paraphrasing John Michell, to liken the situation to the story of the mysterious disembodied hand which materialized at the court of King Belshazzar in the biblical book of Daniel.[6] If, instead of marvelling at the meaning of the writing which the fingers etched onto the palace walls, everyone had simply gasped and said *"Heck, what's making that floating hand work?,"* we might think them a little odd. Yet the research community's intense concentration on the mechanical aspect of the circle phenomenon equates to the same thing in some eyes.… While there has been equal attention given to divining the meaning and significance of the designs, this metaphor does say something about the heartfelt efforts which have gone into trying to define this area. Although enthusiasts may need no convincing of the circles' special qualities, the fact is the world seems to need dogmatic scientific authentication of anything before attention will be given. In terms of waking new people up to the crop circles, scientific investigation has its part to play.

The Hunt for Energy Traces

Putting the man-made argument aside only really leaves room for unusual "energies," gravitational forces or forced air pressure as being responsible for laying down the stems in crop circles, whether intelligently directed or produced by natural conditions. Some believe it is a combination of these processes.

If undefined energies are involved, one would expect them to leave some kind of detectable vestige. It is just this kind of hope which has fired, among others, the work of W C Levengood in the US. Levengood's discoveries of physical traces on affected plants have led him to believe that some kind of microwave energy is being applied, produced by spinning atmospheric vortices of electrically-charged ion plasma, which ties in with Dr. Terence Meaden's earlier observations made in the 1980s.

The Levengood Discoveries

When, in 1990, eminent biophysicist William C Levengood, based in Michigan, USA, was first sent samples of circle-affected crop by Pat Delgado for analysis, his interest was instantly aroused by what he found, which could not, in his opinion, be attributable to human intervention. In the years since, aided by sometime colleagues John Burke and Nancy Talbott (operating as BLT—Burke, Levengood and Talbott), he has examined thousands of samples from many formations around the world and identified several uniform effects.

Visually recognizable traits are grossly enlarged or elongated nodal joints (the "knuckles" on corn-type plants) and the presence of "expulsion cavities" in the same areas, where moisture seems to have exploded outward leaving

Members of the Southern Circular Research team gather crop samples to be sent to W C Levengood in the USA, in this case oilseed rape from a double-ringer at Southease, East Sussex, May 8, 1995. Photo: Marcus Allen

Bent and swollen wheat nodes at Mannings Heath, West Sussex, July 31, 1996. Nodes are often severely elongated in circle-affected crop, which W C Levengood believes is evidence of a high energy being applied. Photo: Andy Thomas

inconsistencies of development, or they grow at a vastly increased rate. Experiments by others have shown some plants grown on in generations from circle-seed appear to flourish faster than controls, are more resistant to disease and give more yield, as if genetically altered.

The Levengood effects are generally more noticeable with circles formed in immature plants (when still green and developing), but remain present in certain riper stems. Tests with mechanically flattened or trodden crop have failed to reproduce these observations, carried out under rigorous scientific protocols. Samples from a formation secretly (and controversially) created by a team led by prominent researchers Karen Douglas and Steve Alexander in 1995 to test the reliability of scientific analysis were examined by an unsuspecting Levengood and, tellingly, produced none of the above anomalous results. Other known man-made formations since investigated, made in a variety of circumstances (some as specific experiments) have failed to yield any notable differences from controls. Of all the many crop glyphs tested by BLT since work began, the majority *have* demonstrated the extraordinary effects defined by Levengood....

Other anomalies have been noted. There are some arguments about the significance of nodal bending, often found in circles, which is impossible to effect by physical pressure. It can occur as a result of "phototropism," where fallen stems grow back up to the light from the node, but it is also seen in swathes which have clearly been *specifically* curved from the nodes to create certain shapes in the floor lay. Two Wiltshire pictograms in 1993 even appeared to show traces of meteorite dust inside, speculated by Levengood to have been drawn down from the upper atmosphere by one of the ion plasma tubes he believes plays a role in circle creation, although this line of inquiry was particularly challenged by cynics.

Debunkers, inevitably, have attacked the BLT results as naive and subjective, but have yet to provide any evidence to disprove the findings. Levengood, well-respected in his field, has tightened up his methods and protocols considerably in recent years (most denunciations are still based on minor deficiencies in his early work) and the observations remain consistent. Certainly his work has been taken seriously enough to feature as a published paper in a hard scientific journal, *Physiologia Plantarum*, in 1994 and even appeared in the British agricultural magazine *Farmer's*

visible holes. But it's the less obvious effects which most indicate the involvement of a non-human cause: At a cellular level, the nodal area is riddled with tiny perforations and the cell wall pits inside the bract tissues which encase the seedheads are often abnormally swollen, causing the embryonic seeds in young plants to become notably stunted in growth or absent altogether. Surviving affected seeds planted on in germination trials show marked differences with control samples taken from just a few feet outside of a crop circle, going to extremes in both ways—either they don't germinate at all or do so reluctantly, with noted

Weekly in 1995. Levengood's work and that which has followed from it within BLT and beyond (see, for instance, details on Dr. Eltjo Haselhoff's book in Appendix A) is the nearest anyone has yet got to the long-sought and all-encompassing "litmus test" which might be able to determine *scientifically* beyond doubt which formations are man-made and which are not. But other attempts have also been made to find such a method....

Clayton, West Sussex, August 22, 2000: an excellent example of nodal bending creating curvature within one swathe of crop, each stem being bent at both nodes (still visible despite harvesting). This is NOT achievable by manual crushing. Photo: Andy Thomas

Searching for the Litmus Test

Radiation was the first residual energy seriously looked for in crop circles, but no firm and repeatable results were ever verified despite promising work carried out by Marshall Dudley and Michael Chorost in the early 1990s. Traces of several unusual radionuclides (or isotopes) were apparently detected in soil samples taken from one or two pictograms. Unfortunately, doubts over the reliability of the checking procedures and the inability of any later formations to yield similar results ultimately left this work out in the cold.[7]

Soil sampling was briefly revived in 1995 when the Center for Crop Circle Studies (CCCS) commissioned ADAS (Agricultural Development and Advisory Service), a division of the UK Ministry of Agriculture, to run tests on a number of formations. The results, the importance of which have admittedly been exaggerated since, were tentative but intriguing; amongst other anomalies (never openly detailed), a curious increase in the nitrogen/nitrate ratio was apparently detected underneath several glyphs. Sadly, if rather predictably, when news broke to the media, the department of ADAS which had carried out the tests was almost immediately shut down after, as rumor had it, an MP filed a complaint that government bodies shouldn't be wasting precious time and resources (although CCCS had paid for them) on such nonsensical frivolities.[8] Conspiracy theories, perhaps justifiably, abounded. This effectively ended that line of enquiry and due to the high expense of running the experiments it has yet to be revived by private laboratories.

Other investigations into different aspects of physical effects have been conducted over the years, but with few more conclusive findings. Colin Andrews initiated tests with crystallized plant samples, which appeared to show significant changes inside affected crop in 1990, but no apparent follow-ups were made and the validity of the work was doubted by some.[9] *Project Argus,* an investigation set up by CCCS in 1992 to cover all aspects of scientific research into unusual effects produced a lengthy report which showed some tantalizing glimpses of hard results (particularly in the electromagnetic realms), but was so technically termed and dismissed so quickly that most people filed it away and any promise was promptly forgotten. Work with electrostatic volt meters has been more productive,

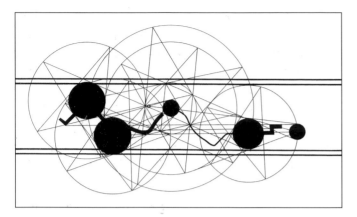

The extremely precise geometrical qualities of some crop formations astound, suggesting their source either abides very closely by natural mathematical laws or that some kind of premeditated intelligence is involved. The notion that such non-random accuracy could be tramped out by hoaxers in dark fields severely stretches the credulity of many observers. These diagrams demonstrate the complex tangents, harmonic proportions and geometrical alignments present in just three pictograms, as extracted by Wolfgang Schindler, who, together with John Martineau, has carried out extensive research in this area. Counterclockwise, from the top: 1. Milk Hill, Wiltshire, July 16, 1992. 2. Barbury Castle, Wiltshire, July 17, 1991. 3. Chilcomb, Hampshire, July 9, 1990. Diagrams: Wolfgang Schindler

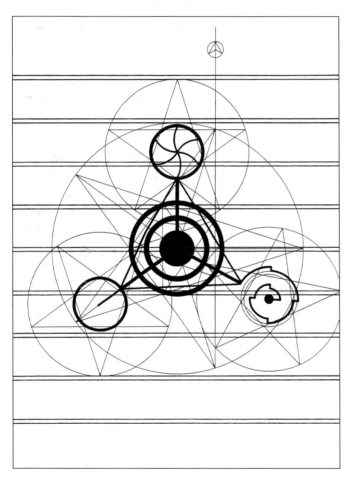

showing distinct anomalies in natural electrical fields at circle sites, but as reliable readings can only be obtained just before dawn, willing experimenters have been hard to come by in large enough numbers. Magnetometers have also given varied results. Cost is the main barrier to more scientific work being carried out on the crop circles in general, and unfortunately universities and other establishments which might provide research and funding have so far been repelled from any involvement due to the stigma of ridicule which seems to surround the phenomenon.

Thus, aside perhaps from biological analysis, an all-encompassing litmus test remains elusive. All manner of other methods have been tried, including infra-red photography and more esoteric methods such as dowsing (see Chapter 4), but many are handicapped by their subjectivity and uncertain repeatability.

Bending Space

One other process by which the plants may be laid down is that instead of a pressure-force, *space itself* may be bent by gravitational means, thus taking with it anything in the vicinity, ie. stems, which then recline afterwards, continuing to grow like nothing ever happened, blissfully unaware that they have been flattened as such. In this case, given that science assures us that space and time are one, one might look instead for time-dilation effects as well as physical traces; curiously, there have indeed been a number of documented time-anomalies in crop circles (see Chapter 3).

Perfection and Imperfection

One of the most astounding features of the phenomenon is the extraordinary accuracy with which many of the designs are executed, enabling them to conform to complex geometries which could not be applied if the patterns were randomly tramped out in a field (see panel). In addition to the genius of the internal logic, they are sometimes positioned at exact tangents and alignments with local features in the landscape, as at Stonehenge in 1996 (page 58).

One of the most comprehensive enquiries into this area was made by John Martineau, who identified several consistent geometrical features in many of the agriglyphs he subjected to analysis. His findings are summed up neatly in the introduction to his work *Crop Circle Geometry* (see Appendix A), quoted here with the kind permission of the author:

1. *When there are two or more circles it will often be the case that the line between the two centers, or a line from the center of one to the edge of another, or a tangent drawn just touching both circles, will be due north, south, east or west. If one of the cardinal directions is not thus indicated then 45 or 60 degrees will be.*

2. *When there are three or more circles it will often be found that lines can be drawn which either just touch three or more circles or which also pass through the centers of circles.*

3. *In the case of a pair of circles, if two lines are drawn tangenting both sides of both circles then it will often be the case that the angle formed between these lines is 30, 45, 60 or 90 degrees. Similar simple angles (simple in as much as they are simple divisions of a circle) may be found by examining the angle between the two lines drawn from the center of one circle which tangent each side of another. Check too the angle formed by the crossing of two tangents between two circles.*

4. *The proportions between concentric radii and features in crop formations are often defined by simple fractions (specifically diatonic ratios) or simple geometric proportions. These proportions all have their graphical equivalents and these, when superimposed on to the formations in question, seem to explain the position and size of other features including grapeshot circles.*

5. *The distances between circles and rings in any given formation are very often whole number multiples of radii present in that formation. In the case of rings or arcs, the center-line (average of inner and outer radii) is the radius which usually harmonizes most elegantly.*

6. *The geometrical characteristics of crop circles can be extended to stone circles and even the solar system. Whoever the circlemakers are, they know their stuff!*

Those who insist the formations are nothing more than the works of human jokers are often bereft of the mathematical knowledge necessary to make valued judgements and fail to understand the highly skilled and convoluted actions and equations which would be required to create many of the patterns. Just drawing some of the more complex designs efficiently on paper would be an effort. Transferring these to the fields would demand extensive calculations and staking out—trampling them "freehand" would be impossible. Quotes from surveying companies have suggested that given several days and many man-hours, such glyphs could be planned, measured and laid out correctly (without taking into account crop-laying qualities), but most arrive overnight or in times and conditions which would never allow for such preparation. The complex NBC television hoax demonstration of 1998 (Chapter 4; superficially impressive, but replete with tell-tale deficiencies) was constructed in six hours, far longer than the summer hours of concealing darkness allow. A car emblem made for Mitsubishi later that year by the same team took *two days* to complete ... (see Chapter 2).

Some of the numerical data extracted from detailed surveys of formations seems to carry information which goes beyond visual interpretation of the designs. For instance, the geometrical area (not the laid crop) produced by the four circular components of the famous triangular pattern at Barbury Castle, Wiltshire in 1991 was found to have a total laid area of 31,680 square feet. The figure 31,680, according to John Michell, is of huge significance to numerologists in *"arithmetic, cosmology, ancient theology and temple architecture."* Among other things, the number 3,168 was *"emblematic of Lord Jesus Christ"* to the early Christian scholars.[10] Other formations have yielded similar startling findings in the numbers alone. Professor Gerald Hawkins, celebrated author of *Stonehenge Decoded,* has discovered clear correlations with crop circle measurements and the Diatonic Scale (a mathematical table which can be converted into music and equates to the white notes of a piano), something which could not happen simply by accident, although his calculations rely on very accurate figures having been taken in the original surveys.

It is hard to know what to make of some of these intriguing observations and "cosmic coincidences," however, they do strongly suggest that the patterns are not just happy accidents, but are devised with extreme skill and finesse whether by intelligent direction or the inherently harmonic cycles of some bizarre natural force.

Nevertheless, it would be a lie to suggest that mistakes are never made even in some of the finest designs, and occasionally kinked paths and geometric wobbles are discovered in otherwise perfect works. Again, the Barbury Castle triangle of 1991 provides a good example. In amongst this work of genius is a clearly bent line making up part of the inner triangle itself, which appears to have got too close to the second ring and has veered outward to accommodate it. However, its creators (?) seem to have been aware of this *before* they embarked on making the line; instead of simply getting to the ring and crudely fudging it, the corrective kink is expertly achieved by two straight lines effectively approaching one another from very slightly different angles. (Some have speculated that the kink may even be an integral premeditated part of the design.) Nearly all crop circle researchers accept the authenticity of Barbury Castle, yet many oddly condemned the Oliver's Castle "snowflake" of 1996 in the wake of the video controversy (see Chapter 2) because it had similar geometrical flaws in a couple of places. Though they do often reach sublime heights of accuracy, the formations seem to be more artistic and organic than architectural. There is evidence to show that some shapes are laid with deliberate distortions to allow for topographical features and gradients so that they *appear* correct at the most viewable angle, be it in the landscape or from the air (an art noted in ancient carved hill figures). Some, however, are more obviously askew than others and a certain level can be reached where even the most giving of observers have to consider human error as the obvious cause.

Most "circles," incidentally, are actually ellipses when measured and are rarely a uniform diameter when readings are taken from different directions, sometimes varying by several feet. Perhaps "crop ovals" would be a better description.

Where and When

Over the years many have attempted to pull together a number of observations which can be conclusively drawn about the behavior of the phenomenon in terms of where and when crop formations manifest, with—as seems par for the course—variable results.

Dr. Terence Meaden, a qualified meteorologist, believed that certain atmospheric conditions were necessary for the instigation of the plasma vortices he felt were creating the crop patterns, generally *"dry, quiet, weather."*[11] However, not to denigrate some of Meaden's otherwise excellent work in defining the possible mechanics of circle formation, developments challenged this observation given that a number of agriglyphs later provably appeared on nights of wind and rain. He also believed that nearly all circles appeared close to hills (aiding the creation of vortexes). Given that "close" in these terms could mean anything up to several *miles* downwind of a hill and that in many parts of England hills are hard to avoid on this scale, this judgement was difficult to verify.

Other attempts have been made to pin down repeatable qualities which might point towards some kind of answer to the crop circle mystery, but if there are any definitive correlations most of them remain uncharted and far more detailed databases need to be maintained.

The Geological Connection

One relationship that does seem sound is the observation, first made by Brian Grist, and later verified by Steve Page and Glenn Broughton, that certain geological strata seem to attract crop formations, in particular aquiferous rocks which retain water, mainly chalk, greensand and limestone.[12] This is an assertion of huge potential significance which has been surprisingly overlooked. Mapping and comparing the general distribution of circles in southern England with geological charts showing aquiferous strata demonstrates a remarkable parity between the two.[13] Given that dowsers believe underground water plays an important role in the charging of what they call earth energy (see Chapter 4), this connection supports their contention that crop circles are created by something tapping this natural force.

The geological link throws up a conundrum for the cosmic intelligence theory because it seems to suggest that any outside sentient force is restricted by our planet's geophysical qualities as to where it places its crop communications. If we are dealing, as some have supposed, with an all-powerful extra-terrestrial hierarchy, what is stopping it creating designs anywhere it likes? Why is it restricted to aquiferous areas if the circles are made with a superior technology? Either, in this scenario, the intelligence is trying to draw our attention to these places, or it *isn't* all-powerful and needs to utilize geophysically-generated earth energies to perform. Otherwise, this connection may suggest that the source of the crop circles is rather closer to home and part of our own natural system rather than from something *out there*.

Wider Patterns

Aside from geological considerations, it has often been wondered if the distribution of crop circles in the landscape may form patterns when joined like dot-to-dots. Glimpses of significance have been gleaned from such exercises, but drawing conclusions from the results is difficult. Three

The general distribution of formations can sometimes be aligned with features in the landscape—or with each other, as with the 1991 "whale" formations. This one at Beckhampton, Wiltshire was joined by two near-identical designs, each placed at the three corners of a perfect isosceles triangle covering several miles. Photo: Andrew King

identical whale-like pictograms from 1991, for instance, formed a perfect isosceles triangle across several miles when linked with lines on a map. More triangular genre-clusters were identified in 2000. (See Chapter 2.) Alignments of formations with ancient sites and ley-lines (as opposed to energy lines) have been noted on many occasions, sometimes creating remarkably accurate geometric patterns.

In addition to geographical observations, others have even tried placing all the different pictogram shapes into variations of visual, date and place order to see if a code will emerge. Some of the results have been interesting, but frustratingly inscrutable (page 170).[14]

One thing which quickly becomes obvious when the wider picture is considered is that Wiltshire is without doubt the central heart of the phenomenon, and the majority of the large complex patterns have consistently graced this area with only one year—1995—where the focus seemed to shift to other counties (mainly Hampshire and Sussex). With Stonehenge roughly at its center, this region has become known to researchers as the "Wessex Triangle" because of the general shape of distribution. The further out from here one goes, the sparser the amount of formations and, with some exceptions, the simpler they become, with regional themes seemingly being expressed in sequences of designs particular to certain places. This throws up further questions as to why a premeditated intelligent force should target specific areas of one country in this way.

Chehalis, Washington State, USA, July 10, 1994. Despite the presence of many huge fields, the USA receives only a small proportion of formations each year. Though regional styles are expressed across the globe, the laying techniques are identical and biological analysis finds the same effects in nearly all of them. Photo: ilyes

Other nations have their own distribution patterns too, but none of them has yet matched England in either numbers or general sweep of design although some are now catching up. Germany is probably the next country down the list to boast some of the more exquisite glyphs seen over the last few years. Only very rarely are exact matches for designs found from one country to another; mostly indige-

nous characteristics predominate, though the observable construction techniques appear to be remarkably consistent, as are the effects discovered by W C Levengood who has examined samples from around the world. Numberwise, countries on the European continent are the most circle-favored; larger ones like Canada, with huge fields available, only notch up twenty or so events each year, demonstrating that size is indeed not everything. The earth energy theory (see Chapter 4), tied in with the aquiferous connection, could account for the notable features of geographical distribution and it may just be that the central core of such a power grid happens to be in England.

Eye-Witnesses

The strange and seemingly "paranormal" effects experienced within and around crop circles, and the many theories which might explain this extraordinary mystery are explored in Chapters 3 and 4. But for all the debate and false accusations aimed at it, recounted in doses throughout the next chapter, be in no doubt whatsoever that there *is* a real phenomenon for the following reason if not for all the others. Although such instances are rare, there have been enough documented eye-witness accounts of people having *watched* crop formations appear out of nowhere to render irrelevant arguments to the contrary.

The fine details described vary, but there may be many different ways a circle can form depending on conditions. Largely, most speak of the same thing—a hugely powerful but very local and selective force like a wind hitting the field and spinning the crops down extremely rapidly, within ten to twenty seconds or less. Most of these events have happened either in the very early hours of the morning or early evening. Sometimes sound and light phenomena are involved and the lights in the sky seen on so many occasions above places where formations are subsequently found are almost certainly a part of this process. One couple in Surrey, Vivien and Gary Tomlinson, even had the disconcerting experience of having a small pictogram appear around them in 1989. Thrown by a strong force into standing crop from a nearby path, they described a tall glowing funnel reaching up to the sky and small "mini-whirlwinds" dancing around their feet, spinning the stems down at an incredible speed. In 1991, Martin Sohn-Rethel and his family, walking on downland near Iford in East Sussex, were almost knocked off their feet by an invisible force, which then moved on into the adjacent field. As Martin watched, a perfect circle was swept down in front of him in no more than *"five to ten seconds."*

More recently, in 2001, BLT Research co-founder Nancy Talbott became the first circle researcher to officially view the creation of a formation, as three thin tubes of light descended into a Dutch beanfield, leaving a steaming ellipse with an emanating T-shaped path.... (See Chapter 2.)

There are around two dozen such first-hand daylight accounts on record, not to mention the many sightings of aerial phenomena coming down into fields on nights when new formations appear. Naturally, many of these witnesses have been ridiculed and accused of perjury by skeptics, yet none of them, often previously unaware of the phenomenon, has had anything to gain from sharing their experiences and no reason to lie. *They* know something incredible is happening.[15]

The Voyage Begins ...

So, with the basic nature of what is actually appearing in our fields explored, we can embark on a voyage through the remarkable history of this evolving phenomenon and some of the outstanding events which have surrounded it....

NOTES

1. As an example, two concentric rings appeared in grazing grass at Sennen Cove, Cornwall on January 31st and February 7th, 1997. (*SC,* issue 62, March 1997) See also Chapter 2.

2. Reported in *SC,* issue 18, June 1993, and further discussed in issue 21, September 1993.

3. Dr. Terence Meaden's *The Circles Effect and it's Mysteries, Circles from the Sky* and Andrews and Delgado's *Circular Evidence* embody the most comprehensive observations in this area.

4. The Felbridge, West Sussex, pictogram of 1995 displayed this effect and is examined in detail in my books *Fields of Mystery* and *Quest For Contact.*

5. Michael Chorost discusses construction lines at length in his excellent article *Hoaxing Doesn't Explain It, The Cerealogist,* issue 6, Summer 1992.

6. The Bible, *Daniel 5,* v 5–6.

7. Recounted in Montague Keen's book *1991—Scientific Evidence for the Crop Circle Phenomenon.*

8. The whole sorry tale is told in *SC,* issue 47, December 1995.

9. *Crop Circles—The Latest Evidence,* Pat Delgado and Colin Andrews, page 42.

10. *Geometry and Symbolism at Barbury Castle,* John Michell, *The Cerealogist,* issue 4, Summer 1991.

11. *The Crop Circle Enigma,* Chapter 8, *Crop Circles and the Plasma Vortex,* G T Meaden, page 85.

12. *The Aquifer Attractor,* Brian Grist, *The Cerealogist,* issue 5, Winter 1991/2, *The Underground Connection,* Steve Page and Glenn Broughton, *The Circular,* issue 33, December 1998. This is arguably one of the most important observations yet made about the crop circle phenomenon and hasn't received the coverage it deserves.

13. The maps in *Fields of Mystery* show clearly how, in the county of Sussex alone, the majority of formations which have appeared there hug the chalk South Downs.

14. Wolfgang Schindler has done some of the best work in this area, outlined in *SC,* issue 28, April 1994, pages 5–7.

15. The Surrey couple's experience is described in detail in *Quest For Contact,* and the incident at Iford, East Sussex is recounted in *Fields of Mystery.* There are a number of good accounts recorded in the books of Dr. Terence Meaden.

View across the huge "snail" motif, Alton Barnes, Wiltshire, July 9, 1992. Photo: Grant Wakefield

2. FROM GENESIS ... TO REVELATION?

One of the most striking aspects of the crop circles is that they have clearly evolved since their first sporadic appearances throughout history. This evolution has been marked by a growing interest in their development from researchers, the public and the media, particularly in the 1990s with the advent of the pictograms, tempered with denial and doubt in the face of astounding evidence. This chapter puts the main sequence of events into chronological order, outlining the history of some of the most notable crop formations and the extraordinary stories and controversies surrounding them....

The Early Years

In the Beginning...?

Quite where the history of crop circles really begins is impossible to say for sure, but it has been theorized they may have been with us in some form or another since prehistoric times. Evidence for this is elusive, but there have been a few tantalizing correlations between the geometry of certain stone circle complexes and crop patterns. This has led some to surmise that perhaps awe-struck tribal peoples came across swirled markings in early cultivated grain or wild grass and saw fit to preserve the site of these gifts from the gods with sarsens or raised embankments.[1] The resemblance of many cultures' ancient symbolism to specific crop glyphs has reinforced this idea, but there is no way of discovering the truth.

Prehistoric speculation aside, some reports come down to us from history which strongly suggest the circles have been part of our landscape for several centuries. Some of these accounts may be buried in folklore and talk of "fairy rings" as at Assen, Holland in 1590 where grass was reported as having been "trodden down" in a ring by mysterious ethereal dancers. However, history makes us wait until 1678 before the first clear record of what appear to have been crop circles comes to light....

Devil's Advocates

It's almost hackneyed to seasoned researchers now, but it would be impossible to document this history without highlighting the tale of the "Mowing Devil." Recounted in a pamphlet issued on August 22nd, 1678, and subtitled *Strange*

The ancient temple of Stonehenge, Wiltshire, as seen from the adjacent fractal formation which appeared July 7, 1996. Some believe stone circles were erected to mark crop circle sites. Photo: Andy Thomas

"The Mowing Devil," as illustrated in the original pamphlet of 1678. This is the most compelling reference to what certainly appear to be crop circles from historical times.

News Out of Hartford-Shire (Hertfordshire, England, to us), this astonishing tale, told in quaintly archaic language, tells of a farmer who approached a local laborer with a view to having him harvest his field of oats. When the price quoted proved rather higher than expected, this led the farmer to exclaim that *"the Devil himself should mow his oats before he should have anything to do with them."* That night, according to the pamphlet, the sky over the farmer's field was seen to be *"all of a flame"* and when the field was observed next day, it seemed as if the Devil himself had indeed popped round and harvested the field; *"If the Devil had a mind to shew his dexterity in the art of husbandry, and scorn'd to mow them after the usual manner, he cut them in round circles, and plac't every straw with that exactness that it would have taken up above an age for any man to perform what he did that one night; And the man that owns them is as yet afraid to remove them."*[2]

Many believe this is the first historical reference to a crop formation. Some have expressed doubt, but the evocative account and the familiar-looking features in the picture which accompanies it seem so close to today's observed effects, what else could these "round circles" seriously be? Even allowing for the fact they are described as having been "cut" as opposed to laid, the precise placing of the fallen stems and mention of the sky being "all of a flame" ties in neatly with the beautiful floor lays of circles and sightings of strange luminosities we are now familiar with.

Other Circular Ancestry

Even putting aside the Mowing Devil, there are enough good accounts of crop circles in the years since 1678 for us to be fairly sure that the phenomenon has been with us for much longer than the limited recent period some would have us believe.[3] There are several documented sightings of crop circles from earlier this century in particular. Terry Wilson, in his work *The Secret History of Crop Circles,* has uncovered records of almost three hundred pre-1980 formations, at least twenty-five of which appeared before the Second World War.

West Sussex had a typical early potential sighting of a formation in 1932 at Bow Hill, near Chichester.[4] Complete with a photograph, this account tells of four rings which appeared in barley. Although they are put down to being archaeological ditch-marks showing through, the photo and descriptions of the stems inside being "lodged" and "beaten down" suggest crop circles more strongly. This is demonstrative of the general source of several early reports, but some are less ambiguous. Researchers at Southern Circular Research (SCR) have heard many tales from people who grew up on farms in the 1920s and 30s who remember formations appearing then and who recall their grandparents having spoken of them from the previous century. Not all of these accounts are of simple circles either. One lady talks of a series of triangular markings which were found swirled into her father's fields, and some reports even sound suspiciously like early descriptions of what would become known as "pictograms" when they burst onto the scene in a big way in 1990.

Other stories bridge the decades; one man together with his brother and sister, as another typical example, actually found and entered a crop circle in the mid 1950s between Epsom and Mickleham in Surrey. While there, they experienced a strange "rainbow" effect shimmering in the air above it. It wasn't until 1997, when confronted with photos of the modern phenomenon (at one of my talks), that he thought to mention it to anyone. There are more sporadic cases in the years leading to the 1970s and not just in England. Tully, at Queensland, Australia saw a little spate of circles in 1966, or "UFO nests" as they were dubbed, connected with sightings of strange lights and objects.[5] More would be discovered here throughout the 1970s.

Despite such reports, however, it's clear that crop circles

were rare before the latter part of the 20th century. Throughout the war years, for instance, despite extra aerial activity, only RAF Tangmere in West Sussex appears to have recorded any formations in photographs (as documented in my book *Fields of Mystery*). Yet something suddenly changed and increasing numbers began to be noted as the years rolled by. This apparent leap in figures was initially put down to a greater awareness of the phenomenon and a growth in those actively looking for circles. In retrospect, this expansion was clearly more than illusion. It was an evolution which would begin to show in more than just quantity.

The 1970s

The Warminster "Flap"

It wasn't until the 1970s that the crop circle phenomenon as we now know it really began in earnest. Those formations which first began to gain attention were the ones which appeared in the area now seen as the traditional center of all circular activity—Wiltshire. The possible reasons for this area's attraction are discussed elsewhere in the book, but, at its most basic, such beautiful enigmas seemed perfectly at home in an area packed with prehistoric monuments and ancient—and modern—mysteries. One of the modern ones was a spate of UFO sightings in the Warminster area, site of one of the "flaps" which seem to pop up from time to time in different parts of the world. It was entirely appropriate that one of the first official "early" documentations of crop formations took place here on August 15th, 1972, when UFO researcher Arthur Shuttlewood and American journalist Bryce Bond actually claimed to have witnessed the creation of a circle before their very eyes at Star Hill. Other shapes were subsequently found nearby.[6]

The Evolution Begins ...

Throughout this decade, increasing amounts of circles began to be discovered, and not just in Wiltshire. Sussex and other counties were also visited by the phenomenon. As time went by, it wasn't just single circles that were being found; several were clustered in one field in some instances and a number even seemed to give the impression they had been symmetrically placed in a pattern....

One of the earliest confirmed sightings of what would

From simple circles something quite unexpected would evolve.... Some circles would continue to appear in their purest form, however, as here (one of four) at Ovingdean, East Sussex, July 27, 1996. Photo: Andy Thomas

become known as "quintuplets" or "quincunxes"—a circle with four smaller surrounding satellites at regular intervals—was found at Headbourne Worthy, Hampshire in 1978,[7] although there had been rare reports from as early as the 1950s. There would be many such designs in the years to come, with the quintuplet one of the most regularly recurring patterns. Together with continuing reports of lights in the sky seen over fields which subsequently gave birth to circles, the superficial resemblance of this configuration to the landing pads of NASA lunar craft gave rise, for the first time, to the notion that some kind of cosmic intelligence might be involved. In time it became clear that the circles were far more than depressions left by descending extra-terrestrial spaceships and the hypothesis would give way to a more subtle twist on the idea of other-worldly contact.

Up to this point interest in the circles had been restricted largely to village gossip and short reports in local newspapers. With shapes like these beginning to appear, it was inevitable that some would begin to take a deeper look at what was happening in the fields around them....

The 1980s

The First Researchers

At the beginning of the decade which would see the crop circle phenomenon develop from a mild curiosity into an international mystery and all-consuming passion for some,

Three formations in close proximity at Westbury, Wiltshire, August 1987, the quintuplet still clearly visible after harvesting. Note that the circle on the far right has been overlapped by another, while the top circle in the photo seems only semi-formed, possibly due to the intersecting tramlines. Photo: Dr. Terence Meaden

theories about what was causing it were thin on the ground. Besides the fringe flying saucer speculations, those ideas that existed, understandably, were largely weather-related. The first serious investigation of the circles was undertaken by Dr. Terence Meaden (also known as George Terence Meaden), a qualified meteorologist who quickly became convinced the circles were the result of a natural atmospheric effect he christened the "plasma vortex," an electrically-charged spinning column of air. As *rings* began to be found around circles and the symmetrical quintuplets began to proliferate, this theory was continually fine-tuned to accommodate an increase of what looked suspiciously like premeditated *designs* to others who were beginning to climb aboard the circle-seeking wagon.

By now, the formations had gained the attention of a group of people who would, in time, be instrumental in igniting the flame of global interest. "Cerealogy," the popular study of crop circles, had been born. Amongst other cerealogists, the most prominent was Pat Delgado, a "retired electro-mechanical engineer," soon joined by another electrical engineer with an interest in the circles, Colin Andrews. Together with light aircraft pilot "Busty" Taylor, all worked together with Meaden and a few friends in a small network. Delgado and Andrews, to Meaden's dismay, quickly began to explore more paranormal realms in their quest for an answer to the enigma, becoming convinced that some kind of intelligence was involved. Attracted by the enduring reports of luminosities, the world of ufology had already leapt into the fray and by the end of the 80s a growing army of characters and investigative bodies—often with egos well to the fore—were on the trail of the crop formations. As all these disparate groups of many opinions and agendas struggled to come to terms with each other's views and methods of investigation, it became increasingly difficult for them to present a united front, splitting into different camps competing to find an answer to something that would remain eternally resistant to being nailed down in any way.

Healey's Comet

As more people were drawn in, so media coverage began to increase. One quintuplet in 1984 found itself the center of attention because of the celebrity politician who photographed it, inadvertently acting as a catalyst for spreading the word wider. An amateur cameraman in his spare time, when the Labour MP Denis Healey (now Lord Healey) spotted the five symmetrical circles near his home at Alfriston, East Sussex, his photographic instincts were aroused. When word got out that a prominent public figure had snapped something rather unusual, Denis soon found his composition reproduced in a tabloid newspaper (dubbed "Healey's Comet") and for the first time in such a big way, the circles were thrown into the public

An early quintuplet at Alfriston, East Sussex, July 27, 1984. This was photographed by Labour MP Denis Healey and thrown into the limelight. The lines between the circles were made by visitors. Photo: John Holloway

domain, questions openly being asked about their origins.[8] Soon, other papers and journals like *Fortean Times* would take up the pursuit.

All Change

In time, the quintuplets began to develop rings connecting their outer satellites. The "Celtic crosses" were born. Some were more elaborate than others, with several rings in some cases, often no more than a foot wide, and the circles would vary in their proportions from pattern to pattern. Other configurations became familiar sights; "triplets" (one large circle with two smaller companions either side), circles with many rings, even ones laid out in a triangular fashion. All seemed to stretch the basic weather theories to breaking point, and the increasing reports of bizarre incidents, lights, sounds and smells in and around formations challenged the notion that these shapes were just inert impressions in the fields. They almost seemed to be *alive,* radiating energies which profoundly affected some who entered them (see Chapter 3).

By the late 80s, hundreds were being reported each year in counties across England, and sporadic sightings trickled in from abroad. It looked as if some of the designs were trying to break their circular bonds. A number began to

From the quintuplets came ... the celtic crosses, the satellite circles linked with rings. Upton Scudamore, Wiltshire, June 29, 1990. Photo: Michael & Christine Green

exhibit emanating rectangular pathways. These would point the way to the massive leap in the complexity of the phenomenon which would take place in 1990.

The Public Eye

In 1989, Delgado and Andrews published the first ever crop circle book, *Circular Evidence,* to a public which unexpectedly took to these new riddles with gusto. The title was a huge success and in many ways single-handedly laid the way for all further research and the many subsequent commercial enterprises which would follow, with talk of paranormal phenomena and tiny hints of the circles' portentous importance to humankind. Terence Meaden's book *The Circles Effect and its Mysteries,* which appeared shortly after, eschewed any such talk and kept to scientific approaches. Rightly or wrongly, it met a more muted response as a result. A media storm was about to break and Delgado and Andrews were quick to capitalize on their new-found fame, setting up *Operation White Crow* with full publicity in June 1989. Based at Cheesefoot Head, a regular circle site in Hampshire, this was the first serious attempt by anyone to capture the elusive evidence that the phenomenon needed for full credibility; a video of a crop formation appearing.

Around sixty or so people took turns in manning round-the-clock shifts to keep an eye on the field below the camp at the famous Devil's Punchbowl just off the A272. However, detection gadgets and monitoring equipment seemed

Colin Andrews (center) surrounded by colleagues, journalists and camera crews for *Operation White Crow* at Cheesefoot Head, Hampshire, June 1989. Photo: Dr. Terence Meaden

to act as a disincentive and after a week and a day the project was abandoned without a result. Though *White Crow* failed to achieve its aims, some rather strange tales transpired, and, on the final night, a group of participants found themselves pursuing a mysterious "trilling" sound (which had been noted at formations before—see Chapter 3) around darkened fields where circles subsequently formed unseen later that night.[9]

End of an Era

The second phase of the phenomenon (the first being simple circles) came to a dramatic close with the appearance of a pattern which would drop jaws and signal the end of the weather-related plasma vortex being a credible theory in its simplest form.

At Winterbourne Stoke, Wiltshire on August 12th, 1989, the last circle of the year appeared. What shocked observers was that it was laid in *four quarters,* each segment swept outward in a different direction, only a small central area being swirled in the more traditional manner. Clearly no mere spinning vortex had created *this.* Though few realized it at the time, with this event, the game-plan had changed and the mystery was to take a huge leap forward when the stems of the following season began to push their way upwards....

1990

The Pictograms

The Winterbourne Stoke event had been a jolt to those investing in weather-bound explanations, but no-one was prepared for the shapes which began to appear in 1990. Although there is evidence to suggest a small number of complex patterns had appeared before, there's little doubt that this year was the major turning point in the development of the crop circles. It's easy in retrospect, with complicated designs now a familiar sight, to forget the terrific impact of what became known as the "pictograms."

There were the circles people had become used to, there were the rings ... but this time bound together by rectangular paths in long symbolic chains. To many, these strongly suggested a premeditated source. The first official pictogram appeared, appropriately given the previous year's efforts to video formations there, at Cheesefoot Head, Hampshire on May 23rd; a dumbbell of a large circle and

A circle laid in quarters of different lay directions at Winterbourne Stoke, Wiltshire, August 21, 1989. This marked the end of an era ... and the beginning of something quite extraordinary. Photo: Dr. Terence Meaden

a path which changed widths part-way down, leading to a disconnected circle (page 103). The most profound aspect of the design was the four unattached rectangular boxes, aligned two each side of the central shaft like number 11's—which especially excited numerologists for whom the sequence 11/11 held deep significance. With this sudden jump in evolution it seemed that anything could happen ... and it did.

Other pictograms began to appear in the weeks after, each seemingly a variation on the same theme, but developing as they went, culminating in what was the most astonishing event yet. On July 11th, the residents of Alton Barnes, a small Wiltshire village in the beautiful Vale of Pewsey, awoke to find a huge and elaborate motif etched into a vast field overlooked by the old burial mound Adam's Grave (page 104). Effectively two of the designs seen in previous weeks stuck together in a long line with added claw-like appendages, this breathtaking inspiration was around 550 feet long and quite the most ambitious formation ever seen. It would eventually be interpreted as representing everything from a dragon to meteorological weather symbols. Strange accounts of humming sounds that night and cars that wouldn't start in the village next morning, whether relevant or not, all added to the mystique. On the same night, a very similar and equally large glyph appeared at nearby Stanton St Bernard.

The media soon found these events on its news desks and the crop circle legend was born, the Alton Barnes pictogram emblazoned across the pages of more than one major newspaper. Other impressive shapes followed, but this would take all the glory. The farmer opened the field up to the public and charged admission, encouraging several thousand visitors to travel down to see this new wonder for themselves. Anyone untouched by the phenomenon so far could no longer remain unaware that something extraordinary was occurring in the fields of England and by now beyond.

Alien Nation

Those who up to now had just speculated on the notion of cosmic intelligence being responsible became firm converts at this point despite the pleas from some that nature *could* still produce such effects, although they weren't yet quite sure how. Everything seemed to boil down to just two things at this point, despite a plethora of other plausible theories (discussed in Chapter 4), which were publicly ignored—either this was all some incredible prank, which many, at this point, found hard to believe (although skeptics *were* getting louder) or ET was finally phoning home. Or phoning us, anyway. Even the press was talking about alien messages from the stars. Were these incredible shapes the product of some extra-terrestrial intervention, and, if so, what were they trying to tell us? One newspaper even offered a cash reward of £10,000 for anyone with proof of how the circles were made. How different their tone would be just thirteen and a half short months later.

Noughts and Crosses

Despite the arrival of the pictograms, there were still some old friends manifesting in the fields. Quintuplets continued to be discovered, and their descendants, the Celtic crosses, grew ever bolder. One such quadruple-ringed design at Bishops Cannings, Wiltshire, even found itself being superimposed with another celtic cross three weeks later, overlapping the outer ring of the original. Simple circles were still being discovered and many imaginative variations on ringed circles delighted their now growing audience of researchers and casual spectators. Bizarrely, a number of formations appeared to be randomly splattered with many tiny circles, dubbed "grapeshot," the function of which

would forever remain a mystery. Their role would be curtailed and streamlined somewhat in later years.

Operation Blackbird

Unbowed by the disappointment of the previous year, Delgado and Andrews decided to mount another attempt at videoing a crop pattern forming. This time, they based their efforts at Bratton Castle, Wiltshire, an area of activity since the early 1980s, and set aside three weeks from July to August in which to net their prize. With an even bigger media splash than before, the newly-christened *Operation Blackbird* enjoyed sponsorship from the BBC and other organizations, including aid from the British Army with manpower and detection equipment.

Tents and vehicles line the hill overlooking Bratton Castle, Wiltshire, for *Operation Blackbird,* July 1990, a venture dealt a cruel blow by unknown saboteurs. Photo: Dr. Terence Meaden

Just two days into the project on July 25th, a hugely excited Colin Andrews announced live to the nation via the BBC breakfast news that their cameras had finally captured the long-sought visual evidence of a formation appearing under anomalous lights. He soon regretted not having looked at it closely before doing so. When subsequently examined, the crude pattern of lines and circles was apparently man-made, with a *Horoscope* board game and wooden crucifix deliberately left inside to leave no doubt (although some claim to this day it was a real circle, which had been added to as a spoiler). With TV cameras following every

The formation at Bratton Castle which ended the crop circle honeymoon ... an apparent hoax created to defuse interest in the phenomenon by publicly humiliating researchers. Photo: Michael and Christine Green

move, a much humbled Delgado and Andrews had to admit to the world that they had been duped. The lights filmed on the night the hoax appeared—also seen by others outside the encampment—were never satisfactorily explained, but attributed by the media to torches of those responsible (!) or the passing overhead of Richard Branson's hot air balloon. (Another formation did appear in front of the *Blackbird* cameras a few days later, but was too far away for anything useful to be picked up. Unsubstantiated rumors persist that successful footage was eventually taken during the weeks of the operation, but kept secret for unknown reasons.)

To this day the perpetrators of the Bratton scam are unknown. Various suspects have been implicated, including even pop music radicals the *KLF* (who later carved their logo into a field), but many consider that the military themselves were responsible, given their presence at *Blackbird*—and temporary absence the one night the hoax appeared. With the public furor over the phenomenon and all its cosmic implications, perhaps things were seen to be getting out of hand by authorities worried about the effect such high-profile paranormal events might have on a normally docile population. Some were by now openly talking of alien communications and the potential raising of human consciousness. What better opportunity to very publicly demonstrate to the world, using the platform Delgado and Andrews had made for themselves, that crop circles might be nothing more than a joke, to defuse the tension?

Whoever made the Bratton design, it certainly had its desired effect. The press suddenly adopted a more cynical attitude than they had just a month before, and the expanding bubble of interest deflated a little. This would be the last such high-profile circle investigation project to be attempted. In future, researchers would be rather more careful about how they went about their work and who they invited along.... (The following year, a similar but much more low-key attempt was made by another group, *Project Chameleon*. This time two formations did appear in full view of cameras, virtually next to the equipment caravans ... but there was a heavy mist and nothing was seen. Motion-detectors, however, failed to go off, suggesting no-one had entered the area. The circle-making forces clearly weren't eager to be caught in the act.) Delgado and Andrews' attitudes notably changed too and became far more cautious. Nevertheless, this didn't stop them publishing a second book, *Crop Circles: The Latest Evidence,* at the end of the summer with the cards-on-the-table question "*Could* it be Aliens?" emblazoned on the cover.

The Birth of CCCS

The debacle at Bratton Castle illustrated neatly the need for a more independent and less charismatic investigative body to document and explore the increasingly beautiful and mind-boggling glyphs. In April 1990, a group of socially-connected enthusiasts decided to set up an organization which would serve as an unbiased forum for discussion and data collection. Some of them had participated in a meditative ritual at the ancient mound of Silbury Hill, near Avebury, Wiltshire in 1989, an action which archaeologist and ex-*English Heritage* Michael Green believed may have helped trigger the development of the pictograms.[10]

With Green as its Chairman, the Center for Crop Circle Studies, or CCCS, as it called itself, managed to attract such luminaries as Professor Archie Roy as President and the Earl of Haddington as Patron. As the years went by, branches of CCCS would be set up around the country and other parts of the world, as the formations continued to creep outward. While it achieved good things and helped spread the word of the circles wider, even this body, like the first researchers of the 1980s, would find it hard to keep a group of such diverse personalities and theory-factions united under one umbrella and struggles for ideological and political control of the organization would continually dog its effectiveness.

1991

Whales and Insects

If anyone feared that nothing could better the amazing crop designs of 1990, they needn't have worried. As the next year's batch began to arrive, it soon became clear that disappointment was not on the cards; the evolution was continuing.

The new pictograms, particularly the dumbbell shapes, seemed more streamlined and delicate than their ancestors, and appendages like the "keys" seemed bolder and sharper. Some though, were plain bizarre. Strange "whales," finned lozenges capped with rings at each end (page 105), prompted less the question "What's making these?," but more "What on Earth do they actually *mean?*" One group likened these aquatic-looking patterns to being an abstract representation of the Virgin Mary, a haloed figure standing on the world, as often depicted in Christian art. Many, perhaps importantly, were beginning to interpret the glyphs within their own frame of reference and deriving very different meanings from just one formation. They seemed to represent all things to all people. Maybe this was in itself a major factor in the circles' existence?

Another recurring theme of the year also seemed to suggest life-forms, this time in the guise of the "insectograms," generally dumbbell pictograms with two antenna and sometimes odd "ladders" trailing from the circles. While some speculated that a kind of alien insect intelligence was making itself known, others found these hard to take seriously. Given the growing backlash against the phenomenon from some quarters after *Operation Blackbird,* designs like this hardly helped. But the insect motif wasn't ridiculous to everyone. An environmental message could be read into their appearance. Perhaps the fact that the glyphs were etched into the very food we ate was sig-

nificant. Maybe the medium was the message? After all, it was easy to forget that all these lovely rolling fields which provided the backdrop to the crop circles were in reality poisoned wastelands of over-intensive farming and chemical spray residues. Environmentally-conscious researchers put forward the idea that the insectograms might be saying something profound about the deadly pesticides humans were pouring into the ground year upon year. As the decade rode on, concerns over genetically-modified

Insectogram and "sprouting" ringed circle at Stonehenge, Wiltshire, July 10, 1991. Photo: Richard Wintle/Calyx Photo Services

crops able to withstand more extreme insect-killing chemicals made some look even further into the message of the insectograms. Insects hold the balance of nature and its eco-systems; was something letting us know we were about to irrevocably tip it?

Scripts and Curlymen

Alton Barnes, already the Mecca of the circle world after its 1990 visitation, was revisited by two of the new leaner pictograms (page 155) and in August, just a little way west at Milk Hill, a strange line of what looked like a hieroglyphic script (page 105) arrived seemingly in response to an over-enthusiastic American researcher's words "TALK TO US!" which, a week before, he had stamped out in a nearby field in a fit of pique at the almost wilful obscurity of the crop symbols.[11] The Milk Hill script has since been interpreted to mean many things in every language from Latin to Atlantean.

Another controversial depiction popped up at Amesbury, Wiltshire on July 28th and typified the polarization which was beginning to come to a head between those who held that the entire phenomenon was nothing more than an elaborately-conceived prank and those convinced that here was something of vital significance to the future of humankind. A pictogram of curly pathways looked suspiciously like a matchstick man from one angle. Some argued that this was just suggestive interpretation, but a few asked what was wrong with "the circlemakers" (as "they" were by now often referred to) giving us a picture of a human figure? These clashes would come to a major head at the end of the summer.

News from Abroad

By now, it was clear that the best cerealogical works weren't just confined to the British Isles. In Grasdorf, Germany, a huge complex of chunky pictogram shapes was discovered on July 22nd, arguably the best yet to have appeared outside of England. What further distinguished the event was the announcement that a treasure-hunter had recovered three metal plates buried in the soil underneath. Each plate bore a cast showing the exact design of the formation.... Those initially skeptical found themselves more intrigued when it turned out, on analysis, that the plates were made of almost pure gold, silver and bronze, worth several thousand pounds in material costs alone—quite an expensive

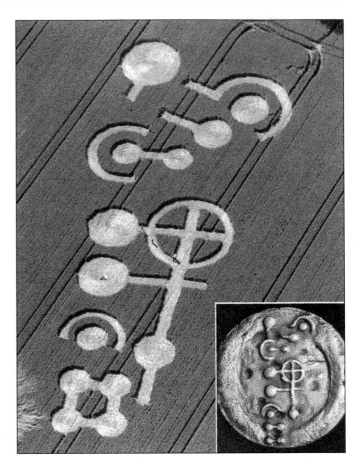

Three precious metal plates (one shown inset) bearing the very design of the formations above them were allegedly dug from beneath this impressive complex of pictograms at Grasdorf, Germany, July 22, 1991. Photos: Michael Hesemann, reproduced from his book *The Cosmic Connection* (Gateway 1996) by kind permission of the author.

prank—but the mystery of their origin still remains.[12] This story provoked a short scare that sightseers might start digging gaping holes into crop circles in the hope of hitting the jackpot, but common sense, for once, prevailed.

The Biggest and the Best

Despite all the previous diversity, no-one was quite prepared for the shocking beauty of the amazing pictogram which arrived at Barbury Castle, Wiltshire on July 17th (page 107), discovered by open-mouthed photographers off to shoot another formation from a helicopter. A huge triangular configuration, it appeared to be a two-dimensional representation of a tetrahedron superimposed with a double-ringed circle and three separate motifs perched on each tip, two essentially circular and one a "ratchet" spiral. Its symbolism seemed so specific that for many this just *had* to mean something. Some noted its resemblance to old alchemical diagrams, others picked up on its apparent reference to the Qabalah, the ancient Hebrew tree of divination, and coincidence-challenging significance seemed to arise from the mathematical data extracted from detailed surveys (page 26). Richard Hoagland and others have even linked its geometrical information with the alleged and contentious artificial monuments they believe adorn the Martian plains of Cydonia,[13] which in turn seem to have geometrical bonds to the nearby Ave-bury/Silbury complex. The stories which surround this glyph, dubbed "the mother of all pictograms" at the time, of loud roaring sounds, descending aerial lights and large dark objects on the night of its appearance, have become legend, although reports of military cordons around the area the next morning are questionable. It didn't stay pris-tine for long—a violent thunderstorm the next night scarred the field with extensive lodging, and the many vis-itors it received left the mother of all pictograms looking old and haggard in a remarkably short time.

As if this astonishment wasn't enough in one year, the circle-making forces then dealt another cosmic slap in the face by delivering a *recognizable symbol.* Several formations had suggested resemblances to known configurations from different cultures, but when a "Mandelbrot Set" casually graced a Cambridgeshire field at Ickleton on August 12th, there was no doubt this was indeed what it was (page 107). The Mandelbrot Set, a bulbous cardioid pattern, named after its discoverer Benoit Mandelbrot, was developed when computer programmers began to experiment with "frac-tals," complex reiterative mathematical sequences. At the center of the resulting swirling patterns appears the Man-delbrot Set, an area of calm which acts like a Moebius strip; when endlessly magnified one continually returns to the same shape. Fractals are not an invention of computers as such, rather, they are a discovery, showing the way the struc-ture of nature proliferates. Quite what the significance of the Mandelbrot was as an agriglyph was hard to say, but other fractal configurations would arrive as the years progressed. Natural force proponents point to the fractal formations as evidence that nature is simply expressing its inherent form in the fields. The fact that this design was

entirely unambiguous, however, was a step forward.

Skeptics pointed out the fact that this symbol had appeared near Cambridge, where universities had worked on fractal science; indeed, a letter in *New Scientist* had even speculated in 1990 as to whether a Mandelbrot Set would eventually manifest as a crop circle. When it did, and at this location, suspicions were aroused. However, anyone remotely familiar with the phenomenon could state with-out any doubt that one didn't just knock out a work this stunning after a boozy night at the student bar. The lay inside was immaculate, the boundary circles separated from the main body by gorgeously thin standing curtains of stems. (The farmer, in a fit of anger, desecrated it by driv-ing a combine harvester through its center only a day after its appearance, and someone later set fire to the inside....) There was something more going on here and this event seemed to fit a mould which by now had been noted on other occasions—that certain patterns seemed to appear in places where they meant something to the people living in that locale. It was an expression of the synchronicity and interaction that would play an apparent role on many other occasions.[14]

The Men Who Conned the World?

At the end of a summer which had seen the most stagger-ing crop formations ever witnessed, it seemed unlikely that anything could knock them from their new pedestal as one of the new wonders of modern times, but in the first week of September something did exactly that. *Today* newspaper (now defunct) screamed the headline "THE MEN WHO CONNED THE WORLD," announcing that ALL of the crop circles over the last thirteen years had been the work of two retired gentlemen named Doug and Dave, one aged 67, the other 62. For the media and the public, the circular honey-moon was over.

Every night of every summer since 1978, Doug Bower and Dave Chorley claimed they had been out constructing crop circles. Beginning as a giggle to "make people think a UFO had landed" their work, they said, had become a cru-sade to fool and discredit the pompous who believed the circles were something of significance. Using nothing more than ropes and wooden poles, they had managed to create huge and beautiful works of art. The mystery was over.

There was, however, a problem with the Doug and Dave scenario. None of it made any sense.

To anyone with even a basic knowledge, it was blindingly obvious there was no way many of the patterns which had been documented could possibly have been created by the methods they claimed. Their mechanical-flattening techniques could never have left the layered weaves of splendor often found inside. The assertion that a simple piece of wire dangling from a baseball cap acting as a gun-sight was enough to keep their lines accurately aligned was just one of the many ludicrous aspects to their story, especially in the pitch dark most glyphs seemed to appear in. Any sacred geometry which occurred along the way was purely "accidental," of course. Doug and Dave clearly didn't have the mathematical grasp to have achieved it and didn't understand the concept anyway, which was obvious as soon as researchers began to question them. The appalling demonstration formations the duo made for the press and television cameras, in a sensible world, should have stopped their gravy train in its tracks, bearing no relation whatsoever to the sublime quality which had hitherto been seen in the fields.

But the media loved Doug and Dave and inevitably the highest profile cerealogists took the brunt of their uninformed taunts. At last all this worrying talk of aliens, new paradigms of consciousness and the like, could be binned; instead, here was something far more likely—and entertaining—two geriatric eccentrics.

Within just a few days, Doug and Dave's claims had been telegraphed around the world (even to countries which had never previously heard of crop circles) and, to most, an enigma had been solved. The fact that no evidence was available to back up their claims, and many questions remained to be answered, didn't seem to put anyone off. How had they made so many large patterns across such a wide area in one night on some occasions? Who was making the overseas formations? Why didn't the press agency which supposedly issued their story officially exist? What about all the pre-1978 formations? Hadn't their wives objected to them annually going missing every single night from June to August? None of this seemed to matter to the public.

To this day, many believe Doug and Dave were a front for a wider campaign to defuse interest in the crop circles. Rumors abound of a government Cabinet meeting held in 1989 to discuss what to do about this threateningly mysterious phenomenon. No-one knows the outcome, but what better way to distract people's attention from something one can't actually *stop* from happening all around by inventing a discrediting story so bizarre, so moronic—that nearly everybody swallows it, working on the theory that if you tell a big enough lie often enough, it will be believed? The Bratton Castle fiasco of 1990 may have been the first step in a program of debunking which peaked with this escapade. How many circles, if any, Doug and Dave really made is unknown. What was clear was that they had not provided a rational explanation for the majority of breathtaking glyphs which would continue to grace the fields.

Having outed their story to the press, the two alleged authors of the phenomenon claimed they were "retiring," although they would continue to perform their antics in front of cameras and give interviews for at least another year before falling out with each other, reportedly over money. The circles were finished, the casebook closed. Wasn't it?

The world may indeed have been conned, but not, perhaps, in the way most thought.

1992

Business as Usual

Considering Doug and Dave's "retirement" a few months before, how strange it was that in 1992 the crop circles were back for yet another season with all the same qualities seen in preceding years. So who was making them this year?

What *was* missing was the intense media interest, which had dropped like a stone after the announcements of the previous September. Whatever their motives or unseen backers, Doug and Dave had done their work well in diffusing focus from the phenomenon. It was old hat now, nothing more than the work of a couple of wacky old men and no longer worth column inches or TV slots, unless to be cynical. The thousands of tourists who had flocked to Wiltshire in 1990 and 1991 had found other pursuits and were notably absent, leaving just a small core of people out roving the fields, still convinced that something exciting was going on. In a way, perhaps the very fact that hardly anyone was interested and yet *still* the formations were appearing was a useful indication that there was a genuine mystery after all.

Snails and Crescents

The designs of 1992 did seem a little more subdued than the previous year, as if the phenomenon was being marginally sapped by the scaled-down lack of interest, but those who were beginning to note the interactive quality of the circles pointed to this as being a perfectly natural response (which again suggests that human consciousness plays a role in their creation, as indicated by the CSETI experiment below and other work discussed in Chapter 4). In fairness, after the initial shock of the first pictograms, people by now took complex patterns too much for granted and had an unrealistic thirst for miracles which nothing could live up to. In truth, the quality of many of the formations was still exquisite even if there was evidence of a small movement of have-a-go Doug and Dave copycats, some of whose efforts were scrappily obvious.

Alton Barnes, revisited yet again, got a surprise when what appeared to be a gigantic representation of a snail graced the East Field on July 9th (page 108). Although it displayed some gorgeous qualities of lay, some found themselves unable to take it seriously, suspecting human inter-

Inside the "body" of the "snail," Alton Barnes, Wiltshire, July 9, 1992, generally accepted as a genuine formation by most observers who entered it, despite its bizarre configuration (aerial shot: page 108). Photo: Andy Thomas

Croppie legend has it that a would-be "hoaxer," in the wake of Doug and Dave, boasted of how easy it would be to recreate the Alton Barnes snail and popped up the road to Stanton St Bernard to have a go. This was the result, standing in the same relevant part of the design as the photograph of the original. For once, looking at this mess, the evidence supported the hoax story. Photo: Andy Thomas

vention. But why? In a way, it followed on naturally from the insectograms of 1991, which some had thought were snails anyway. Such doubts were typical of the new fear and suspicion which had been sown amongst even some of the remaining researchers in the wake of recent events. The English were forgetting their own heritage though; the snail was once held as a sacred animal by the ancient Britons, and the "dodman," as it was known to them, held deep symbolism. A roughly-laid claimed man-made copy of the snail (for once, believably so—see photos) which arrived at nearby Stanton St Bernard a few days later merely reinforced the impressive quality of the original.

Amongst the many other designs of the year, a shape was then introduced into the circle-making canon which would remain with it ever after; the crescent. This appeared in a variety of guises in this year's pictograms, most notably in what was a close depiction of the astrological sign for Mercury at West Stowell, Wiltshire on August 2nd (page 109). Some crescents tapered to such fine points it was impossible to walk their entire length. For those who had surmised Christian interpretations of formations like the "whales," here were some glyphs which inspired a more Islamic approach.

Music to the Corn Ears

Catching the eye of CCCS Chairman Michael Green, three innocuous-looking lines of irregular grapeshot found in Wiltshire at The Ridgeway, Bishops Cannings and Lockeridge in June immediately suggested notes of music (page 109). Nagged by memories of school hymns, he discovered that the Lockeridge circles persuasively resembled the opening four bars of *Unto Us is Born a Son* (tune: *Piae Cantiones,* 1582; words: G R Woodward). With this and others' connotations, could the crop patterns *really* be heralding the Second Coming, as some believed? Intrigued, Michael commissioned a musician to overlay the three separate grapeshot lines and play them as a single piece on a synthesizer. No further religious revelations were forthcoming, but the slightly discordant, rather melancholy tune was coherent enough to suggest that musical use may well have been the purpose of these circles.

All in the Mind?

On July 24th, certain members of the US-based alien contact group CSETI (Center for the Study of Extra-Terrestrial Intelligence) gathered to conduct a visualization experiment. Usually their work involved flashing lights into the sky in sequences designed to attract UFOs, which they believed could be communicated with in this way. This night, in addition to such methods, they settled into a meditation of sorts and visualized the CSETI logo—three circles in a triangular pattern connected with paths—appearing in the sky and then in a field. As they sat, unseen by them, this very symbol manifested as a formation in wheat at Oliver's Castle, an Iron Age hill-fort near Devizes, Wiltshire. This was just one example of the power of the mind seemingly influencing the creation of crop patterns; others, albeit less planned occurrences, were constantly being recorded, and several more incidences would follow.

On the same night and later the same week, the CSETI team and others were also involved in several apparently major sightings of anomalous lights and flying objects at Alton Barnes,[15] although some later claimed reports were much exaggerated.

Inside the CSETI logo which manifested in the fields at Oliver's Castle, Wiltshire, July 24, 1992, the very night the ET-contact group conducted a meditation visualising its appearance. Photo: Grant Wakefield

The Charm Bracelet

One of the last events of 1992 was also the most complex. On August 16th, in a field adjacent to Silbury Hill, near Avebury, an impressive "wheel" design appeared to give a menu of many preceding motifs all in one (page 108). It became known as "the charm bracelet." Familiar components of various crop glyphs were placed at intervals on a ring, with circles, crescents, cardioids, "claws" and dumbbells all included. A radiating "bow-tie" sat at the center. It seemed to be a summing up of the story so far. Curiously, a gap in the ring suggested a missing element, but this area was superimposed over a water trough with wild grass around it and a mess of downed crop, which looked as though some energy-form had tried to perform there but discharged messily instead. As many dowsers believe the presence of water generates "earth energy," maybe the trough played a role here?

In a scenario that would become familiar in the coming years, Jim Schnabel, a young American with journalistic leanings who had infiltrated the inner echelons of the research community by gaining the trust of individuals (then betrayed to devastating effect on some), claimed to have created this formation, although no evidence was ever presented. In the wake of Doug and Dave, all sorts of people crawled out of the woodwork to claim the hoax crown. Schnabel and a small group of cohorts laid claim to several other designs with equal lack of evidence.

Schnabel *had* been an entrant in a hoaxing competition staged that summer at West Wycombe, Buckinghamshire on the night of July 11–12th by *The Guardian* newspaper and crop circle journal *The Cerealogist* to examine the differences between man-made and "genuine" crop patterns. Most competing patterns (which adhered to a specific design and had to replicate known circle qualities) were made by teams, who spent many hours and used a surprising amount of ingenious but utterly impractical equipment on making a fairly modest-sized variation on a dumbbell. The time spent (see Chapter 4) and the absence of flow and layering convinced many that mass-hoaxing couldn't possibly explain the whole phenomenon, although some of the patterns were superficially neat.

Schnabel was one of the few competition entrants who worked alone. However, when challenged to publicly recreate the Silbury charm bracelet in 1993, his cheeky insis-

tence on not replicating the original design, but instead making an unattractive and rather mechanical-looking play on garden roller and flying saucer silhouettes, simply reinforced to many the unlikelihood of his connection to its inspiration (page 161).

The new post-Doug and Dave attitude of the media was depressingly illustrated by the fact that the circle-making competition was the only cerealogical event widely reported in 1992. *Volte-face* lectures like that described in the introduction to this book and a television program (filmed in 1991) for Channel 4's *Equinox* series hardly helped matters, being heavily biased towards the hoax-hypothesis. The TV company cruelly set up Terence Meaden and Busty Taylor for embarrassment by tricking them into declaring a man-made formation genuine. However, when the circles returned yet again in 1993, recently-diverted eyes began to turn back to the fields when it became clear that fascinating things were still happening out there, even if the research community was increasingly divided on itself....

1993

Suspicious Minds

Given that the mass-media were hardly talking about crop circles at all, let alone hoaxing, it was ironic that by 1993, many in the research community could talk about nothing *but* hoaxing. Because of recent events and the deliberately mischievous behavior of characters like Jim Schnabel in stirring up trouble both in the fields and within investigation groups, issues became severely clouded. The few alleged "hoaxers" enjoyed cultivating an image of being shadowy *agent provocateurs*, spreading largely fictitious, or at least much exaggerated, tales of their exploits, and anonymously mailing defamatory (if entertainingly witty) "news sheets" such as *The Informer*, which would attack prominent personalities in the research community. Fears of being caught out or targeted by these acid renegades led to a sudden reluctance to declare anything genuine. Every formation began to be treated with suspicion by some previously enthusiastic cerealogists who didn't want their pride or reputation hurt, even with no evidence of trickery beyond pub chatter.

By now, *The Barge,* a quaint canal-side pub at Honeystreet, near Alton Barnes, had taken over from the original watering-hole, the *Waggon and Horses* at Beckhampton,

Cheesefoot Head, Hampshire, August 5, 1993. Despite many fine pictograms in 1993, they appeared in a turbulent atmosphere of doubt and suspicion deliberately stirred up by sceptical troublemakers. Photo: Michael Hubbard

to become a central gathering place for circle enthusiasts, complete with a regularly updated bulletin board. An entire subculture sprang up, with "croppies" as they by now referred to themselves, drawn down there for days or even weeks on end, ready to head out to the first new circle of the day. On one hand this was a positive development, forging friendships and bringing like-minded individuals together. However, so addictive did the adrenaline surge of being at the world center of croppiedom become, a number of people began to over-absorb themselves into the seductive atmosphere of the idyllic setting, and actually going out to examine crop circles began to take a back seat. "Bargehead" casualties began to appear and beer and

gossip took over as the prime motivation for spending time there. This provided a perfect and contagious breeding-ground for deadly rumor, which haunts the scene to this day. So easily stirred into hoax-paranoia were some that one *Barge*-based group even took to nocturnally patrolling the fields with searchlights from the "Hoaxbuster" mobile—a Ford Capri fitted out with siren and flashing beacon (ironically, they later became hoax claimants themselves). Those wishing to cast doubt on the genuineness of the phenomenon knew by now that all they had to do was head for Honeystreet and *claim* to have made something—or claim it on someone else's behalf with "inside knowledge." Bar-room prattle would do the rest. No-one actually needed to expend any energy making formations to become a "hoaxer." (Yet, despite this, still the fields were being graced with fantastic designs of skill and imagination.)

From this point onwards, a clear divide began to appear within the cerealogical community. After years of prominence and pedestal treatment, some of the first-generation researchers, in the murk of misinformation and absence of any clear answers to questions posed several years before, were beginning to seem jaded and disillusioned, their stars no longer in the ascendant. The publication of Jim Schnabel's book *Round in Circles*, an amusing but unkind and misleading attack on *"the secret history of the cropwatchers,"* which virtually ignored the phenomenon in favor of portraying these original enthusiasts as a bunch of delusional eccentrics, accentuated their dilemma and closed a chapter. Pat Delgado and Terence Meaden had already retreated almost completely from public life, hurt by Doug and Dave and the *Equinox* program respectively. Several of those remaining were edging towards outright skepticism, confused by their failure to find solutions and dismayed by the new disrespect shown them, bemoaning the loss of a mythical "golden age" of cerealogy when they had the limelight to themselves. Some even began to inform farmers that the formations on their land were "known hoaxes" and that no-one else should be granted access (a despicable practice which occasionally occurs even now). It was as if the old pioneers wished to break their favorite toy so that the fresh breed of researcher, seemingly unsullied by the weight of a past they hadn't personally witnessed, couldn't play with it. Such was the reversal of positions that some believe to this day that certain leading lights were "got at" by unknown authorities and ordered or bribed to debunk what they had formerly enthused over.

But in an act of appropriate balance, saddened by the sight of their one-time mentors being sucked into skepticism and recriminations, newer arrivals to the scene carried the torch of open-minded inquiry onwards, learning a few lessons from the deposal of their predecessors. Besides a vocal minority poisoned by the disaffected pioneers, these newcomers seemed less set on finding a definitive answer to the crop circle mystery, a pursuit which had caused some of the problems of the past. The need to be seen making big steps forward always seemed to cause figureheads to make huge and suspiciously sensational pronouncements, or hint at breakthroughs and shadowy intrigues, which were invariably never followed up, but nonetheless promoted to reassure their audiences they were on the way to wrapping the whole circle conundrum up. Those who continued this approach through the 1990s began to feel isolated as time went on, yet actually stepped it up as a defense mechanism when apprentice minds, who were by now spending more time in the fields than they were, began to question their authority. The next generation of researchers seemed happier to accept the crop formations for the beautiful puzzles they were, collecting data and making measured observations, without the pretense of *really* understanding what was going on. Even so, games of one-upmanship and ego struggles would continue to raise their heads from time to time.[16]

Meanwhile, Back in the Fields ...

The formations themselves, happily, were continuing to do their thing, blissfully detached from whatever trivial distractions may have been consuming the research community.

Some of the major designs were suddenly moved out into the provinces this summer. West Sussex had a huge spate of activity in the Sompting area, a kind of mini-Alton Barnes of the south coast, throwing up two gorgeous Celtic cross designs among others, and the Sussex CCCS investigation team (now Southern Circular Research) became the most prominent research group, conducting several ambitious communication experiments.[17] Meanwhile, up in the East Midlands, another branch of CCCS was also becoming highly active and on July 7th received one of the best pictograms of the year as a reward, a highly elaborate

The first of two perfect Celtic crosses at Sompting, West Sussex, June 23, 1993, which became the "Alton Barnes" of the south coast due to the number of glyphs appearing in the area. Photo: Andrew King

Second of the Sompting 1993 Celtic crosses, June 28, as seen from a nearby track. Photo: Andy Thomas

crucifix of circles, rings and pathways at Charley Knoll, near Loughborough which seemed to bear a resemblance to the Northern Cross star constellation (page 110). Other formations would appear to give more specific astronomical information in 1994. The gifts of advanced designs to these regional teams was another sign of the interactive quality of the phenomenon, which seemed to react accordingly to the amount of activity generated towards it in any given area.

Wiltshire wasn't ignored, however, and just below the white horse carving at Cherhill, what became known as the "hands of friendship" (two variations on dumbbells linked in the middle by interlocking half-rings) was taken by some as an offering of peace from the circlemakers (page 110)! More ominously, depending on one's religious persuasion, an emblem of what looked like a cluster of three sixes — ie. 666 — arrived near West Overton, and several visitors recorded detrimental health effects inside it (page 110). How much of this was simply the power of suggestion was uncertain but, uncannily, the Ordnance Survey map reference for the formation was 130 666.... Just up the hill from this at East Kennett, a simple ring was made rather more ingenious by the fact that it encompassed an entire T-junction of roads, the ring split into three segments in three separate fields. Where it met the grass verge, this too was flattened, although the tarmac seemed untouched. A large configuration nick-named "the spaceship" later materialized in the same field as the ring's main section.

The T-junction ring and adjacent pictogram at East Kennett, Wiltshire, 1993. The ring appeared July 11 and the "spaceship" (as it was dubbed) July 25. The long path between the two was made by visitors. Photo: Andrew King

Lights, Action ...

With reports of substantial anomalous light sightings at Alton Barnes from 1992 still fresh in people's minds, particular emphasis on seeking such phenomena was made this season. The whole area of downs overlooking the Vale of Pewsey drew many waterproofed and wellingtoned adventurers with flashlights, snaking up the road to Adam's Grave from *The Barge* to spend their nights signalling to the sky. In fact, most wound up spending their time ecstatically flashing messages to other lights across the valley, which appeared to flash back, unaware that all they were doing was attracting the attention of identical anoraks with the same intentions. The hills above Alton Barnes became a mass of winking lights and false excitements.

Some genuinely odd sightings were made, however, and peculiar luminosities and objects were seen over Cherhill the night the "hands of friendship" pictogram appeared. And despite the best efforts of active debunkers, who allegedly released a number of glowing balloons to bait the flashlight brigade, unquestionably weird and inexplicable aerial phenomena *were* seen around Alton Barnes.[18]

The Bythorn Mandala

The most staggering event of the year was left until last. In a field still standing at Bythorn, Cambridgeshire, a stunning ten-petalled "mandala" encompassing a pentacle arrived on September 4th (page 111). The most impressive aspect of the design was that it seemed to be a subtle reversal of the usual pattern etched *inward* into standing crop, and instead was a flattened circle with bits left *standing up* to create the effect. Most who witnessed it were suitably amazed and strange tales of mysterious crunching footsteps from invisible entities were recorded by people who meditated inside it one evening....

The mandala did have its detractors, however, in what became one of the less proud episodes in research history. Hoax-paranoia had produced all sorts of odd people claiming to have made formations in 1993, and the Bythorn mandala wasn't spared the rod. Except that in this case a number of CCCS organizers actually believed the story of a 19-year old that he had created the pattern by himself with a piece of rope and a broken camera tripod with only two legs (a bipod?) which had acted as its anchor. From this action, it was alleged, had come this gorgeous design, replete with some excellent examples of sacred geometry—an accidental feature according to its supposed maker. The evidence presented for this was so thin as to be invisible, but CCCS made the mistake of holding a closed meeting where the formation was put "on trial" to decide its status (see also Chapter 4). It turned out to be a watershed, splitting the council irrevocably, where those who had been growing progressively more negative were forced to reveal their new colors, and those who defended the genuineness of the mandala were backed into a position of all or nothing, leaving total polarization between people who had previously been friends or at least colleagues. It said something about the power of the circles that arguments over their origins could have this kind of dramatic effect.

Nevertheless, the excellence of the mandala design and its style of creation pointed the way to the following season which, together with other techniques old and new, would use standing patterns in flattened circles again and deliver some of the most striking imagery yet seen in the fields.

1994

The Circles That Weren't ...

It seems incredible, given the astonishing range of especially huge, fantastic designs, which were proving them false even as they were being written, that several major English newspapers ran stories in 1994 declaring that the crop circle phenomenon was officially over, having closed with Doug and Dave's "confessions" in 1991. And this despite the raised publicity profile of rock singer Reg Presley this year, whose personal interest in UFOs and crop circles was instantly picked up on as newsworthy when one of his old songs became a massive hit for the band *Wet Wet Wet*. This almost wilful ignorance of what was really occurring in the meadows of England and beyond was a perfect illustration of how the media could blinker itself to that which it simply did not wish to see, in the light of the fact that 1994 was the best year yet for the agriglyphs.

The impact of the first pictograms and their subsequent development in 1990 and 1991 had left some observers disappointed with what they saw as the comparatively lackluster efforts of the following two years, even if this was partly an illusion caused by enthusiasts simply getting used too quickly to the new phase of the mystery and having

unrealistic expectations. Exaggerations of the numbers of formations in the early years of the 90s didn't help either. In truth, from 1990 the figure had settled into around two hundred and fifty or so reported events globally each year on average, a statistic which would remain fairly steady throughout the decade. Even so, there was certainly a new zest and ambitious flair to the patterns of 1994.

Early Hints

A taster of the lively energy of the summer to come was hinted at as early as February, when two thin rings appeared in soil and green shoots, one near Silbury Hill and another at West Kennett just opposite the end of the stone avenue at Avebury. It couldn't be coincidence that a major formation, the first of what would become known as the "galaxies," would materialize on this very spot later in the year.

The first true batch of designs arrived in the same area in a field at West Kennett, near The Sanctuary, as early as April, in the glowing yellow canvas of oilseed rape. A celtic cross with an extremely thin, almost invisible ring, a circle and a standing crescent all clustered together in the same field, promising much for the future.

Scorpions and Bubbles

The design which appeared just across the road from Silbury Hill on May 23rd surprised everyone. Although its basic components were largely a Celtic cross and circles, they were laid out in the shape of something very like a scorpion, with a long tail of diminishing roundels. Crescents provided pincers and a sting at either end. Emblems depicting life-forms had been seen before, but this and its 1994 brethren were particularly sophisticated versions of insectograms. In truth, only the first really resembled a scorpion, but the name stuck for the other designs with tails of circles, although it was eventually replaced by the more appropriate "thought bubble" (which characters think with in comic strips). Again, an environmental message was read into the life-form types by some; it was this summer that a controversial experimental pesticide was introduced for testing which used real scorpion venom as a major ingredient, against the advice of certain scientists.... Was the scorpion symbolism in the crops connected?[19]

The very best of the scorpions/thought bubbles was, without a doubt, the vast 400-foot-long pattern which provided such a spectacular sight from the A361 road to

Devizes, at Bishops Cannings, Wiltshire (page 112). It appeared on July 15th, the same night as a similar design at nearby Wilsford, and another at Ipsden, Oxfordshire. Even the most narrow-minded observer driving past this vista couldn't ignore such a sight without feeling slightly impressed. Although some believed it resembled a dragonfly larvae more than a scorpion, it was clearly in the same series as its Silbury predecessor and was stunningly executed, illustrating once again that this phenomenon was NOT a joke, whatever or whoever anyone thought responsible. To turn out such sublime symbolism virtually every night of every summer to this degree showed apparent intent far beyond a simple prank, a huge grasp of mathematical geometry and a deep understanding of multicultural symbology which seemed to strike a chord in just about everyone, appealing to many different people in many different ways.

The farmer thought it a bad joke though—or wanted it to be. Boards were erected around the field with angry missives to the effect that anyone entering to view this product of pure vandalism would be firmly dealt with. This was a ploy which would be used by other circle-plagued farmers

Wilsford, Wiltshire, July 15, 1994. Formations can impress on several scales: 1. aerially; 2. from the roadside where their size is sometimes more appreciable; 3. inside a large component of the pictogram, or 4. at an intimate level— the tiny grapeshot which ended the huge tail of circles was in some ways as impressive as the totality, in that something had gone to the meticulous effort of creating a gorgeous little circle, no more than a foot across, which mostly went unnoticed. A Dutch couple videoed a brilliant arcing light in the large ring when filming it from the road (see Chapter 3). Aerial photo: Michael Hubbard. Internal photos and road shot: Andy Thomas

over the years, although some, as at Alton Barnes, were happy to accommodate visitors, sometimes charging for entrance. By now, a condition known as "circle rage" had been diagnosed in some landowners. The agricultural community was, understandably, becoming very upset at the increasing areas of circle-flattened crop and the subsequent mess caused by visitors. The source of the phenomenon was almost irrelevant; damage was damage and no message from the stars or evidence of an incredible force could make up for lost revenue. The National Farmers' Union decided that the easiest answer to plump for was the hoax hypothesis and announced a reward of several thousand pounds for information leading to the prosecution of the perpetrators. To this day, only one person has ever appeared in the dock (page 85), because *no satisfactory evidence of hoaxing is ever generally produced to justify a prosecution,* despite a number of open claims (and the NFU have quietly forgotten the reward). Which says it all, really.[20]

The "head" of the Bishops Cannings motif had already featured as part of an elaborate insect which arrived at Barbury Castle on July 7th, which, while clearly being another life-form, could also be looked at as orbiting planets or phases of the moon (page 112). Astronomical interpretations were also applied to the non-scorpion thought bubbles, which appeared in several other counties this summer, notably at East Dean, near Chichester, West Sussex and at the aforementioned Ipsden, Oxfordshire (pages 112 and 159). In the weeks they were forming, the fragments of comet Shoemaker-Levy 9 were tumbling into Jupiter's turbulent atmosphere to great media attention. Photographs beamed back by the Hubble space telescope and other probes showed long chains of cometary fragments strung out like a necklace, recalling strongly the tails of circles on the bubble formations. The crescent-moon version at East Dean went one further by strikingly resembling the shape of one of the dark scars left by the impacts on the Jovian surface....

The Galaxies

Continuing the potential astronomical theme were the spiral-armed formations which became known as the "galaxies." Standing tufts, rings and crescents inside a central flattened area strongly suggested some kind of star map. Despite this obvious connotation, it would not be until 1998 that they were positively identified as astronomical

diagrams—with dramatic implications (see page 73).

The first in the series didn't survive long. Appearing at West Kennett on the very spot of the February soil ring, opposite the Avebury stone avenue, this 330-foot formation found itself being cut down on the same day it arrived, July 1st. Conspiracy theories abound; military personnel reportedly turned up and cleared visitors out of the field, moving in with their own equipment and cameras. Whatever they found inside, the conspiracy believers held that it was so important that such information couldn't be

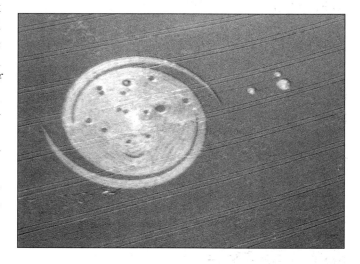

The first of the "galaxy" formations, West Kennett, Wiltshire, July 1, 1994. It wasn't to last very long.... Photo: Michael Hubbard

The first galaxy after its "haircut" by the farmer. Conspiracy or simple visitor-thwarting by the farmer? Photo: Michael Hubbard

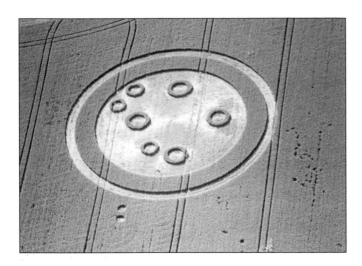

A galaxy of rings at Froxfield, Wiltshire, August 24, 1994.
Photo: Andrew King

allowed to reach the public, and the farmer was ordered to cut the heart of the design out—which he did, eliminating the floor lay with a combine harvester. An equally likely theory for its destruction, however, is that the farmer himself was incensed with the idea that several hundred pairs of eager feet would soon be traipsing into his field to visit this new wonder and decided to remove anything that might be of interest—others would occasionally try the same ploy. Ironically, the gaping hole left in the field actually drew *more* attention than the complete galaxy might have done.

Whatever the reason the first galaxy was removed, it didn't do anyone any good, as a few weeks later, on July 23rd, another, more finely created version popped up to replace it at West Stowell, just a mile from Alton Barnes (page 113). This was an exquisite creation and a joy to behold. Walking inside was like strolling across a gigantic pinball machine, the crop layered and plaited, flowing like water around the standing areas. It was impossible to reach the ends of the spiral-arm crescents, as the paths became too thin to continue along. Other galaxies followed in 1994. There was no way any human could have created these formations with the methods usually claimed and even old hoax-claimants began to speak in reverential tones about a mysterious "A Team" of circle creators which must exist, of which even they knew nothing. Some began to concede that there must be a genuinely paranormal phenomenon at work after all. It was notable that, realizing the tenuous position 1994's incredible glyphs were putting them in, a

few regular hoax-apologists who wrote for various journals now began to speak about the human teams *adding* to an existing mystery instead of actually *being* it, although hardened debunkers would hold fast to the end.

Other Stunners …

There were many unbelievably gorgeous and fascinating designs in 1994. A nest of interlocking crescents at the foot of Oliver's Castle, Wiltshire was as fine an example of the accuracy involved in crop circles as anything, the tips of the standing crescents coming down to the width of *one stem* (page 113). The lay of the inner ring was at one point interrupted by a perfect swirled circle in the middle of an otherwise counterclockwise flow (an effect also noted at the Wilsford thought bubble). Chapter 5 talks more of this formation.

The longest formation ever seen … at the time! Ashbury, Oxfordshire, July 26, 1994. Photo: Michael Hubbard

Froxfield, Wiltshire, August 4, 1994. The apparently simple geometry of this "flower of life" design is deceptive. Each ring that makes up the pattern is of quite a different diameter, yet all interlock perfectly. Photo: Michael Hubbard

Ashbury, Oxfordshire broke all records on July 26th by having the longest pictogram then recorded—almost a quarter of a mile long, a thin design of rings and circles. Around June 21st, Birling Gap, East Sussex produced one of the more controversial events; a duo of ovals, one of which lay in two halves with flat edges of identical length either side of power cables which crossed the field, were distinguished by having been laid from only *halfway up the stems*. Unaesthetically pleasing, but unhoaxable, these were dismissed instead by some as the work of birds, despite the farm manager's denials, long used to real rook damage.[21] At Froxfield on August 4th, a huge "flower of life"-type mandala dropped a hint of the almost-grand finale of 1994 to come. A complex of overlapping rings, its beauty was mocked by some as being nothing more advanced than the most basic of geometry until it was discovered that each ring *was a different diameter from the one next to it* by several feet—yet the design interlocked perfectly to the eye, which was where its true genius lay.

Caught in the Web

The most shockingly beautiful crop design of 1994—and possibly of all so far—materialized quietly over two nights, August 11th and 12th, directly below the northern embank-

ments of the Avebury stone circle (page 114). Beginning as a huge flattened circle, the standing template of a web shape surrounded two inner rings. The following night, the strands of the web were filled in, leaving the most gob-smacking symbol which had ever appeared. Nothing as sophisticated as this had ever been seen and, like the Froxfield flower, its geometry was ingeniously subtle. To create perfect arcs, as seen in the strands of the web, would require the locating of very accurate center points (like placing the needle of a compass on a page, any would-be hoaxer would need to use a stake or someone holding a rope at this stage). The arc points, however, when calculated, moved up *several feet* to create each strand, instead of all having a single anchor-mark. This means the exact position of every point would have to have been worked out *separately* without the creators miscalculating once—and the Avebury web was perfect. To cap it all, the first two arc points were in the standing crop outside of the circle itself—so where was the mess which should have been left by people trying to find their centers, or the trails through the field? The web was a fine example from a number of formations over the years, which require geometrical marker points being placed *outside* the laid area of the pattern itself, in standing unaffected crop, with no visible traces....

Specters Recede

1994 had been a renaissance year for the phenomenon, when the spectre of Doug and Dave and other jokey wannabe hoax-contenders who had haunted the scene so fatally the two years before had finally been consigned to the backburner by a collection of the finest agriglyphs yet witnessed, even if the media wanted to pretend they didn't exist. To many eyes, the veracity and ingenuity of the crop circles themselves had spoken their defense against accusations of being nothing more than the art of pranksters. One glance at the new developments left any observer in no doubt that something important was going on. Those who still adhered to the hoax view would have to change the nature of their explanations for the motivation and ability of the alleged construction teams—and very noticeably did so. Now the claimants would alter their supposed intentions from being there just to catch out the pompous with silly crop patterns, to becoming pompous themselves, portraying their supposed exploits as meaningful attempts to make the world a better place through their enlightened "art." The paranormal phenomena which seemed to surround the circles, like luminosities, strange energies and other bizarre occurrences, were no longer denied by the "hoaxers," but acknowledged as evidence for how important their work was, in that it could actually stir up these type of unexplained effects. Clearly, higher forces were working through them; or so they claimed. This sharp change from being pranksters to saintly channels of other realms left many unconvinced. It simply reaffirmed to some that the role of people physically making crop formations was just a small part of something far stranger, which was coming from *somewhere else.*

An expression of the new feeling of solidarity and belief in an untarnished phenomenon led to the setting up of *Project Sky* throughout 1994, where scattered groups of researchers gathered at their favorite regional sites at synchronized times to meditate and "commune" with whatever was behind the circles. They used the opportunity to give thanks for the finest season to date.

The summer closed with a last cryptic emblem showing what might have been thirteen phases of the moon or a curled up scorpion within a ring (page 114), as if the creature-like symbols which had paraded themselves across the fields of 1994 were going back into hibernation, ready to emerge once more the next year, metamorphosed into whatever their new form would be. ...

1995
Deceptive Spirals

When a formation arrived in young barley at Beckhampton, near Avebury on May 29th (page 115), it seemed to herald yet another year of blockbusters for the Wiltshire region. But in the same way that what appeared to be a configuration of concentric circles was, on closer inspection, an amazing continuous spiral moving out like grooves on a vinyl record, the promise it seemed to hold was not to be fulfilled in this area, but in Hampshire instead.

For the first time, Wiltshire would have fewer circles in 1995 than some other counties. Although its neighbor took most of the plaudits, other counties would also get a fair share, with Sussex having as many formations as the usual ancestral seat, treated to some of its best ever designs and boasting one of the first of the year on May 8th at Southease, East Sussex, a simple double ringer with *half* a grapeshot.

1995 saw Sussex play host to some of its best ever designs, as with this "Catherine wheel" in young barley at Alfriston, East Sussex, May 31. Photo: Michael Hubbard

The Iron Age hill-fort of Cissbury Ring at West Sussex, site of an important communication experiment and *Project Sky* the year before, played host, appropriately, to one of the most impressive ring variations ever seen, a huge series of concentric but off-center loops like a hypnotic tunnel into the Earth (page 115). The subsequent arrival of an elaborate dumbbell, triangle and circle next to it made this one of the largest complexes recorded. A spectacular "Catherine wheel" motif at Alfriston, East Sussex, an intricate pattern nearby next to the famous Long Man of Wilmington chalk carving (page 115), and the appearance of rings and circles at Felbridge, West Sussex (page 152) apparently in direct response to a meditation experiment (see Chapter 4), helped make 1995 a very special year for these counties.[22] It was as if Wiltshire deliberately wound down to allow other areas to shine.

The Quintuplet of Quintuplets

Hampshire shone the brightest, however, with a dazzling array of exquisite glyphs. Yet one that really should have knocked people off their feet virtually passed without comment, as if to illustrate just how far the phenomenon had taken its devotees without them realizing it.

When the quintuplets had first appeared nearly two decades earlier, they had almost gone unnoticed, but once aware, people marvelled at their complexity and waxed

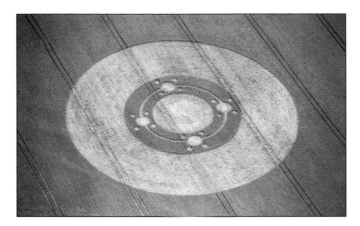

Telegraph Hill, Hampshire, June 12, 1995. Hampshire, like Sussex, had a good year in 1995, but by now people were growing so accepting of the designs that this "quintuplet of quintuplets," an elaborate descendant of its simpler predecessors, barely raised eyebrows. Imagine the shock which would have greeted this just ten years before! Photo: Steve Alexander

lyrical about their potential implications. Yet by the time Telegraph Hill, near the old haunt of Cheesefoot Head, delivered a beautifully swirled quintuplet on June 12th actually *made up* of four quintuplets connected by a ring, surrounded by an even wider ring, it barely registered with some. By now it was just another crop pattern. It was the perfect example of the learning curve the designs had taken us on. That something of this sophistication and beauty could now be seen as nothing more than the latest installment of something expected, taken for granted, demonstrated that most croppie observers had developed a heightened sense of open-mindedness, a willingness to accept the incredible. Imagine the furor had the quintuplet of quintuplets appeared thirty years before! If the formations were indeed building blocks in a communication process designed not to frighten, they had been highly effective. If they were just the outpourings of some natural process, then the leap between the early configurations and something of this order showed that a force of some kind was substantially increasing in momentum by the year. The skeptics believed this sort of evolution showed nothing more than the hoaxers proliferating and improving their craft, yet the *techniques* for laying the crop down remained remarkably consistent with all the effects noted years before. A long time for the same people to keep such a large mystery going.

Out of the Shadow

In the shadow of the previous year's stunners, it was not surprising that some saw this year's efforts as disappointing in comparison, but in reality there were as many masterpieces as ever, mainly in Hampshire. A kind of sequel to the Oliver's Castle crescents of 1994 arrived at East Meon, accompanied by a smattering of grapeshot. A strange but lovely "jellyfish" visited the Devil's Punchbowl at Cheesefoot Head, but was later joined by the harshly mechanical-looking words "LETISS FOR ENGLAND" (meaning Le Tissier) and an ungraceful (but explanatory) footballing stick-man, which made for a useful comparison. What looked like a broken loop of someone's major intestines surrounding concentric rings at Dunley, near Litchfield had its center perfectly aligned with a line of pesticide discoloration in the crop. Composer Andrew Lloyd-Webber even got treated to a formation on his land at Kings Clere, a circle with five standing radiating arms inside, faring better than what the then Prime Minister John Major got treated with near his residence at Chequers, Buckinghamshire—an ejaculating male member (which we'll assume wasn't genuine....) Wiltshire wasn't entirely bereft of pioneering techniques though—the first clear outlines of squares appeared in a motif at Winterbourne Bassett.[23]

The "intestines" at Dunley, near Litchfield, Hampshire, July 6, 1995. Note the line of crop discoloration which crosses the center of the formation. A number of designs have seemingly placed themselves in alignment with such markings, for reasons unknown. Photo: Andrew King

Squares at Winterbourne Bassett, Wiltshire, July 23, 1995. Described by the famous US psychic Darryl Anka, channelling the apparent ET "Bashar," as the most important formation ever to appear—if we can decipher it! Photo: Steve Alexander

Eye Spy

One of the more intriguing events of the year was inevitably the most controversial. A huge and complex "eye" design was discovered on July 7th at Long Marston, near Stratford-on-Avon, Warwickshire and enthralled those who witnessed it (page 66). However, it also turned out to be the adopted logo of a pop band called *Pitchshifter,* who had been playing at a nearby festival that same week. Naturally, this was enough proof of human origins for many. But two things didn't add up; a) all who entered and studied the eye at close quarters were convinced of its genuineness, and b) the members and management of *Pitchshifter* clearly knew nothing about their logo's appearance in the fields. When informed, they actually went to the lengths of placing an advertisement in the music press with a photo of the formation and a telephone number for anyone with information to ring. No-one ever claimed responsibility, not even the usual suspects eager to claim anything. Instead of mystery PR hoaxers, could it be the circle-making forces had thrown up a symbol—as they had done so many times on other occasions—which meant something specific to that location? The discovery of the logo's resemblance to an old Aboriginal symbol threw new intrigue into the fray. Though the doubters would doubt forever, others became convinced this was an example of the interactive and synchronistic quality observed so many times with the crop circles, a view that would be compounded by almost identical events at the same spot two years later....

The Asteroids

If the "galaxies" of 1994 had suggested an astronomical theme, it was certainly continued this season by the dawning of the year's major genre—"asteroid belts," huge loops made up from many grapeshot of different sizes, sometimes with fine rings and circles at the center, resembling orbiting planets. Of the several variations, all in Hampshire, two stood out as the most impressive.

Ninety-nine circles made up one design at Bishops Sutton on June 20th, which strongly hinted at being a diagram of a solar system (page 115). Some speculated that "they," the intelligent forces which might be behind the phenomenon, were showing us their home planet. Others even wondered whether it was a representation of *our* system, but only work conducted in 1998 would decide this (see page 74). The huge formation which appeared at Longwood Warren, near Cheesefoot Head, however, clearly *was.*

The most fantastic pattern of the year appeared to show the orbits of the four inner planets in our celestial neighborhood, surrounded by a beautiful necklace of over sixty touching circles portraying what might be our asteroid belt (page 115). Each orbit was marked by a thin standing ring superimposed by a further small ring to mark each planet, with even the off-center eccentricities of their movements included. The central ring clearly represented the sun. A work of high art and true genius. One thing seemed to be missing though—the Earth. We had an orbit, but not a ring depicting our planet. This worried some. Convinced that the crop circles were warnings of forthcoming apocalypse (see Chapter 5 for thoughts on this), speculation was immediately rife as to the meaning of this spectacular chart. But cooler conclusions quelled fears when astrophysicist Jazz Rasool compared the formation with planetary charts and pointed out that it represented a snapshot of the positions of our inner planets on June 26th, *the day it appeared*—as seen from beneath what is known as the "ecliptic plain," rather than from above, from where diagrams of the solar system are usually depicted. Why Earth wasn't shown was unclear.

What was so important about this date that the circle-making forces chose to highlight it? Jazz believed it might have significance to the arrival of comet Hale-Bopp in our system. Hale-Bopp would come and go in late 1996, early 1997, with a little hysteria, but without mishap, providing a marvellous sight in the night skies. However, the later work of astronomer Jack Sullivan would throw new light on the possible meaning of the Longwood Warren glyph.... (See page 73.)

Early Finish

The circle season unexpectedly came to a halt at the end of July. Normally one could expect almost another month but, with one or two exceptions, extremely hot weather drove the combines out early and the canvas was lost all too quickly. As a result, 1995 was down in numbers of formations, and enthusiasts prematurely found themselves marking time. In the same way Wiltshire had been given a bit of a holiday, many croppies found themselves with August off as well and had to find something to do with themselves instead—like living normal lives.

1996

Redistribution

Given the phenomenon's sudden relocation to other climes in 1995, anyone booking their holidays in Hampshire for this year would have been sorely disappointed when most of the big stuff returned to Wiltshire, leaving Hampshire and Sussex virtually bereft after their boom year. But what arrived back in the old fold challenged 1994 in its breadth and saw the boundaries and parameters of the crop circles leap forward in several ways, taking everything up yet another level.

The first formation of the year hinted at rebirth and the promise of what would follow; Girton, Cambridgeshire received a sprouting bulb motif on May 14th (page 116), to be followed with another on June 12th. The first, in oilseed rape, was more basic, but the second showed a long, flowing shoot preparing to blossom, with tapered ends emanating from an attractive radially-laid circle in green barley. The promise would not go unfulfilled.

DNA

When a strange but impressive serpent-like squiggle appeared at Froxfield, Wiltshire in 1991 (page 106), a number of people noted its resemblance to a diagram of a broken human chromosome, wondering if perhaps the phenomenon was heralding—or procuring—the arrival of some kind of genetic change for humankind.

Five years later, those with this view felt vindicated by the arrival of a 648-foot chain of eighty-nine spiralling circles back in the East Field at Alton Barnes on June 17th (page 117). Emerald barley flowed like water, and each circle—even tiny ones no more than a few feet across—had a standing central tuft. There could surely be no coincidence that it strikingly recalled the double-helix of a human DNA strand (although some felt it also suggested a "sine" soundwave). Was this once again telling us something

Standing center in one of the spiralling grapeshot making up the "DNA" pattern, Alton Barnes, Wiltshire, June 17, 1996. Photo: Andy Thomas

important about the effect the agriglyphs and other factors of world change might be having on our race, including the potential bombshell of our own tampering with genetically-modified crops? Or, bearing in mind the work of W C Levengood and the discoveries he was making about biological changes taking place inside the circle-affected crop, still routinely processed through the food chain, was it beyond the realms of possibility that these effects could be passed on to humans in such a way as to influence genetic development (page 171)?

One of the farmers of the East Field was by now used to being visited by the circles in a big way and had become convinced that there was something more going on here than just a man-made prank. With this in mind, she challenged the would-be "hoaxers" to show how clever they really were by recreating the DNA pattern in a public demonstration directly alongside the original. No-one took up the offer.

Incredibly, this became the first ever crop circle to be featured in the most paranormally-skeptical of journals, *Nature* magazine, intrigued at the appearance of a biological symbol—which says something of this formation's impact.

The Stonehenge Fractal

One of the most significant circle events of all time took place on July 7th in the southerly field adjacent to the A303, the busiest road in Wiltshire, and opposite Stonehenge, the most visited ancient monument in England.

There were many extraordinary things about the shape which appeared there (page 116). It was a fractal known as a "Julia Set," a centipede-like pattern of 151 circles resulting from the same series of reiterative calculations that produces the Mandelbrot Set. 915 feet from top to tail, its spiral sweep was a representation of the "Golden Mean" in sacred geometry. The order in which the size of the circles grew and again diminished followed the "Fibonacci Sequence."[24] When checked on a hunch by Michael Glickman and Patricia Murray, the whole design was found to be aligned with the north and west edges of the field—a line could be drawn from where they met, directly through the centers of the middle circle and two either side in the curl of the spiral. Two further lines could be drawn from the corner to tangent the outermost circles of the fractal, at perfect 36 degree angles. They also discovered that the largest circles were at the highest point of the field, which was very slightly domed, the smaller ones tailing off down the slopes. Clearly, there was no randomness of execution here. And yet, the most amazing aspect to this formation was the time it appeared: between approximately 5:30 P.M. and 6:15 P.M. one *Sunday afternoon*.[25] A forty-five minute period in broad daylight and in full view of traffic flowing east along the A303.

How was this known? A pilot was flying over the ancient stones at about 5:30 P.M. Used to seeing crop circles from the air, he swears there was no formation present. A few minutes earlier, at about 5:15 P.M., a Stonehenge security guard (clearly we need protecting from the stones) walked to the southern part of the complex and looked down into the relevant field. There was nothing unusual there, nor had there been all day. A farm worker also confirmed the absence of any shape there throughout that Sunday. Yet by the time the pilot came by again shortly after 6:00 P.M., the massive fractal had appeared....

Given the lengths of time taken to create the relatively small patterns in the 1992 hoaxing competition, that something this large, with so many extraordinary mathematical qualities, could be created by humans in such a short interval beggared belief. Rough calculations showed that just to have created random circles would have taken whatever number of bodies making around three every minute or less—without allowing for the many *hours* which would be needed to lay them out so accurately. To have performed such an incredible feat in full daylight without being seen would be impossible anyhow. Other daytime manifestations of formations had been reported before, but never so prominently as this.

Even the media picked up on this event, the story making its way onto television and into the press. After such a long hiatus of interest, at last the phenomenon was making its way back into the limelight. The farmer, initially reluctant, was persuaded to open the formation up to visitors—for a couple of quid per head. The party atmosphere subsequently born and the wave of euphoria felt by many of the estimated *ten thousand* sightseers enticed inside by a sign on the A303 ("See Europe's Biggest Crop Circle!") illustrated that for all the media skepticism and indifference, the public, offered the chance to experience the real thing for themselves, could see there was something going on which couldn't be ignored. For many, the circumstances surrounding the arrival of the Julia Set provided the final proof that hoaxers were not the answer to the crop circle mystery.

Not that this stopped two of the usual landscape art-claimants crawling out of the woodwork to declare this glyph their own. They hadn't done their homework though, and geometrical explanations for how they created and positioned the shape would have made it impossible to execute with such methods. The claim that the witnesses were mistaken and it had been made the *night before* and no-one noticed it in such a prominent and well-flown place until teatime the next day was merely the silliest of several slightly perturbed skeptics' desperate attempts to explain this one away.

The Best of the Rest

Of the many beauties of 1996, a few stood out that little bit further. In one of the few non-Wiltshire examples of excellence from this year, Essex was host to a striking flower emblem of seven overlapped circles and rings with three central standing crescents at Littlebury Green (page 116). In the renewed media alertness to the phenomenon, this even managed to make it to the front cover of a free paper given out on trains, *Commuter News,* with the somewhat (or not?) misleading headline "ALIENS LAND!"

The longest formation of all time, approximately 4,100 feet long, Etchilhampton, Wiltshire, July 29, 1996. Photo: Andrew King

Close-up of the "Pegasus" motif accompanying the long pictogram at Etchilhampton. Photo: Andrew King

A "vesica pisces" of two overlapped standing circles at Ashbury, Oxfordshire, drew a few adherents as the best formation of the year, beautiful in its simplicity (page 116). Another fractal, this time caterpillar-like with the individual circles squashed together, accompanied a stunning motif of rings and crescents, both standing and flattened, at Liddington Castle, Wiltshire (page 117). Each had extraordinarily complex lays and swirls.

A record was shattered at Etchilhampton, Wiltshire on July 29th when the longest formation ever recorded (the previous contender being Ashbury 1994) managed to virtually touch both ends of the same vast field, being approximately 4100 feet long.... A long, thin chain of small circles linked with extensive pathways snaked out into the distance. It took around twenty minutes to walk from one end to the other. Alongside these paths and circles was a teardrop shape and a flattened circle with what appeared to be a stylized flying horse contained within a standing triangle at the center. Other records would be broken as the season ended....

With the expansion of the Internet, information from other countries became more easily available and each year seemed to bring further evidence that the circles were occurring on a much wider scale than hitherto suspected, even if England remained the most active focus. Many previously quiet nations began to announce crop formations, and in 1996 the Czech Republic and Holland, as just two examples, reported much increased activity, while America boasted the earliest account of the season on March 9th, with some spindly native-American-looking symbols at Laguna Canyon, California, in scrubland by the side of a highway construction site.

Flaked Out

On August 11th, the arrival of a 300-foot six-armed "snowflake" below the Iron Age hill-fort of Oliver's Castle, Wiltshire, was the prelude to a storm which would rip through the research community. Later that day, a young man turned up at *The Barge* with a video purporting to show the snowflake appearing out of nowhere under a series of glowing white lights, and a controversy was born.

He claimed he had been out looking for circles and UFOs at dawn, gazing out across the fields from the top of the hill, when his attention had been drawn by a strange light. He had begun to film with a hand-held camcorder and as he did so, captured the creation of the pattern as lights soared swiftly in arcs above the surface of the crop. The entire sequence was just eighteen or so seconds long. The snowflake was seen to appear, stems falling smoothly and gracefully into place, within seven....

Taken initially as the first ever video evidence of a formation appearing, it seemed that at last someone had managed to capture what *Operation Blackbird* and all the other similar attempts had failed to do. It was certainly an impressive piece of footage and corroborated other eye-witness reports of circles forming, in terms of speed. The lights were very similar to ones filmed on other occasions (see Chapter 3), and at first there seemed no reason to doubt the video's authenticity....

Just a few weeks later, however, and opinion quickly began to turn sour. With little more justification than paranoia at that point, word began to spread that the sequence was faked, a special effects bonanza designed to catch out and discredit researchers. The fact that the alleged cameraman became reluctant to speak about his experience and vanished shortly afterwards was enough in the eyes of many to condemn the video as an elaborate hoax, together with disputes raised about lighting conditions, wind speeds, and other uncertain aspects. Yet many questions remained as to the odds against a con man being on the scene of the new formation so early in the morning to obtain the raw footage and how he could have created such a sequence so

The Oliver's Castle "snowflake," Wiltshire, August 11, 1996, as seen from a similar viewpoint to that in the controversial video which purports to show it appearing. Photo: Andy Thomas

well and so quickly with only a day in which to tweak it to look as if the snowflake were appearing. Analysis of the sequence by experts turned up inconclusive results, most saying there was no evidence of tampering. But a few vehemently argued otherwise, pointing out discrepancies in the overlaid "fields" which make up video images, despite only having copies to view, not the original footage, which some declared left their findings void. Attempts to replicate the video with personal computers as test comparisons were alarmingly crude.

At the time of writing, despite many loud claims to the contrary and supposed "confession" rumors (the video has generally been dismissed), no satisfactory evidence has come forward to conclusively prove it a hoax, but with the cameraman, allegedly a video effects designer, still remaining elusively enigmatic and the master tape still unavailable, nothing to prove it genuine either.

The fuller story of the Oliver's Castle video and its implications is told in the epilogue to my book *Quest For Contact.* Suffice to say that, like the 1993 Bythorn mandala debacle before it, the controversy polarized researchers' views and forced some participants in the debate, perhaps unhealthily, onto one side of the fence or the other. It outed those growing (inexplicably) more skeptical towards the phenomenon, a disease which seems to strike those frustrated by the lack of answers, highlighted the egos of those who believed only *they* could tell the difference between genuine and hoaxed formations (in view of the skepticism towards the video, later arguments degenerated into questioning the authenticity of the snowflake itself) and forced some supporters of the video to become "defenders of the faith," opening them to accusations of croppie fundamentalism. Only a few managed to keep the middle ground to look at both sides of the arguments and thus became targets of abuse from either camp. Perhaps the arrival of *potential* final proof for the veracity of the phenomenon was a little too much when it came to it, given that the video was dismissed long before there was any serious reason to do so. A proven sequence of a formation appearing out of thin air, it seems, would be too much not only for hardened skeptics, who would then have to revise their cherished beliefs, but also for casual believers in a metaphysical source, for whom unequivocal evidence would suddenly bring the true ramifications of the circles too close to home even for them.

All of which illustrates once again the profound effect the circle phenomenon has on people; a positive one which opens up minds to new questions and alternative insights, but also a dangerous one for those who get too close, crystallizing the lighter and darker sides of human nature just a little *too* revealingly.

Yet, at the end of the day, the video sequence actually raised the profile of the phenomenon further in the media, with several television programs broadcasting the sequence. Some members of the public, unaware of the vicious arguments surrounding it, simply took it at face value as evidence for a genuine phenomenon. If the video *was* a fake contrived to discredit by showing how gullible enthusiasts could be, it failed in its intent on the wider scale and only added to the rich tapestry of mystique around the crop circles. Whatever its status, at the very least it provided a pretty good artistic representation of what it might look like to witness such an event.

The snowflake itself was much hated by the farmer; angry at its desecration of his land, he prematurely drove his combine harvester through the center in a fit of pique. By doing so, he inadvertently created the first formation visitors could drive directly into from a nearby track, as two researchers discovered,[26] saving the long walk from the edge of the field....

Windmills of the Mind

But who really needed video evidence to show something very special was occurring, when patterns like the one which crowned this season were being discovered?

The massive creation found at Windmill Hill, near Avebury, on July 29th (page 118) was many hundred feet across and, in one more record-breaker for the year, contained 194 circles—the most ever found in one design at that time. Glowing aerial phenomena were seen in the area the night it formed. Its configuration was truly awesome. Another fractal, similar to the Stonehenge event, this one, appropriately, resembled a huge windmill, a triple Julia Set with three long arms of diminishing circles. Each had a standing central tuft and the sequence of their floor lay alternated clockwise to counterclockwise throughout.

A perfect equilateral triangle could be drawn by geometrically linking up the mathematical centers (not the tufts) of the three small circles which hugged the middle. Incredibly, moving up through the next three largest and the next three and so on, equilateral triangles could still be created by linking their centers. This process could be continued until reaching the very tips of the elongated arms, where *still* a perfect triangle could be drawn. If just one of the circles in this pattern had been misplaced even slightly, this geometrical harmony would have collapsed. Its execution was faultless, its inspiration divine (literally, to some observers).

A stroll through its endless maze cut to the heart even deeper. Whatever perpetrated such shocking beauty either obeyed some incredible natural law to the letter (nature is fractal, after all) or displayed an extreme mathematical grasp and the gift of instant draughtsmanship (imagine even marking this out with chalk on a car park) way beyond the means of any board and roller crunchers, despite their claims, made even against this marvel.

Approached by enthusiast Rod Bearcloud, a US surveying company stated that to mark out the triple Julia Set to this degree of accuracy would take three to five days, adding two days for "calculation time" and another *three* if working at night.... Their man-hour charge would be around three thousand dollars. This appeared overnight—the same evening as the record-breaking long pictogram at Etchilhampton.

With the Stonehenge daylight appearance, the longest

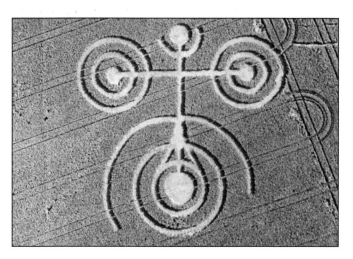

In 1997, Surrey received the most complex pictogram ever seen in the county, at West Clandon, August 2, yet it went unnoticed until this picture was taken and was never explored on the ground to anyone's knowledge. Photo: Michael Hubbard

ever formation, the Oliver's Castle controversy, and now this staggering pattern, there was a sense that things were moving forward, that the stakes had been raised even higher.

Circles Supreme

The fractal formations, and their ancestral predecessors the thought bubbles and asteroids, threw into relief an aspect of the phenomenon's evolution which was becoming apparent—after the rectangles, triangles, claws and other hard-edged pictogram shapes which accompanied circular qualities in the early part of the decade, the circle had been reinstated as the major component of the designs. Now the elaborate shapes were often *made up* of many different-size circles, instead of a specific shape being created wholesale. This thread of development would continue into 1997 but with a few new twists. Circles would continue to dominate, but triangles weren't beaten yet.

1997
Early Alarm Call

In the months when crop circles usually remain a distant dream of summer past and a tantalizing seduction for the season ahead, Cornish enthusiasts found themselves called to arms unexpectedly when, on January 31st, an unusual 37-foot white ring was discovered in grazing land at Sennen Cove, near Land's End. Not only was this the earliest a formation of sorts had ever been discovered, out here on the very tip of England it was probably the westernmost event yet reported on these shores. Rather than laid flat, the grass was pale and shrivelled, yet weeds in amongst it were unaffected. The landowner swore nothing had been placed in the field to make such a mark and the horses which usually occupied the field were reportedly nervous about going back in once the ring had appeared. A week later, another ring appeared, this time *inside* the original....

The Barbury Flower

One of the first conventional patterns of the year was a gorgeous floral design of six petals and a ring which appeared back at Barbury Castle in oilseed rape around April 20th (page 118). It seemed to hold a promise and a prophecy for the rest of the season in that for a spring event its design was remarkably advanced. Usually the phenomenon started simply and built up, but here it had jumped in the deep end, as if in preparation for some early deliveries. The prediction inherent in its geometry was that, like the majority of 1997's major configurations, this was a design contained within a set boundary. Gone were the days of elongated, sprawling pictograms; instead mandala-type approaches would dominate, designs essentially held within a circle.

Work carried out by Barry Reynolds showed that to have correctly placed each outer arc of the flower would have necessitated that the one next to it was *already present*. In other words, the petals must have been created simultaneously, or very extensive and perfectly-placed construction marks would have been crucial. There was no sign of such lines in this case. Interestingly, the outer shape was an exact match for the 1996 Littlebury Green mandala. Then, in the same week the Barbury flower formed, a new design also arrived back at ... Littlebury Green. As ever, the question of whether anything of import could be read into this or not, frustrated accordingly. The new Essex formation, this time a large rape ring with a smaller ring and cleavage-like V-shape superimposed upon it, got landed with the nickname "the cosmic bum," but revelations that in fact the V was the astrological sign for Aries, the small ring appearing to show the current position of the planet Mars in relation to it, restored its credibility.

The Tree of Life

Since the famous Barbury Castle triangle of 1991 which had resembled part of it, observers had been waiting for the arrival of a full "Qabalah" in the fields. On May 4th it finally turned up in oilseed rape at Burderop Down (page 119), not far from the site of its semi-predecessor. The Qabalah, or the "Tree of Life," is an ancient chart of divination, originating from Hebrew wisdom, used by several "occult" sciences as *"a map defining creation and the origins of spirituality"* according to Debbie Pardoe.[27] For this to turn up as a crop glyph was, for some, a most important development due to its significance in various belief systems.

On the other hand, its very familiarity as a known symbol, one of only a few undebatably recognizable patterns over the years, inevitably caused the typical accusations of fakery from those unable to accept that the phenomenon could speak so clearly, pointing to the fact it was aligned to tractor tramlines as evidence. But a number of major pictograms of yore, generally accepted as genuine, had adhered to tramlines, so what did that mean? (See Chapter 1.) One researcher decided he knew better than the phenomenon itself how it should operate and even issued an imaginary diagram of what the Qabalah *would* have looked like had the *real* circlemakers been responsible!

Aesthetically, the Tree of Life was not the most beautiful of agriglyphs, but it was one of the most distinctive. The fact that the swirls of the individual circles which made up the Qabalah turned in the directions one is supposed to follow through the tree, and that two paths slightly kinked were also ones which had specific significance to Tarot readers was enough to convince some of the formation's worthiness.

As if to allow time for the implications of this to sink in, things then took an unexpected rest, with only a couple of lesser designs appearing over the following four weeks....

Home from the Holiday

After a somewhat daunting wait, in which some began to seriously fear the crop patterns had said all they had to say with the first few of the year and retired, the tension was ended with a flood of startling emblems which would then continue unbroken for the season.

On June 1st, an elaborate Chinese puzzle of segmented shapes within what was in effect a ringed triangle arrived in immature barley at Winterbourne Bassett (page 119). Striking in appearance, what gave it its distinctive look was that only the central circle and outer perimeter were conventionally swirled; everything else was mostly laid in straight lines, recalling the quartered Winterbourne Stoke circle of 1989, which had heralded the beginning of a new era. The barley was so young that within just two weeks the motif was almost invisible again, where the stems had simply grown back up.

Just over a week later, on June 9th, a huge snowflake pattern within a hexagon proved that whatever energy had triggered the huge fractal at Stonehenge the year before was not exhausted yet. This beautiful configuration was on almost exactly the same spot, and, although it bore no visual resemblance to its ancestor, amazingly it contained the same inherent geometry. In the way that the fractal centipede followed the Fibonacci Sequence in the arrangement of the spine circles, the 174 (!) grapeshot circles which studded

Stonehenge and the hexagonal "snowflake," Wiltshire, June 9, 1997. Note the similarity of the formation's size to the embankments of the henge itself. Photo: Steve Alexander

the branches of 1997's design also followed the same sequence.[28] The hexagon was another first for the crop circles—only in a man-made communication experiment in 1992 (by two Germans, Joachim Koch and Hans-Jurgen Kyborg) had such a shape ever been used. It would reappear later in the season around a complex of radiating crisscrossed paths at Cley Hill, near Warminster (which began as a single circle and expanded a week later), not far from where Arthur Shuttlewood claimed to have watched a circle forming over two decades before. 1997 seemed to be consolidating the previous summer's mood for moving things forward. Unfortunately, after the carnival atmosphere which had surrounded his field for the Julia Set, the Stonehenge farmer grew hostile this time and forbade public entrance, convinced that lightning couldn't genuinely strike twice in the same place—even though the same field had played host to an insectogram in 1991. Someone should have told him that recurring events on the same spot were a major part of the phenomenon, as other areas across the country had discovered. And was it any accident that after the furor over the "snowflake" formation at Oliver's Castle the year before, 1997 was host to what looked like several … snowflakes?

The hexagon returns at Cley Hill, Wiltshire, July 14, 1997. The rectangular patch of thistles at the bottom of the picture was completely untouched by the flattening process. Note how the lay of the hexagon leaves the radiating paths deliberately uncovered. Photo: Steve Alexander

Hampshire Renaissance

Not all the action was confined to the usual arena. After 1995's rush of activity in Hampshire, it had been virtually deserted in 1996, but saw something of a comeback this season, generally in the traditional area around Winchester where a dozen or so events occurred. Notable among these was the world's chunkiest quintuplet at Headbourne Worthy, site of one of the very earliest types in 1978; nineteen years on, this revisit was a sobering reminder of how far things had come, the components now four large ringed satellites superimposed over the edge of a massive central circle.

In the wake of the previous summer's Oliver's Castle shenanigans, the repercussions of which continued to resonate in 1997, the new-found polarization and subsequent insular judgements of some researchers led to some unfortunate over-confidence in pronouncing verdicts on formations. A ring of twenty-nine circles around a radially-laid circle at Shorley, near Cheriton, which recalled the asteroid belts of 1995, had its reputation tarnished when the same prominent documentor who hadn't liked the Qabalah refused to include the two mottled spokes (which linked the ring to the center) in his drawings, believing them, purely from visual observations, man-made additions. This set a dangerous precedent—if people were to start omitting bits of designs they didn't personally like

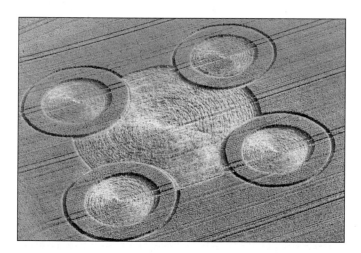

A chunky descendant of the quintuplets, a decade and a half on. Headbourne Worthy, Hampshire, July 7, 1997. Photo: Karen Ryan

from diagrams, where would it end? Entirely blank pictures to show suspected hoaxes? After protests, the Shorley diagram was amended to include the spokes, albeit in a margin note....

Another Hampshire event would suffer its own unfortunate association, when a ring with thirteen inward arcs and two grapeshot, dubbed the "pastry cutter," at West Meon was later visited by the one and now only (Dave Chorley having passed away earlier in the year) Doug Bower, who made a small and scrappy pattern next to it for BBC television's *Country File*. Bower, despite credibility having been somewhat dissolved by all the astonishing formations which had appeared since his "retirement," was still known to pop up on various programs in attempts to reinstate the Doug and Dave myth, and here interviewers tried to catch out researcher Lucy Pringle by seeing if she would declare his handiwork genuine. Luckily, the quality of the hoax spoke for itself and she refused to play along. Six years on from Channel 4's *Equinox* program, some TV journalists still seemed to lack the vision to see that something a little more significant than retired gentlemen's japes was going on in the fields of the world.

Global Expansion

Indeed, tracts of farmland across the globe were increasingly being treated to what England was long used to, and around a third of 1997's total number of formations were found in other countries. Of these, Germany and Holland had perhaps the most impressive efforts (page 119). Two astonishingly ingenious designs, one a labyrinth and the other a sacred maze, came down at the Germanic towns of Bodenhausen and Burghasungen respectively, both glyphs very reminiscent of ancient rock carvings. The Netherlands' best event of the year, at Dreischor, Zeeland, was also its most debatable; recalling the 1996 Windmill Hill fractal, this appeared to be an inverted triple Julia Set, with the largest circles on the *outside* (page 119). Visually attractive, the lay was simplistic though neat. Was this because it was, as claimed, the work of local villagers, who assert they spent several days planning and constructing the design as an experiment to see how good a man-made formation could be, impressing themselves with how hard it was and how long it took? As ever, claims they could prove their authorship because they lodged a copy of the plans with a lawyer *before* constructing it, came to noth-

July 7, 1995 . . . An "eye" formation appears at Long Marston, Warwickshire, which just happens to be the logo of a pop band playing nearby that week. . . . Photo: Jeremy Kay

July 16, 1997. . . Another logo of another pop band appears at the same spot, with an astonishing 3-D quality to it. . . . Elaborate PR hoax or interactive synchronicity? Photo: Steve Alexander

ing because neither evidence, the diagram nor the lawyer were ever publicly produced to anyone's knowledge.

Sneaky Pimps?

On July 16th, on virtually the same spot as the "eye" of 1995, a highly ambitious broken doughnut or "torus" was discovered at Long Marston, Warwickshire. In an identical situation to the eye, this impressively-laid descendant was also the logo of a pop band who had been playing at the Phoenix Festival nearby, this time the, er, *Sneaker Pimps.* Again there was no evidence of hoaxing; indeed, the configuration, laid as if to show perspective, was a highly skilled execution. The construction of the design looked as if a circle had been laid and then smudged in a loop to create a quite breathtakingly three-dimensional effect with an inner eye-shaped "ring," which by coincidence, if such a term could still be used with crop circles, recalled the outline of its predecessor. Once again, perhaps either the circle-making forces were playing mischievous games or the thought patterns of those at the festival had somehow coalesced to create it in ways which experiments had shown possible, as at Oliver's Castle in 1992 and Felbridge, West Sussex, 1995 (see page 152).

Two Sides of a Coin

In another, earlier, potential expression of synchronous interaction, the phenomenon's favorite area was revisited yet again when Alton Priors (adjacent to Alton Barnes) received a 300-foot "torus knot" of its own (page 118) on July 11th, eve of a major croppie gathering at the nearby village hall the next morning. Resembling a ball of string, twelve overlapping rings around a central circle, like the Long Marston event this had a three-dimensional quality to it. The rings were unruly inside, but in such a way as to defy explanation. In most of the rings the crop was swept outward to the sides, and, where paths crossed, whatever had created it had seemingly struggled to maintain coherence, stems falling in all directions and then suddenly correcting themselves in a manner inconsistent with man-made techniques, especially where tractor tramlines intersected. Standing curtains of crop marked the lines as they crossed the central circle—a feature noted before (see Chapter 1).

As if to show another side to the circle-making coin— some lays are rough but complex, others neat but straight-

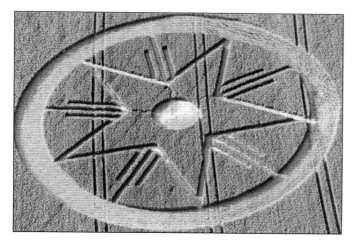

Striking emblem at Bishops Cannings, Wiltshire, July 13, 1997. One of the neatest crop lays of the year. Photo: Karen Ryan

forward—another pattern appeared the same weekend on July 13th, just up the road at Bourton, near Bishops Cannings. This was a five-pointed star within a large ring. "Sunburst" paths emanated around a small central circle. Equally stunning to see, this had been created with quite a different finish from the Alton Priors torus, although one feature remained the same—pronounced standing curtains at a point where the tramlines traversed the ring (page 18). The laid crop in this was one of the neatest examples seen.

The Mayan Countdown?

In the same field at Etchilhampton which hosted the world's longest pictogram in 1996, two of the crispest and most striking emblems of the year arrived on August 1st (page 120). Eyes were most often drawn to the ringed six-petalled motif, a model of geometric perfection, but equally important might have been the separate but adjacent very unusual circle containing a standing rectangle divided into 780 (!) small square boxes, twenty-six along one side, thirty along the other.

Researcher Michael Glickman immediately christened this formation the "Calendar Grid" because, for all the world, it seemed to resemble just that. Taking this idea a little further, he surmised that if one took the side of twenty-six boxes as meaning twenty-six *weeks,* that would give six months—roughly the time period crop circles usually appeared every season. Calculating twenty-six times thirty

Silbury Hill and its fractal companion, Wiltshire, July 23, 1997. Photo: Steve Alexander

would then give fifteen years. Fifteen years from 1997 would take us to … 2012—the date the ancient Mayan calendar comes to an end (in our reckoning) and a time when many expect tumultuous planetary events to occur as one era closes and the great cycle of life begins again.... Much has been written about this date by New Age philosophers. Could this design have been a countdown, an advent calendar to point us to the importance of 2012?

Geoff Stray, 2012 expert, deepened the slightly disturbing connection further when he later realized that the Etchilhampton grid is divisible by exactly three "Tzolkins"—grids of thirteen by twenty squares that form the Mayan sacred calendar. In his influential booklet *Beyond 2012*, Geoff also points out that when the containing square is included to make 781 units, yet another meaning emerges: *"781 is the number of 'bits' in Maurice Cotterell's 187-year sunspot cycle, which Cotterell has related to the Mayan great cycle, ending in 2012. The accompanying six-pointed whirling star would then represent the six rotating magnetic fields of the sun (two polar and four equatorial) that cause the sunspot cycle."*

Given the many times seeming solar symbolism has occurred in the cropfields, particularly in the two years which followed, and the significance of sunspot activity to the rise and fall of civilizations, as highlighted by authors like the aforementioned Cotterell, perhaps some kind of vital direct information was being communicated in these formations? With solar activity seemingly being anticipated by crop circles, as revealed in 1998 by the late discovery of a date prediction from a 1994 formation, and its eventual fulfillment in 2000 (see pages 73 and 80), the Etchilhampton events of 1997 may have been more prophetic and meaningful than many guessed at the time.

2012 connections have since been discovered in other formations. Indeed, the fractal wave which generates a Mandelbrot Set, seen as a formation in 1991, closely correlates with a specific date timeline, measured by global events, which indicates 2012 as the "terminal point" of the wave.... (For a fuller explanation of this, and an excellent summing up of the whole 2012 phenomenon, readers are strongly advised to source Geoff Stray's website at *www.diagnosis2012.co.uk.)* Something to ponder.

Return of the Fractals

The three formations which most caught the public imagination in 1997 were undoubtedly the ones which saw fractal geometry return to the fields—but this time with triangles as their major components instead of circles, although circles would still be an integral part of the designs.

The first of these arrived on July 23rd in a field overlooked by Silbury Hill, the center of so much activity since everything took off. A recognizable configuration known as a "Koch Snowflake," this six-pointed star-like emblem

Ingeniously plaited grapeshot in the Milk Hill "Koch Snowflake," Wiltshire, August 8, 1997. Photo: Andy Thomas

was effectively made up of many increasingly smaller triangles. Where the circle-making forces appeared to feel tiny triangles would become messy at the perimeter, 126 grapeshot circles had been substituted, each with an immaculate lay. Walking inside this huge expanse of flattened crop, it was impossible to see the pattern of the flow. Only the aerial photographs resolved the floor lay into an incredible geometrical spider's web. A group of people on Silbury at dawn for the summer solstice had asked for a formation in this very field. It seems they were rewarded. But the best was yet to come.

On August 8th, one of the most impressive crop glyphs yet to have appeared graced the fields below the white horse chalk carving at Milk Hill, near Alton Barnes (page 120). A column of light was seen coming down from the sky on the night it formed. Almost identical to the Silbury snowflake, this was distinguished by the presence of a central six-armed flower. In all, the fractal contained a record breaking 198 circles—the most yet included in one design. The central grapeshot in particular were stunningly created. It was as if every technique ever seen had deliberately been included in one circle or another. One had been twisted into a sausage-like plait and exquisitely spiralled, another had been wound up into a cone of crop with a hole at the center into which a whole forearm could be lost (page 15). Other imaginative variations peppered the formation.

One of the US surveyor companies contacted by Rod Bearcloud (as with Windmill Hill 1996) was asked to quote the time required to lay out an identical Koch Snowflake in a crop field. Estimated completion time was four to five days, adding two and half more if "calculation time" was to be included, and another *four* if the work was to be carried out at night. The man-hours they charged would cost almost four thousand dollars. 340 separate points of reference would need to be staked out, as the fractal would be impossible to create accurately without them.

One might think, in the face of something as geometrically astonishing and sublime as this that any talk of it and its cousins of the season having been knocked up overnight as a casual piece of landscape art would die in the throats of those who dared speak it. But life went on as ever.… A few days after its appearance, a crew from *Sky TV,* oblivious that someone else had already claimed it anyway, arrived with an old cohort of Jim Schnabel and had

him make a few grapeshot of his own around the perimeter of the Milk Hill snowflake, the inference being that if four or five minor random circles could be conjured up so easily, well, so could the rest of it have been.… No-one was asked to recreate the whole fractal, needless to say. However, the claimants of the Stonehenge '96 Julia Set would go on to attempt something in a similar vein for NBC TV cameras in 1998 with very mixed results and under beneficially unrealistic conditions at that (Chapter 4).

1998
A Wheel of Fire

Aside from a modest eclipse motif in rape (two ringed circles, one smaller one overlapping the other) at Weyhill, Hampshire on April 19th, the first major design of the year came down on May 4th in the field north of the West Kennett Long Barrow, near Silbury Hill, and could be seen clearly from the A4 road (page 121).

It appeared to represent a 130-foot-diameter ring of rope—or a wheel of fire, thirty-three tongues of what might be flames revolving in a seemingly clockwise direction. Many people pointed to its resemblance to the "Beltane Wheel," a Pagan symbol, and thirty-three is considered a numerologically sacred number in what is known as the "Master Sequence."

Following the Etchilhampton "calendar grid" of the previous year, and its possible sun cycle connections, it is interesting to note that this also had Mayan echoes, recalling that civilization's symbol for the sun.…

This was a very rare pattern in that it incorporated no circular components in its design at all, beyond the overall ring effect. Work by Martin Noakes showed that the geometric construction required to create the wheel did, however, involve circular geometry, each "flame" needing either four circles or eight overlapping rings to be marked out *before* final execution, a painstaking sequence that takes many hours to effect accurately on paper alone. A containing or linking ring would be also be needed for correct placement of the overlapped rings, yet none was present either as part of the design or as an underlay.

Despite these meticulous requirements, the formation appeared to have arrived within two and a half hours— an impossible time-frame for such a sophisticated work.

A photographer attempting to capture moon-set and sun-rise was actually present at the Long Barrow the night the wheel was formed. He was there from sunset until midnight, next to an untouched field, and then returned again after 2:30 A.M. He heard and saw nothing while there, yet became aware of the formation's adjacent presence as the light rose. The short period of his absence would not have been enough time for anyone to construct such a design.

Negative Positive

The early months of the 1998 season did produce some rather wonky and unaesthetic designs, which left some dubious as to their origins, but no-one need have worried—the impressive stuff was soon to return.

As a remedy to the less impressive doodlings, some beautiful examples of what one would usually expect soon began to arrive. Two literal negative/positive images of each other appeared simultaneously in Wiltshire at Furze Hill and Clatford on June 22nd. At Furze Hill, four vesica pisces-like overlapping circles in wheat created a central motif of standing petals and a central lozenge-shape, while at Clatford an near-identical effect was created, but with overlapping *rings* in barley creating the petals and lozenge as flattened areas instead of standing.

Meanwhile, at Clanfield on June 19th, a cluster of what looked like different-size bubbles around a double ringed circle began what would be a recurring Hampshire motif, whereby circles are superimposed on a circular perimeter, formed only as rings on the outside, but as full flattened

The first ever seven-fold geometry design. Danebury hill-fort, Hampshire, July 5, 1998. Photo: Frank Laumen

circles on the inside. This type of design would be seen several times in the county over the next three years, culminating in the best example at Bishops Sutton in 2000 (page 85).

At Sixes and Sevens

One number never geometrically played with by the phenomenon until this season was seven, though its coming had been predicted by researcher Michael Glickman, who had been observing the trajectory of the circles' numerical development.

Finally, a seven-fold design graced the fields on July 5th below Danebury hill-fort in Hampshire, a perfectly balanced wide ring with seven curling wave-type shapes around its edge. This was the beginning of a full celebration of seven-fold geometry in 1998 which would raise yet more expectation about future numerical evolution.

On July 9th, back in the East Field at Alton Barnes, now well-used to such innovations, a second seven-fold Hindu-looking mandala was discovered (page 121), waves of multi-directional crop flow creating a beautiful, shimmering jewel of seven shallow petals with many tiny circles dotting its perimeter. With no internal standing features and just two very thin rings visible within the lay itself, at 300 feet across it was the largest single expanse of flattened crop ever found in one formation (more than 6,000 square meters!), a sea of horizontal stems which boggled the mind. It didn't stay pristine for long; high winds and heavy rain soon demolished its crisp edges, reducing it to a rather unpleasant-looking splodge for later visitors.

A third seven-fold was to come, however....

More Eye-Witnesses

Military helicopters were seen flying very low over the field on the night of the East Field mandala's arrival, and some reports speak of the helicopters seemingly chasing small balls of light, something seen before in this area.

As if disappointed that the elements had so efficiently destroyed the beauty of the first Alton Barnes seven-fold effort, a further pattern of such geometry then arrived just south of East Field at Tawsmead Copse, Alton Priors on August 9th (page 121). This employed a chunkier, less rounded but no less impressive perimeter, still with many tiny grapeshot around it (173!), and featured a large central standing component with 14 points, repeating the behavior of the second "Koch Snowflake" fractal of the year before (page 68), which likewise added a central motif absent in its predecessor.

On the night *this* complex offering appeared, two separate parties appear to have actually witnessed its creation beneath further light phenomena activity. Two American women from Vermont, Naisha Ahsian and Lili Ruane, watching the fields from Knap Hill to the north in the very early hours of the morning, saw luminosities spiralling over the field where the formation was found waiting for them the next morning. Meanwhile, four other independent observers, Nikki Saville and her brother, together with two others, were also watching from Adam's Grave, the barrow which overlooks East Field: *"While watching the lights, two people joined us, a couple in their early thirties, from a nearby town. We all watched as three lights split from the first and moved around the field. The moonlight lit up the ground. We could make out a shape appearing in the field."* [29]

All of which is testimony once again to the fact that many crop formations have nothing to do with human artists, but plenty to do with light phenomena.

Revenge of the Pentagrams

The five-pointed star at Bishops Cannings in 1997 (page 67) was the precedent for three major formations to embody inventive variations on pentagrams in 1998. Like the group of three seven-fold mandalas, these also came as a trilogy (genres of formations often seem to come in threes—the "whales" of 1991, the "galaxies" of 1994, the fractals of 1996 and 1997, etc.).

The first to appear, at Beckhampton on June 20th in the same field as the 1995 spiral, was a striking development of the symbolism seen in the Bythorn mandala of 1993 (page 111)—ten petals surrounding a standing pentagram with a central circle, the whole outlined with scalloped edges.

The second in the series, however, went yet further. On July 4th at Dadford in Buckinghamshire, the mother of all pentagram formations was discovered not far from Silverstone motor racing track (page 122). What was most astonishing about this variation was that it was a *double* pentagram, one superimposed upon another, which appeared to be peeping out from "behind," with a ring further "behind" that. Around it, intriguingly, were three small glyphs which appeared to be what some called a Hindu

One in the 1998 pentagram series, Beckhampton, Wiltshire, August 8, 1998. Photo: Frank Laumen

"Ganesha" symbol, an ankh cross and what might be a (T-shaped) flying bird.

Observing previous pentagram formations, Michael Glickman had noticed that in every case one point of the star would point precisely south. At Dadford, the overlapped pentagrams ensured that two points were able to aim precisely south (in the underlying one) *and* north (in the overlaid one).

This overlapping of pentagrams was repeated in a similar way on August 8th, again at Beckhampton, but this time the masked pentagram was larger than the foreground one, its points reaching out to the perimeter of the enclosing flattened area. Behind *that,* in this version, was also a pentagon, which again had been prefigured at Bythorn in 1993.

Once again, the evolution of the designs was being laid out in a very plain—and exciting—manner, taking the symbolism logically onwards, step by step, leading to constant anticipation as to what might follow.

Return of the Creatures

After the very clear "lifeform" designs of 1994, there had been a lull in such symbolism, but it returned overtly this season.

The Lockeridge area gave birth to two such clear examples. One, nicknamed a "dragon," though it resembled more of a larval creature, appeared on July 10th and was a bizarre form of "thought bubble" with grapeshot antennae (on the same spot as the Lockeridge "whale" of 1991). It boasted an impressive floor lay and was unusual in that its largest circle lacked a conventional swirl, but was laid in straight lines from two separate angles. Thin curtains of crop separated the antennae circles, though they were quickly trodden down by visitors.

At Beckhampton (in the same field where the third pentagram of the year would appear), what some saw as a strange scorpion or manta ray-type design turned up on July 21st, comprising a 150-foot motif of overlapping circles, rings and crescents with a long 250-foot tail of fifty-one grapeshot circles, culminating in a lozenge-shaped cluster of further small circles (page 122). Others interpreted it as a fertilized egg beginning its process of initial growth. Once again, military helicopters taking an interest in aerial luminosities were reportedly witnessed on the night of its arrival.

Almost a month on from the other Lockeridge lifeform, on August 7th another very strange "creature" pattern was discovered one field to the east and was clearly a relative of the Beckhampton "manta ray," but this time a squat jellyfish-type affair of overlapping rings, circles and semi-circles with a short triangular tail leading to a cluster of grapeshot (page 122). Some named this "The Queen." Others saw it as a spaceship....

Hoaxing Hi-Jinx

Naturally, the season could not be allowed to pass without the annual outings of human circlemakers, but 1998 seemed particularly busy on the media front. This year, not content with its mini-revival of geriatric hoaxer Doug Bower the season before, the BBC program *Country File* tried again, filming Bower making a quartered circle with the help of the usual circlemaking team now wheeled out each year to perform their duties for the cameras, who also created their own artistic effort. The formation they made (at Milk Hill on July 25/26th), as ever, was initially attractive to the undiscerning eye, but lacked important geometrical subtlety.[30]

The same team also declared a July four-fold mandala at Silbury Hill theirs through *The Guardian* newspaper, which ran two fairly damning articles on the circles, though several researchers disputed the claim. Doubters sharpened their knives further when they went on to create a modest car motif for use in a Mitsubishi advert on the 9th and 10th of August at Alton Barnes. The fact that it took *two days* of sweaty and reportedly ill-tempered hard labor to complete in broad daylight, with no need for time-consuming stealth, said everything about the sheer time and effort needed to

Man-made car created for Mitsubishi advertisement, Alton Barnes, Wiltshire, August 9–10, 1998. This took an astonishing two days to complete in broad daylight.... Photo: Werner Anderhub

create man-made formations, when so many other patterns have arrived in very short periods of time. (Given the high payment made to the human circlemakers by Mitsubishi, and other commercial circle sponsors since, one has to ask why more of these many mysterious hard-working folk who are supposed to be out there don't try to take advantage of such lucrative work...? It's nearly always the same people involved every time. Where are all the others? What philanthropists they must be, so generous to give of their time and sweat and never look for glory or recompense!)

In an ironic twist, local police were called to guard the field with the car design overnight. Despite this, rather amusingly, someone managed to slip under their gaze and added some belching exhaust fumes of their own....

The *Country File* program was screened early in 1999 and was, predictably, a ridiculous hymn to the "life work" of Doug Bower and those "inspired" by him, resurrecting long-deflated myths as fact while inventing some new myths of its own. Needless to say, the alternative view and any facts and figures which might balance this propaganda were virtually ignored.

Astronomical Discoveries

It had been said by many people back in 1994 that the so-named "galaxy formations" (pages 51 and 113) were clearly star maps. Yet it was not until 1998 before anyone took the time to actually translate the positions of what were clearly stars and planets into a definitive interpretation.

When amateur astronomer Jack Sullivan approached Southern Circular Research with his ideas, it was immediately apparent he had hit on something very important, and together we began to investigate further. Using the astronomical computer program *Red Shift 3*, Jack discovered that the West Stowell "galaxy" of 1994 clearly showed a conjunction of the planets Mars, Saturn and Jupiter (the three rings) superimposed over a map of the star constellation Cetus (the small standing tufts). A particular phase of the moon (the small crescent) was also depicted. Comparison to star maps showed that this was an alignment which was indeed due to take place in that part of the sky at midnight GMT on the cusp of April 6–7, 2000![31]

The formation's depiction of this was compacted (to enable it to feature within one circular frame), but irrefutable. To show star positions so accurately as to be able to tell the exact time from them … what precision! It beggared belief that such a work could have been created by a man with a garden roller in one hand and a star chart in another, in pitch darkness.

The importance of this date and the accuracy of the interpretation was solidified when Jack Sullivan looked at the other two "galaxies" of 1994 and found that they depicted the same alignment, but from slightly different zoom perspectives and with different emphasis upon individual elements of the charts. Remembering that the first galaxy was wilfully destroyed by the farmer (which some believe was part of a conspiracy to erase a pattern of great importance—see page 51), something obviously thought it important enough that a second and third attempt had to be made to replace the prototype.

Encouraged by such positive results, Jack went on to look at several other past formations in an astronomical light and discovered other plainly predicted dates within their configurations.

An examination of the planetary positions in the Longwood Warren solar system design from 1995 (with the missing Earth—see pages 56 and 115), when looked at from *above* the ecliptic plain rather than below, as Jazz Rasool had done with his previous reading of the formation, revealed a date of January 16th, 1998 as the next time they

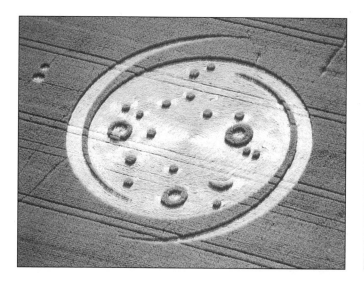

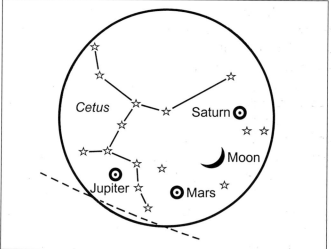

The West Stowell galaxy of 1994, seen with its counterpart star chart showing an alignment of planets in Cetus (shown upside down from the astronomical norm for better comparison with the photo; the dotted line is the ecliptic plain). The formation has compacted some of the features (and there are further stars in the tail of the real Cetus which the design does not include, as they fall outside its boundary), but there is no doubting the correlation. Photo: Steve Alexander.

would fall into these places—just gone by when discovered! At this point, the "missing" Earth had been directly next to Venus, in "inferior conjunction" (closest approach), which at least answered the puzzle of where it ought to be, even if the significance of the date remained a mystery in this case.

Continuing this work, another 1995 "asteroid" glyph which appeared on June 20th at Tichborne, Hampshire, was found to be another unarguable depiction of our inner solar system, showing an alignment of planets due to occur on September 6th, 2003....

So we had a number of predictions, but the most insistent (as shown in three formations) was clearly that of the galaxies. There would be a two-year wait to see what would transpire on the night of April 6/7th, 2000. Would something significant occur in that constellation? Some celestial event, perhaps? Was it the alignment itself or just the date which was important? Was a killer comet coming from that direction? Or was it of more astrological, metaphysical significance? (See page 80 to see what transpired.)

The comet interpretation was a likely contender as far as some were concerned, since an unaesthetic but curious formation which appeared on June 15th, 1998 at Lockeridge appeared to actually depict what might be a comet with a curved tail approaching an orbiting planet....

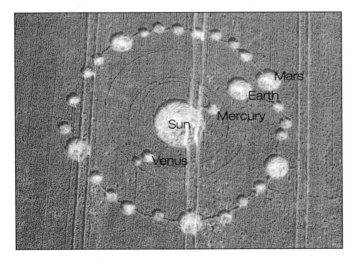

Tichborne, Hampshire, June 20, 1995. It took until 1998 for it to be realized this "asteroid" glyph was another depiction of our inner solar system showing an alignment of planets due to occur on September 6, 2003.... Photo: Andrew King

Certainly, whatever the galaxy formation meant, Jack Sullivan later discovered that the Bishops Sutton "asteroid" design (page 115) of June 20th, 1995 (same night as the Tichborne solar system) appeared to record the trajectory of Comet Bradfield, which came to closest Earth approach just a month later on July 26th, 1995—yet no-one in the astronomical community knew of the existence of Comet Bradfield until *after* it had passed and was picked up in August! Thus, the crop formation had accurately depicted a contemporary celestial event which our scientists were not then themselves aware of.... (Curiously, researcher Wolfgang Schindler later claimed that if the Bishops Sutton formation is superimposed on the Longwood Warren solar system, to scale, elements fall into place so that the position of the missing Earth in the latter is revealed. Was one pattern a puzzle, and the other a key...? If so, the subtlety of this phenomenon is once again shown to be astonishing.)

Dawning Realization

With 1998's discoveries and developments, it suddenly seemed there was far more solid information contained in certain formations than some had perhaps realized. With the recurring play on seven-folds and pentagrams, there was clearly a geometric lesson being laid out for us, but with the discovery of the accurate data and importance contained in what had originally been seen as just vaguely astronomical patterns, it was suddenly clear that we had to start paying much closer attention in future....

1999

Eclipse Predictors?

The first major design of the season to draw the breath of the cerealogical world appeared at Middle Wallop, Hampshire on May 3rd (page 123). A long line of circles and rings ordered into nine major components gave a very strong impression that what was being conveyed were the steps of a total eclipse. The symbolism, together with the brilliant canvas of yellow oilseed rape, seemed to suggest an eclipse of the Sun rather than the Moon. With a very rare total solar eclipse due to cross the south-western part of the British Isles on August 11th this very summer, many saw this pictogram as an acknowledgment of that coming event.

A number of other eclipse-like formations which appeared in the early months of the season seemed to reinforce the view that something felt the impending celestial event was of a significance worth noting in the fields. Another early arrival at Avebury Trusloe on May 23rd seemed to draw on biological symbolism, however; a "fried-egg" lined with squiggly balloon shapes within a 250-foot circle, surrounded by twenty smaller circles, suggested a fertilized human egg to some.

The Menorah

Over the years, a number of religious-looking symbols had provoked speculation about their meaning, but there seemed little doubt that the pattern of eleven circles and curved paths which appeared at Barbury Castle on May 31st (page 123) quite clearly represented, with a few small differences, a very important sacred icon from the Jewish faith; the Menorah. A symbol traditionally said to have been given directly to Moses from God and encapsulated as the holy lamp holder used in Jewish festivals, its importance on numerological, mystical and religious levels is paramount in Judaism and other cultures beyond. The formation didn't go unrecognized—the *Jewish Chronicle* newspaper gave it front page coverage!

The Menorah also has symbolic connections to the Qabalah, or "Tree of Life"—which had also appeared at Barbury Castle as a crop formation in 1997 (page 119).

The use of the number eleven was not without significance. Though it was not eleven-fold geometry in the strictest sense (as hoped for and predicted by Michael Glickman), the deployment of eleven circles was a step towards it, taking the geometrical lesson which had been unfolding over the years yet further on.

Another, smaller, glyph of a pincered and tailed double ringed circle which accompanied the Menorah formation also intrigued. At first thought to be some kind of insectogram or "scarab beetle," Michael Glickman pointed out, as a far more likely solution, its resemblance to composite symbolism representing the tools which traditionally accompany the Menorah; the oil-filled lamp used for kindling it, the wick tongs and the "snuff dish" for burnt wicks....

Blast from the Past

Alton Barnes, by now well-used to the attentions of circle-seekers, produced yet another challenge in 1999, one which

Avebury Trusloe, Wiltshire, May 23, 1999. Biological symbolism or a "fried-egg"? Photo: Andrew King

plainly harked back to a former symbolic era, as if to remind the blasé of just how far the phenomenon had come since the first pictograms arrived to shock the world barely a decade before.

On June 12th, a hugely long chain of older pictogram shapes linked together and spanning over 1000 feet arrived in the East Field (page 122), with an accompanying 350-foot long serpent-like design a few hundred feet away. Like a summing up of the late 1980s and early 1990s, everything was there—rectangular boxes, keys and claws, insectogram ladders and antennae, plain circles, celtic crosses and more, all excellently executed in beautifully flowing barley, with the tramlines as its spine in the old-fashioned style. (For good measure, a more contemporary "Ganesha" emblem was thrown in too, as seen most notably at Dadford the year before.)

Like condensed chapters from earlier times, these amalgamated glyphs forced the circular community to appreciate just how quickly the extraordinary developments of design had occurred in the early years of the 90s—and of the vast symbolic distance traversed since.

Most amazingly, the night these two formations appeared, the fields were being watched by a group of researchers on the overlooking downs. Seeing nothing, all but one left at 2:30 A.M., while a sole individual stayed, but fell asleep. No sounds disturbed the sleeper. Yet the duo of massive formations were discovered by the farmer at first light, around 4:00 A.M.—allowing just an hour and a half in

Three-dimensional cube at Allington Down, Wiltshire, June 23, 1999. This is also a Tibetan meditation and healing symbol known as "The Antahkarana." Photo: Frank Laumen

West Overton, Wiltshire, June 23, 1999. The most overt use of hexagons yet seen in a formation. Photo: Werner Anderhub

which these formations could have been created; an impossible time-frame for people given the many hours man-made demonstrations have shown are necessary for human construction. Yet another example, if one were needed, of crop glyphs appearing under time and circumstances which rule out mundane skulduggery.

A Year of Invention

As if happy that we had been satisfactorily reminded of the phenomenon's ancestry, the crop circles moved on to new themes, creating some of the most beautiful and unusual designs yet seen.

An Egyptian theme seemed to be suggested by a winged disk emblem which appeared below Silbury Hill on June 19th, while what might have been a three-dimensional cube at Allington Down on June 23rd actually turned out to be a mirror-image of a Tibetan meditation and healing symbol known as "The Antahkarana."[32]

The following night, June 24th, an intricate lattice of ten hexagons connected with very thin paths and clusters of serrated grapeshot appeared at West Overton, calling to mind a crystalline molecular structure. This remains the most overt use of hexagons (introduced only in 1997) yet seen. If folded up into a three-dimensional object, the design produces an octahedron.

Hampshire had a slew of neat floral-style mandalas throughout the summer, nearly all marked with two small standing "blobs" contained somewhere within each design—a Hampshire "signature" seen in years since. Meanwhile, Kent had a number of very sophisticated crop glyphs, worthy of more central areas' activity.

Another record was broken on July 16th at Windmill Hill, when a further formation in the standing-square-within-a-flattened circle series produced the most circles yet seen in a single formation—288 grapeshot arranged around the edge of the square in double and triple rows, creating a four-cornered cross.... Two weeks later, on August 4th, its counterpart (both were effectively fractals based on diminishing squares) appeared at West Kennett next to the long barrow, without the surrounding circle and this time inverted, the cross composed as standing areas in *flattened* crop with an outer fringe of 156 grapeshot.

Silbury Hill was awarded a rather sharp-looking four-fold fractal with jagged edges on July 24th, while on July 29th Avebury received a unique design of a triangle of thirty-three standing circles, with grooves cut at strategic angles to create the impression of six three-dimensional cubes leaping out from them when seen from above. While this astounded many researchers, others thought it rather rough in construction, causing much confusion (still unresolved) when the usual suspects came forward to claim they had made it for the *Daily Mail,* though the evidence for this was far from clear.

The gorgeous fourteen-pointed star which appeared at Roundway on July 31st, however, was widely acclaimed as the most beautiful, if not the most complex, of the year's designs (page 123). The total area of flattened crop covered more than 6,000 square meters! Resembling the splash made by a drop of water, seven 72-foot circles on protruding tapered paths were interspersed with seven 32-foot smaller examples. A continuous clockwise path swept around the entire perimeter, creating the circles, continuing back along the shafts, up again and into the next circle, and so on. Some of the best center swirls yet seen were found here and the middle of the whole pattern was marked by a low 7-foot-diameter ring of crop built-up within the actual floor lay. From the air, the vision created was very striking.

Four Mandalas

Four Wiltshire-based circular mandalas stood out in particular as prime perfect works of the phenomenon in 1999:

A nine-pointed star of angled triangles with a central swirl of crescents (and a nearby "Ganesha" symbol) at Cherhill on July 18th (page 123) was so precisely and crisply formed that it was as though a huge stamp had impressed itself on the ground. The lay was meticulous and the clear execution of the whole design staggering.

Next day, July 19th, as if the phenomenon was still not content with such perfection, the stone quoit of Devil's Den, near Avebury Down, received a temporary companion in the shape of quite the most elaborate mandala ever to have appeared. Furthering the new use of the number eleven through a repeated sequence when counting the lines of circles across its diameter, this busy (almost over-busy!) amalgamation of a six-pointed star superimposed on a hexagon, with a central design of rings and many circles, left observers breathless at its ambition. However, it was soon damaged by a selfish photographer in a helicopter which came down so (illegally) low that the downdraft actually flattened some areas of the pattern. The crudity

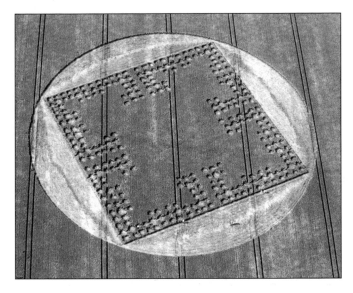

July 16, 1999 ... An emblem of 288 grapeshot appears at Windmill Hill, Avebury, Wiltshire.... Photo: Frank Laumen

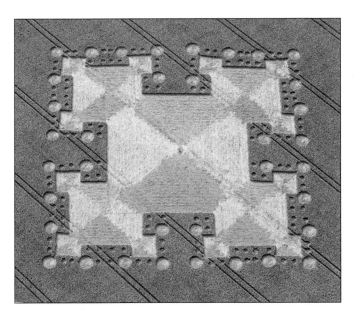

August 4, 1999 ... A reversed counterpart of the Windmill Hill formation appears at West Kennett, Wiltshire, without the surrounding circle and with the pattern inverted! Photo: Frank Laumen

of the mess it left put paid, incidentally, to any theories that simple circles might be made by helicopters!

On July 21st, Liddington Castle received a complex and unusual three-fold pattern which had a look of a designer-garden with low hedges and rectangular walkways, while on July 28th a staggeringly beautiful emblem arrived at Beckhampton, which appeared to show a single ribbon folded six times over on itself in a ring, giving the striking illusion of three-dimensionality (page 124).

With such formations, it was becoming clear the phenomenon was reaching to new heights hitherto undreamt of....

Seeing the Light ...

With each year producing yet more sightings of balls of light and other luminosities connected with crop formations, 1999 was no exception.

On July 4th, a group of researchers were gathered for a night watch above the chalk horse of Rockley Down, Wiltshire, overlooking Hackpen Hill. Shortly after midnight, a sprinkling of small lights were spotted over the field below, followed soon after by what looked like a shaft of light, or searchlight beam, scouring the field. Then all was dark again. The farmer has suggested the searchlight may have been from fox hunters, sanctioned to be in the

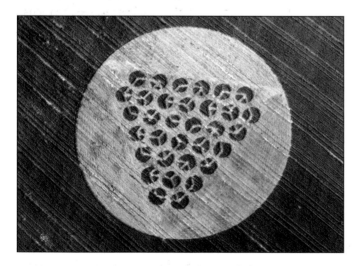

Avebury, Wiltshire, July 29, 1999. A clever optical illusion of cubes, controversially claimed as man-made for a UK newspaper, but disputed by some. Photo: Frank Laumen

area that night, but the other lights remain a mystery. No field intruders were found by the hunters. Next morning, in the area where the lights were seen, an astonishingly sophisticated crop design (page 123) was waiting....

A perfectly-formed triple-armed spiral of thin paths and a central area (which defies textual description) gave the impression of a twirling galaxy or whirlpool. From the inside, as with many designs, it was impossible to guess the exact nature of the pattern, which required very subtle geometrical construction and unusual curves, as circle diagram-makers discovered when they attempted to reproduce it on paper!

With the imminent important eclipse drawing nearer, some saw a curious resemblance of this formation to "saros-cycle" diagrams showing the paths drawn across the Earth's surface by the Moon's shadow during a total solar eclipse. (Curiously, the spiral curves were also of the same type used within some ancient stone circles, as discovered by Gerald Hawkins.)

More sightings of aerial phenomena accompanied the surveillance of a very crisp emblem of three interlocked crescents within a thin standing ring, which was discovered at Barbury Castle on July 23rd. As Donald Fletcher, a visitor from London, filmed the formation from the top of the Barbury downs, he spotted a large glowing sphere, around a foot across, travelling towards the flattened area. As it came across the formation, the light dipped into it briefly before taking off across the fields, accelerating at an alarmingly impressive rate, much as the light in Steve Alexander's famous sighting behaves (page 131).

On the same day, US researcher Patricia Murray was also filming the formation from a similar spot on the downs. Leaving the video camera running on a tripod for a few minutes, she was amazed to see, on later viewing of the footage, that she had captured the passing of *many* balls of light over the formation (some seeming to rise from the floor lay), identical to Donald Fletcher's.... They were also present in still photographs she took that day. (See video images on page 130).

Basket Case

On the morning of August 6th, researchers Werner Anderhub and Andreas Müller were out exploring early at 6:15 A.M., when they spotted quite the most wonderful and unexpected creation at Bishops Cannings—a seven-armed star of radiating standing rings against a bed of flattened crop (page 124). What distinguished this pattern above all others was that the laid crop between the arms had gone down in a series of overlapping rectangular swathes, giving the impression of a basket-weave or checker board. The striking effect was an unusual twist on the usual methods of floor lay. At the exact center stood a standing tuft of seven stalks for a seven-fold design. Within the rings of the arms themselves, superb sculptured swirls offered an artistic counterpoint to the checkered lay. Despite a slight geometrical error in the spacing of the arms, there was no doubt this was one of the most unusual formations to date. The two ground researchers managed to survey the formation in quite some detail and, shortly after, Ulrich Kox was flying on early reconnaissance and took photos and videos of the new arrival as he spun above it. It was lucky he did.

Barely three hours after its discovery, outraged at this latest affront from what he saw as nothing more than creative vandalism, the farmer took a combine harvester and cut a path through his field to the basket-weave. Once there, he proceeded to destroy the formation forthwith, in anger or exasperation at the thought of the visitors it might generate. And so this rarity of cerealogical occurrences was lost in a single morning. Such a lay has not been repeated

Highly elaborate mandala at Devil's Den, Avebury Down, Wiltshire, July 19, 1999. This was later damaged by turbulence from a descending helicopter. Photo: Frank Laumen

in as accomplished a manner since. Though its untimely destruction has perhaps given the formation an exaggerated mythical quality it might not otherwise have had (some Internet obituaries about its loss to humanity were slightly over the top), it remained a strong topic of conversation among researchers for some time to come—and the unspoken battle between cerealogists, keen to see the focus of their interests preserved for longer, and the agricultural community, eager to dissuade such fascination, intensified accordingly.

The Season Eclipsed

Just when it seemed the 1999 season was going to reach a peak of hitherto unseen proportions, it was interesting to note that from the total solar eclipse of August 11th, seemingly depicted in the early symbolism of the year, things unexpectedly quieted down. The eclipse passed with massive media coverage, but without apocalyptic events. Yet the formations which appeared around the country in the weeks after seemed restrained and less numerous, though plenty of fields remained standing. Some speculated that the earth energy grid had been somehow subdued by the celestial process, leaving a slight sense of anticlimax, though, in truth, few could really complain after such a summer of inventiveness.

Beautiful motif of interlocked crescents at Barbury Castle, Wiltshire, July 23, 1999. Two separate videos were taken of light phenomena within this formation (see images on page 130). Photo: Frank Laumen

Just one last big glyph came, on September 1st at Avebury, an eight-armed star with an exquisite double radial burst in the central circle and a number of remarkable swirls elsewhere. The Greek symbol for Pi lay nearby, leaving a curious mathematical note hanging at the end of a season—and of a decade—of wonders no-one could have dreamt of just ten years before.

2000
A New Decade

In 1990, that new decade had been marked by the crop circle mystery bursting into the international media with a flurry of then utterly extraordinary patterns etched into the fields.

As the century entered its (true) last year, and another decade began, expectations were high that the phenomenon would take another quantum leap into something new. It didn't quite happen like that, but the continuing progress of its serene upward curve ensured that the marvels of the 2000 crop circle season were no disappointment. First of all, however, there was a prediction to be dealt with....

The Galaxy Legacy...?

In 1998, astronomer Jack Sullivan had discovered that the three 1994 "galaxy" crop formations resembled star patterns showing a very specific conjunction of planets—Mars, Saturn, Jupiter and the Moon—which would occur in the constellation Cetus at midnight GMT on April 6–7, 2000. Speculation had been rife as to what would occur on that date, if anything. Finally, the night arrived....

The planetary conjunction itself was considered remarkable enough to make it into the newspapers (which had no knowledge or interest in the galaxy formations). One even carried a story that some believed an unexpected (and, to some, suspicious) computer crash on the English stock markets on April 6th—the first day of the UK's new "tax year"—might have been caused by an unusual energy configuration generated by the astronomical alignment. Others simply ran stories about the visual beauty of the conjunction, which would not be repeated for over three thousand years.

On April 6–7th, 2000, one of the largest solar storms in a century erupted on the Sun, flooding the Earth's ionosphere with particles and creating the widest sighting of the aurora borealis across the UK and other parts of Europe for many years, usually being restricted to more northern regions (hence its more common name of "northern lights"). I was lucky enough to witness this effect as a strange shifting curtain of red light above Alton Barnes.

The solar storm, caused by an enormous flare thrown out by the Sun as it approached its eleven-year peak of sunspot activity, had been measured by some observatories as a G4 event on a scale of 1 to 5—very big, threatening satellite communications and other electronic systems.

So many questions arose.... Was this what the galaxy formations were alerting us to...? Was the storm more significant than we knew, especially given the work of "alternative" scientists like Maurice Cotterell on establishing the link between evolution, the rise and fall of civilizations, solar radiation and sun cycles? (See also thoughts on the Etchilhampton "grid" and 2012 predictions, page 68.) Was this current peak of the solar cycle (a peak in both the short-term and the long-term cycles) having a greater effect on our genes than we knew? Were we flooded this night with something of great value to our growth as a species? Was this, as some believed, a crucial moment in

Bishops Cannings, Wiltshire, June 18, 2000. What at first appears to be a "Chinese puzzle" is, in fact, three pentagrams seen in perspective. Photo: Andreas Müller

our evolution, signified by the galaxy formations six year's previously? And if so, disturbingly, how did the circle-making forces *know* such an event would occur on this date?

The Sun, or symbols that certainly look something like it, has featured regularly as a recurring crop circle motif in recent years. Though we could never be truly sure whether the date inherent in the galaxy predictions coinciding with such a massive solar event was mere chance, many people felt that in the those formations, something, somewhere, was trying to signify something of importance....

Playing Tricks with the Eyes

Perhaps surprisingly, given the anticipation caused by the aurora events and the general expectation of the numerical significance of the year, things took a while to get going. Just a handful of formations graced the fields between April and June, but of these, on May 20th, Alton Barnes yielded up a sign of things to come with a pentagonal design containing an elongated star which played 3-D tricks with the eyes. The era of optical illusion crop formations had dawned and would be followed up with some truly mesmerizing patterns later in the summer. A checker-board grid of standing rectangles within a circle at Windmill Hill on June 18th (page 125) gave the startling effect of producing a near-spherical effect to the eye, while a "Chinese puzzle" emblem at Bishops Cannings which arrived on the same night perplexed at first, but on longer inspection resolved itself into three pentagrams seen in perspective, clinging to the surface of another sphere.

The Hole Story

The Kennett/Silbury Hill area, long one of the centers for cerealogical activity, was very much the major hotbed of circular activity this year, with what seemed like every other field in a square mile being visited by a formation. Some say there was a reason for this....

On May 29th, visitors to the ancient and mysterious Silbury Hill itself were surprised to find a large gaping hole in the center of the mound's summit, marking the entrance to a yawning cylindrical shaft some 33 feet deep. Though this unexpected opening up was almost certainly due, in part at least, to the shoddy workmanship of treasure-hunting exca-

Beckhampton, Wiltshire, June 11, 2000. Reports claim these formations appeared within an hour and a half in early daylight. Photo: David Russell

vators from 1776 who didn't fill in their diggings properly and simply plugged the top, many felt potent forces were released when the plug finally collapsed inward. Strange lights were seen over the Hill by several witnesses in the weeks preceding the hole's arrival. Whatever the real circumstances behind the subsidence, however mundane, those who believe Silbury to be an accumulator of "earth energy" hold that its unexpected opening must have led to a significant release of the focused natural power that fires up this sacred landscape, spawning, perhaps, the rash of crop formations in such a concentrated area.[33]

Hotspot Highlights

Of the cerealogical creations which appeared in the Silbury square mile, one of the first arrived next to the West Kennett longbarrow on June 2nd. Initially unspectacular, with a very messy lay, the triangular outline which appeared there, ringed with twelve flattened smaller triangles, suddenly surprised everyone on June 3rd by transforming itself overnight (page 126) into a quite exquisite emblem of standing and flattened areas, the formerly haphazard lay

The demise of the astonishing "magnetic fields" formation at Avebury Trusloe, Wiltshire, July 22, 2000. Photo: Ulrich Kox

miraculously combed into good order! Though some formations had been known to develop additions on occasion, this stands as one of the most extreme examples of a complete remodeling. Golden lights were again seen hovering over Silbury the night the first stage of the design appeared.

On June 11th, two striking images appeared west of Silbury behind the *Waggon & Horses* at Beckhampton, one a 230-foot eight-pointed star with four thin rings and gorgeous splayed radial lay centers, the other a 150-foot ring surrounding a hexagon, triangle and inner circle. The farmer drove past the field at first light around 3:30 A.M. and has stated there was nothing in the field. The formations were spotted about 5:00 A.M., suggesting they may have appeared within an hour and a half, fully visible in daylight from the A4 road....

Of all the patterns which appeared in the hotspot, the most shattering, if not the most attractive, was another grid, not unlike the 1997 Etchilhampton "calendar," but this time comprising an astonishing 1600 rectangular components, like a circuit board (page 124). It was discovered at East Kennett on July 2nd. With quadranted merging sections of standing squares becoming flattened squares, the geometrical logic of how one would go about laying out such a pattern so accurately in a dark field gave headaches to even the best architects and geometers. On the ground, one could not make head nor tail of how the design worked, especially as crop flowed around each *individual* component of the grid without resorting to criss-crossing lines for its construction. A much cruder heart pattern which appeared alongside it later in the season, though liked by some and a more conventional design, was widely considered (and claimed) to have been made for a wedding ceremony. Whatever its source, it seemed crass and unsophisticated next to such a subtle and complex puzzle.

The Ultimate Celtic Cross

If the chunky quintuplet of 1997 (page 65) had seemed the ultimate development of this design genre, the formation which arrived at Everleigh Ashes on July 19th took the related Celtic cross theme on to an unforeseen further development.

In 1989, the cerealogical world had got a tiny taste of the developments which would rock it to its young foundations the following year when the last formation of that season, at Winterbourne Stoke, was found to be a circle split into four quarters of linear crop lay instead of a conventional swirl (page 36). The Everleigh Ashes formation of 2000 (page 125) saw *four* such quartered circles aligned as a Celtic cross orbiting a round barrow, which had been used as the central component of the pattern, a more direct interaction with sacred sites than had ever been seen before! On the antique mound itself, the grass and nettles had been swirled to complete the effect. An amazing sign of just how things had moved on in one decade.

Magnetic Fields

Some other things had also moved on in recent years.... The very public pronouncement of veteran circle researcher Colin Andrews that he now believed 80% of the current formations were man-made and that the rest were caused by natural magnetism achieved much publicity for the phenomenon, but was met with cynicism and indifference by some skeptics and non-skeptics alike, albeit for different reasons. With no official data produced for scrutiny at that point, this assertion remained simply a personal belief on the part of Andrews. The notion that such a large proportion of glyphs were man-made was severely challenged by several noted researchers; and if it were only the recent years' formations which were made up of 80% hoaxes, why hadn't their numbers gone up accordingly? What, in that view, had happened to the real phenomenon? Why were there almost none of the "simple" kind of patterns—alleged to be the genuine "natural" ones—still appearing...?

Indeed, many formations themselves continued to challenge the idea that humans could create such complexity and beauty in conditions of darkness. The most shocking masterpiece of the year was certainly the breathtakingly fantastic design which arrived at Avebury Trusloe on July 22nd (page 126). A 240-foot staggering series of standing and flattened diamonds splayed outward in a containing circle gave the impression—perhaps ironically, given the Andrews pronouncement—of particles held in magnetic fields. Though the basic geometry behind the design was more straightforward than it seemed at first glance (effectively a series of twenty-nine intersecting lines creating an interference pattern, not unlike what is known as a "Moire" pattern), the predictable inferences made in *The Mail on Sunday* newspaper that it had been man-made were revealed as yet another unworthy and false distraction by a simple glance at the flawed mathematics and sheer naivete displayed in the printed proposed construction method. Even the given dimensions were wrong.[34] The truth was that even seasoned researchers were opened-mouth in awe at the detailed execution of this show-stopper.

But the show didn't stop there, with another astonishing gift formed by similar mathematical principles appearing just a few miles away at Picked Hill on August 13th, a 250-foot "torus knot" of forty-four criss-crossing arcs creating a cluster of 308 chevrons, recalling the center of a sunflower (page 125). For some, this was somehow the most moving and pleasing of the season's efforts.

A Season of Beauties

A stunning array of cerealogical jewels graced the fields in 2000, of which the following are merely highlights....

At Uffington, overlooked by the famous white horse (or dragon) chalk carving on the downs above, a won-

Eleven-fold geometry arrives for the first time in this spoked "turbine" symbol (its center partly laid in the basket-weave effect), Bishops Cannings, Wiltshire, July 25, 2000. Photo: Andreas Müller

Silbury Hill, Wiltshire, July 24, 2000. Note the broken pentagram, its missing petal deliberately set out of place. Photo: Andreas Müller

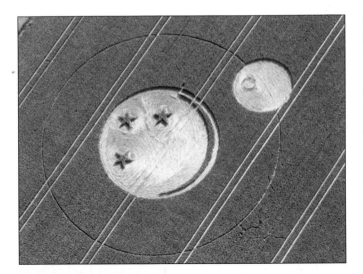

More standing pentagrams in another pattern with seeming astronomical connections, Pewsey, Wiltshire, August 7, 2000. Photo above: Andreas Müller. Internal photo: Frank Laumen

derful "thought bubble" materialized, its head a multi-petalled six-fold flower (page 126). Many considered this the most overtly beautiful of the year's designs.

Eleven-fold geometry, as long anticipated by Michael Glickman, finally turned up properly in an eleven-spoked "turbine" affair at Bishops Cannings, its central circle distinguished by a strip being laid in an echo of the "basket weave" style pioneered by the formation which lay near here for such a short time the year before (one or two others also displayed this effect in 2000).

Opposite Silbury Hill, a very unusual cluster of six

standing pentagrams with "hollow" centers was notable because one of the pentagrams was broken, its missing triangular petal "lying" nearby at a strange angle.

Another quite extraordinary inner lay effect was discovered in a simple ringed circle with a small orbiting standing pentagram at Horton, near Devizes (page 125). Instead of a spiral swirl, there were two centers to the circle; one bare patch splayed the crop out radially, while a perfectly opposite-balanced center gathered that radial burst together again in a tightly bound bundle, like an old-fashioned haystack. The crop was so firmly wound together that it was impossible to separate it. From the air, curiously, the two centers resembled the central part of the Avebury Trusloe "magnetic fields" formation....

More standing pentagrams were found in a clearly-related pattern at Pewsey (below *that* hill's white horse), accompanying a sliver of a standing crescent, all orbited by a very thin ring with a circle superimposed on it. The astronomical feel of this design was accentuated by the fact that an *extremely* thin standing curtain of crop in a small ring within the orbiting circle rather gave the impression, from its position, of representing Jupiter's great "red spot."

Hampshire had more very neat and attractive designs, perhaps best seen in an elaborate "bubble-cluster" at Bishops Sutton, joined a week and a half later by another accompanying design. Kent also continued its rise into more complex territory with a quite exquisite six-fold star at Istead Rise, radiating small circles like a Christmas decoration.

Playing the Triangle

In 1991, it was noted that the distribution of the three "whale" patterns formed a perfect Isosceles triangle (one with two equal sides) across the landscape (see page 27). Ten years later, Michael Glickman realized a similar game was being played again. It became clear, from scrutinizing maps and using global positioning co-ordinates, that several triads of three symbolically-linked siblings with a clear design similarity had been "arranged" in 2000.

Of the four groups of three, the first of these (a trio which each included small pentagrams) formed a triangle with long sides 7.7 miles in length, with an accuracy of 98.77%. Another set (patterns relating to the mathematical value of Pi) formed a triangle with sides of 5.84

Bishops Sutton, Hampshire, July 14 and 30, 2000. The best in a series of Hampshire designs based around half rings and semi-circles, seen here with a companion which arrived two weeks after. (The dark streaks are tree shadows). Photo: Steve Alexander

Istead Rise, Kent, July 29, 2000. One of the county's most elaborate patterns to date, rather like a radiant Christmas decoration. Photo: Andrew King

miles, with an accuracy of 98.1%. A set containing central octagrams formed a triangle of 4.47 miles length, with a 99.2% accuracy, while a fourth set of equilaterals within hexagons managed a triangle length of four miles, with a still-impressive accuracy of 95.4%.

Plainly, there were bigger patterns being formed than just the individual formations themselves. More work may yet reveal other clusters creating important geometric shapes across the countryside.

A Sign of Things to Come ...

On August 13th, a bizarre but compelling design arrived in a field directly opposite the small radio telescope at Chilbolton, Hampshire (page 127). A pattern in the "bubble cluster" genre, it looked rather like some kind of communication dish itself, radiating out—or receiving—bunches of semi-circles and grapeshot. Many at the time remarked that this glyph looked indeed like it had something to say about radiating and receiving, and that its proximity to such a symbol of interstellar watchfulness was surely no accident. Such thoughts would come to a head almost exactly a year later, with two formations in the same field, which would shock the cerealogical and ufological communities....

2001

Doom-mongers Delight

After such a positive summer before it, two things occurred to stunt the enthusiasm of a newly-fired up public in 2001....

There were dire warnings from skeptics about this debut season of the new century. The initial ones came hot on the heels of the first ever, and much publicized, legal prosecution for a man-made crop formation. After years of offered rewards and investigation, the grand total of one man was finally found guilty of making just *one* crop pattern after having made the mistake of faxing a copy of his star-shaped design to a US radio talk show host *before* then making it. When the farmer was informed of this indisputable evidence, he pressed charges and months of investigation resulted in the miscreant being fined the "grand" total of £100 plus £40 costs. Naturally, the skeptics screamed, no-one would *dare* try to create any formations in the wake of this verdict and the result-

The most striking example of the curved triangle designs, Berwick Bassett, Wiltshire, June 9, 2001. Photo: Steve Alexander

Ancient Echoes

The first designs picked up on themes begun in 2000. One recurring motif in Wiltshire was a type of mandala based around triangles with curved edges, with several varied examples appearing, while one formation at Badbury revived the checker-board idea founded the year before, but this time encircled by an "oroborus," a coiled snake eating its tail, which had a flavor of Aztec or Mayan culture, echoes of which had been signified before in the "2012" grid at Etchilhampton in 1997 (pages 67 and 120). Aztec symbolism eventually came big time on June 1st in what for many people was one of the best formations of the year, at Wakerley Woods, Northamptonshire (page 127), a circular segmented complex arrangement of Aztec calendar signs (which in themselves derive from the earlier Mayans). In fact, 2001 saw many ambitious designs in the north of England, though they received far less publicity than those in the usual focus area.

Paranoia's Revenge

Despite these earlier cerealogical offerings, some thought the first thirty or so UK glyphs were slightly lackluster, feeling they didn't match the intense impact and ingenuity of masterpieces from former years. The evolution of the designs was perceived to have faltered slightly, though

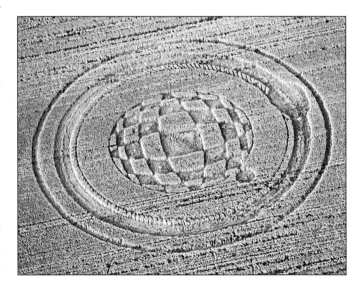

Ancient symbolism returns with the "oroborus," a coiled snake eating its tail, Badbury, Wiltshire, June 17, 2001. Photo: Werner Anderhub

ant national publicity, as the land artists they believed responsible for the entire phenomenon would all stay at home for fear of the law.

More doom-mongering followed when the threat of hefty trespass fines was imposed during the Foot and Mouth disease crisis which afflicted UK livestock over the winter and spring. This, the skeptics cried, would ensure even further that hardly any circles would appear. Even if a few did, no-one would be allowed in.

None of these doomy predictions came to pass, and though the season was later to start than many before it, the first UK formations did actually arrive during the height of the Foot and Mouth outbreak in early May, despite later media claims to the contrary (indeed, a double-ringer in rape appeared directly within a hard-restriction quarantine area on May 11th at Meonstoke, Hampshire). Events had blossomed in full by July, as ever, despite some lingering paranoia and a slight reduction in number. No apologies were forthcoming from the skeptics, naturally. Though access to fields was tighter than before as far as visiting new circles went, the movement restrictions had eased enough by high summer for some farmers to open up their fields without qualms.

not everyone agreed, citing unrealistic expectations on the part of some observers.

But those who believe the phenomenon to be psychically interactive with human expectation pointed out that the seeds of deliberately spread confusion may have stunted the early development of the crop glyphs in 2001. Certainly, for a year begun with such doomy prophecies and low expectations, there was much confusion and hoax paranoia, similar to the feeling which prevailed in 1993— a year which preceded a major renaissance in 1994, lest we forget.

One victim of this grip of doubt was a striking glyph which appeared at Alton Barnes on June 21st, resembling a pyramid with a rayed sun rising above its peak. "Alternative" Egyptologist Adrian Gilbert enthused over its potential symbolism, and observers waiting for the Solstice sunrise from Adam's Grave (the barrow which overlooks East Field) claim it wasn't there when the light first came up, but was when they looked again a little while later. However, the reputation of this formation was damaged by a widely circulated Internet report, describing the lay inside as messy and loudly voicing its view that it was man-made. This unduly negative assessment, made by one person, was soon repeated as gospel throughout the croppie kingdom and the pyramid was dismissed by many without any further consideration—a sad fate for a glyph many felt was attractive and meaningful.

Such paranoia was, of course, boosted with the aforementioned prosecution, one unfortunate upshot of which was that the wide media coverage given to the story brought an unbalanced focus onto the man-made component of the crop circle phenomenon. This was deliberately stirred further by the prosecuted individual by way of a campaign of e-mails, leafleting and further circlemaking.

The creation of several man-made formations for either research purposes or yet more TV shows hardly helped matters. The fact that some high-profile circle researchers were themselves involved in sponsoring some of these projects sat badly with many enthusiasts, and some were critical of their methods, protocols and uncertain motivations, questioning their conclusions. The making of a well-executed direct *copy* of the 1995 Longwood Warren "solar system" for a UK film production (for a fictional love story entitled *A Place To Stay*) further affronted some, though it took—as ever—many hours to construct. To

Alton Barnes, Wiltshire, June 21, 2001. Though the symbolism of this pyramid emblem was acclaimed in some quarters, others oddly found such direct pictorial material hard to take. Photo: Francine Blake

the discerning, the differences were clearly apparent and it lacked the important subtleties which had so distinguished the original.

Hollywood Beckons ...

Despite the subterfuge exercises, there seemed to be a general resurgence of interest in the crop circles from the realm of film and television, with no less than five camera crews from around the world following croppies around in fields, pubs and conferences for video and TV projects, and, in one case, even a cinema documentary by an award-winning filmmaker. This was planned for release in 2002 to coincide with a new dark Hollywood thriller starring screen hunk Mel Gibson as a clergyman dealing with crop circles in America. Whatever its integrity with regard to real-life accuracy (expectations: low!), the eventual arrival of *Signs* (not to mention the aforementioned UK production) would certainly stir up much publicity for the phenomenon as its release date loomed. The summer of 2002, when the fruits of many of the other filmed exercises could be presumed to appear, was expected to be a high-point for awareness of the phenomenon, with both the research community—and the skeptics—poised to capitalize on this.

The Patterns Which Didn't Exist ...

Even by August, some media reports were still stating that hardly any crop formations had appeared in 2001 because of the Foot and Mouth restrictions, reported in a sniggering, scornful tone. The fact that this was utter nonsense, which could have been verified by a simple glance at some of the many Internet reporting sites now available, seemed to pass them by. So, among the many formations which didn't apparently exist in 2001 were the following....

One spectacular recurring trait was a form of star mandala, radiating small standing circles in rays, as at Chilcomb

Another radiating design, at Chilcomb Down, Hampshire, July 15, 2001. Photo: Andreas Müller

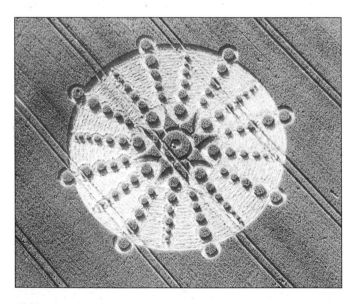

Radiating mandala, Lockeridge, Wiltshire, July 28, 2001. Photo: Andreas Müller

Down, in Hampshire (as seen by many people from the A272) and at Lockeridge in Wiltshire.

Other new surprises and unexpected themes arrived too, such as an ingenious style of interlocking wavy curves begun on July 15th at Windmill Hill, Wiltshire, with gorgeous internal swirls, and continued at Avebury Trusloe in a more complex form on July 22nd.

An unusual floral design, not unlike a "Tudor rose," encompassed by very accurate standing "scroll"-type broken rings was discovered at Beckhampton on July 24th. When a local television company (HTV West) had the usual suspects make an elaborate but highly geometrically flawed mandala in the adjacent field three days later on July 27th, the two made for good comparisons, one having appeared mysteriously and created with obvious care and attention, the other made as a supposedly impressive television demonstration, but botched. A visiting coach party from the Glastonbury Symposium conference (see Appendix A), led by Palden Jenkins, was shown into both formations and told one was known for a fact to be a man-made demo—but not which was which. Interestingly, simply from ground observation and feeling, nearly every person out of fifty visitors correctly picked out the demonstration design. No scientific litmus test, of course, but an interesting exercise nonetheless.

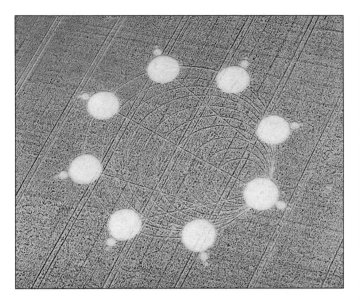

Huish, Wiltshire, August 14, 2001. A multi-dimensional tunnel...? Photo: Werner Anderhub

This unusual design with "scrolls" at Beckhampton, Wiltshire, July 24, 2001 (top photo: Werner Anderhub) was followed three days after by the filmed human making of a design one field away on July 27, commissioned by HTV West (bottom photo: Andreas Muller). Though complex, the geometry of the demonstration is hideously flawed. A coach party, shown both these Beckhampton formations with no prior knowledge, singled this one out as the television demo with little trouble.

Among many other inventive designs, one stood out as being particularly unusual. The pattern which was found at Huish on August 14th appeared to represent a three-dimensional tunnel of thin rings surrounded by eight small thought bubbles, this perspective only confounded by straight lines which ran into each other at strange angles. Many remarked that it seemed to have something important to say about multi-dimensionality. Interestingly, it was later revealed that the basic design of this formation had been secretly anticipated, and drawn, in a vision received by then CCCS Chairman Carol Cochrane months before its arrival in the fields.

Devils and Angels

On July 11th at Great Shelford on the Gog Magog hills in Cambridgeshire, a huge ring with two small central circles was discovered. The diameter of the ring was first claimed to be—spookily, for those still obsessed with negative readings of the number—an exact 666 feet. Though this measurement was later found to be incorrect (it was 674 feet), for some the stigma stuck. Over the next two nights, it grew, initially developing a perfectly-executed internal sacred maze and other small accoutrements, and then a quite mind-blowing multi-ringed square, the corners of which were beautifully curved. Some thought this

"Scorpion" formation at Stadskanaal, The Netherlands, August 1, 2001. Dutch researchers claim the design grew another tail circle while they were examining it. Aerial photo: Hans Hesselink. Close up of additional circle: Robert Boerman

last addition resembled a step pyramid as seen from above. (See page 128)

If the reported diameter of the first formation was seen by a few as a devilish sign, then salvation arrived two weeks later in the same area on July 25th (page 128) in a quite stunning display of three nested crescents filled with over seventy-five radiant thin lines like light rays—it resembled nothing less than a heavenly being lifting up its wings in a display of luminescence and was very quickly dubbed "The Angel." Each long line of radiance, no more than a foot in width, was perfectly straight, leading some, very reasonably, to ask how such straightness could possibly be freely walked by land artists. With the exception—perhaps significantly?—of the twelfth and thirteenth lines, both laid in the same direction, on the ground the lay of the crop was put down in one continuous flow which weaved in and out to create each line, without a break. The total length of this only briefly interrupted flow was around 4,500 feet....

For many, this was dubbed the most beautiful, somehow most optimistic, of all the season's masterpieces.

Events Abroad …

Away from the circus which habitually surrounds the UK crop circle scene, other countries continued be graced with events of their own to explore with rather less stressful intensity. Germany, for instance, was by now regularly receiving clusters of sophisticated glyphs, each as elaborate as many of their UK counterparts, but with their own flavor, despite biological samples showing identical effects inside. A growing troupe of very dedicated German researchers kept tabs on these, while also regularly visiting England to conduct tests and surveys of kinds increasingly neglected by the more blasé UK home front! Interest and research activity in Canada was growing fast too, as increasing numbers of formations came to light. Places as diverse as the Czech Republic, Israel, Serbia and Poland also reported several new crop formations in 2001.

Dutch Courage

The Netherlands, however, produced two of the most notable and astonishing events of the year. With burgeoning cerealogical reports in recent years, it had become the focus of attention for important scientific work into the circle phenomenon. Dr. Eltjo Haselhoff had long been conducting his own studies into physical effects and the link with aerial light phenomena and became, in 2001, after W C Levengood, only the second person to have a contribution on the subject of crop circles accepted in a peer-review scientific publication, in this case their relation to balls of light, printed in the journal *Physiologa Plantarum*.

Dr. Haselhoff found himself part of an intriguing mystery while investigating a "scorpion"-shaped formation at Stadskanaal with a team from the Dutch Center for Crop Circle Studies in early August. As they strolled around the formation, an extra circle appeared even as they surveyed it, though no-one saw it happen—suddenly there it was. Photos proved that it had not been there when they first entered. They began to feel ill effects as they approached it, and decided to leave in case the newly-formed shape had dangerous properties. The batteries immediately drained in two of the cameras present, and a digital camera was later found to have had its data corrupted.

A Historical Sighting

The most extraordinary and significant event to take place on Dutch soil concerned US-based researcher Nancy Talbott, whose BLT Research group had done so much to promote the work of W C Levengood into biological anomalies inside circle-affected crop. In the summer of 2001, Nancy was continuing her investigations into circular appearances and their links with luminosities in a specific area of The Netherlands—and in particular with a young man called Robbert van der Broeke in the Amsterdam area, who seemed to attract both such phenomena around his house at Hoeven. Her findings had found his stories to be true and Nancy was staying at his home conducting further observation and experiments when something quite astonishing happened—for the first time in cerealogical history (officially, at least), a crop circle researcher *witnessed a crop formation appearing*.

There had been around two dozen eye-witness sightings to crop circles forming over the years (page 28), but all of them, in recorded cases, had been members of the public with little or no knowledge of the phenomenon. Cerealogists had witnessed lights on nights when formations appeared before, but, rumors aside, despite many efforts to achieve a firm sighting through surveillance and night-watches, not until now had a member of the research community had such a directly verifiable encounter.

Writing in an article which officially announced the sighting,[35] Nancy describes her amazing experience, which took place on August 21st, 2001:

By 3:00 A.M. Robbert and I had been in the kitchen discussing the crop circles, their possible causative mechanisms and origins, what they might mean, etc. for several hours.... Partly out of fatigue and partly out of frustration I decided to go up to bed, telling Robbert that I was tired of all this "pussyfooting" around and asking, "why can't this phenomenon be more obvious, more direct?"

I was sleeping in Robbert's old bedroom, which is on the second floor at the back of the house, overlooking the garden and farm-field. The bed is placed so that it faces directly out through two floor-to-ceiling glass doors which go out to a small balcony overlooking the garden and farm field beyond, and there are thin, gauzy curtains [see-through] hanging at these glass doors. The farm field is clearly visible from the bed. Robbert was still in the kitchen downstairs.

... At about 3:05 A.M. I heard a few cattle nearby bawling raucously, as cattle do when they are disturbed. From years of talking with farmers and ranchers who have had crop circles (and other unusual events) occur on their properties, I immediately realized that this bawling might be a sign that something strange was afoot.... The cattle quieted down for a few minutes, but at about 3:10 A.M. they started up again....

... Then, at about 3:15 A.M., a brilliant, intense white column, or tube, of light—about 8 inches to 1 foot in diameter—from my vantage point flashed down from the sky to the ground, illuminating my bedroom and the sky as brilliantly as if from helicopter searchlights.... Then this tube of light disappeared and both my room and the outside went dark. While the tube of light was there it was so bright I couldn't see exactly where it was touching down and wasn't sure how close it was.

Approximately one second of total darkness elapsed and then a second tube of the same brilliant white light, slightly edged in a bluish tint, appeared slightly to the left of where the first tube had been. Again, the room and the outside lit up spectacularly, somehow leaving the intense tube of light clearly visible for about one second. Then, after another second's darkness the third and final tube descended to the ground.... The entire light display took five to six seconds;

Actual view from the garden of the house where Nancy Talbott and Robbert van der Broeke witnessed tubes of light creating a formation in a bean field at Hoeven, The Netherlands, August 21, 2001, taken just a few hours after the sighting. Though not visible from this viewpoint, a T-shape path emanates from the right of the ellipse. Photo: Nancy Talbott

When we turned my flashlight onto the field we could see that half of the crop in the downed area was laid away from us and the other half was laid toward us, and I thought I could faintly see steam rising from the freshly-downed beans (which I attributed to the interaction of the tubes of light with a heavy night-time dew covering the crop).

At dawn the next day, from my bed, I could clearly see the new circle, which turned out to be, in fact, an ellipse of about 35 feet in length and 20 feet in width, with a 20-foot-long pathway adjoining the northern edge which ended in a crossbar (like the capital letter 'T').

Some of the more skeptical researchers, impressed, despite themselves, and perhaps a little envious of an experience long wished for by many, illogically stated that this

The house, as seen from within the new formation. Photo: Nancy Talbott

if the bawling cattle are considered to be part of this situation the total time would be about ten minutes.

By the time the third tube of light flashed down to the ground I was half out of bed, yelling to Robbert, who was still downstairs in the kitchen. He, at the same time, was running up the stairs to get me, having witnessed the event from the first-floor kitchen windows. From the kitchen he could see that the tubes of light had hit the bean field, just beyond the fence at the back of the garden, and he reported also that the sky had lit up like daylight when each column of light had occurred.... Neither of us saw anything in the overcast sky from which these tubes of light had originated. Later that night, Robbert reported that he had heard the dog next door barking furiously just prior to the appearance of the light-tubes.

... We headed for the back fence and the farm-field and there, just over the fence about 15 feet into the bean-field — just barely visible in the darkness — was the new crop circle.

sighting proved that only simple formations were genuine—but if an elliptical shape with a protruding "T" bar is classified as "simple," why cannot other, more complex shapes appear from the same processes?

In truth, this highly important and dramatic event was but one demonstration that despite all the intrigues and paranoia which may infect the crop circle community from time to time, a sizeable mystery still remains around this most beautiful of unexplained phenomena.

The Milk Hill Record Breaker

Aside from astonishing happenings to individuals, on August 12th one formation suddenly arrived to rock the cerealogical world—and shake the public from some of its apathy towards the circle phenomenon.

Using a "fractal" style (though not technically a fractal itself) first pioneered at Stonehenge and then Windmill Hill in 1996, the six-armed design, which was discovered perched atop the downs of Milk Hill near Alton Barnes, was the largest single diameter and most elaborate glyph ever to have appeared (page 127). It came on a night of rain, yet was found pristine the next morning, without mud splatters or soil disturbance.

409 circles of many sizes ranging from 70 feet to 4 feet made up the pattern, breaking all records and covering a huge area of around 800 feet. Its scale meant airplanes and helicopters had to fly higher than usual for photographers to take it all in. On the ground, its configuration was almost impossible to discern and appeared simply as a maze of connected circles, some with wafer-thin standing curtains of stems between. Only here and there did undulations in the topography of the field give a little elevation, revealing at the most one arm of the design rolling into the distance. Visitors in another part of the design from you appeared simply as dots on the horizon, so vast was its expanse.

Each circle seemed to be an expert demonstration of varied styles of centers and lays. While some displayed open central splays, others had standing tufts or corn dolly-type nests. One even had a network of three tiny macrame-like rings formed from twisted, folded stems.

But from the air its true beauty and accuracy was revealed. An endless procession of helicopters, microlights and light aircraft spiralled above, hypnotized by this astonishing creation and packed with television crews from around the world. The aforementioned UK movie pro-

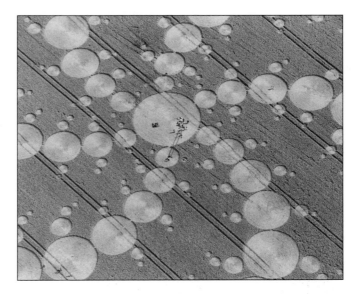

Close-up of the center of the staggering Milk Hill formation, Wiltshire, August 12, 2001. The film crew from the UK film *A Place To Stay* can be seen with camera and microphone booms in the middle. Photo: Werner Anderhub

duction, with joyous opportunism, filmed erotic gypsy love scenes within it, while even the usually acid media seemed impressed. The formation found itself in newspapers and TV news bulletins for days.

Some usually dissenting voices were cowed, too. With an air of humility, one member of the usual human public circlemaking crews even issued a statement expressing severe doubts as to how such a design could be laid down in one night. (Had it appeared over a series of days, it would have been spotted in this busily flown circle-spotters area.)

Though inevitable rumors and fears of double-bluffs rolled around for weeks afterwards, the Milk Hill wonder remained untainted by claims. Had they come, most would not have taken them seriously. After a summer where some had felt the patterns to be rather subdued and the croppie world full of confusion and deliberately spread hoax paranoia, this appeared to be a last-minute gift to test even the most devout skeptic.

Surely, after this, one could expect no more surprises from the phenomenon in one summer? But even as croppies began to imagine they could relax into the UK autumn wind-down, just days later the fields suddenly sprang two more major shocks....

Views from within the huge formation at Milk Hill, Wiltshire, August 12, 2001, showing the scale and variety of this astonishing design. (See also page 127.) Photos: Andy Thomas

The Face of Things to Come...?

On August 14th, and then August 19th, two formations visited the field at Chilbolton, Hampshire (page 128), opposite the radio telescope which had been given a cerealogical companion the year before.

The impact of the first of the new visitations was not immediately realized by those on the ground—and even some of those flying over it at a low level. It appeared to be an unevenly distributed matrix of dots formed by small standing pillars of crop against a flat rectangular canvas of 145 feet by 186 feet. Crop flowed around each individual element; it was not laid as a plain grid. The pattern was diligently photographed and investigated. But when the aerial photographs came back and were held at a distance, the "dots" resolved into something which sent a shiver down the spine—the matrix was a *face....!*

Without a doubt, this was a *picture,* formed as a halftone (like old newspaper photographs) by the accumulation of the standing dots creating patches of "light and shade." From this emerged a heavily-browed humanoid face which was startling to behold.

What was it? An extra-terrestrial face? A human face? A representation of the Turin Shroud? The stone "face" on Mars? Or pop singer Posh Spice, even? The speculation which sparked from this new type of crop formation threw up many wild guesses and deep conjecture which continues at the time of writing. All that could be said for sure was that it was a face of some kind, and the implications of this disturbed, because it seemed to suggest that a more obvious alien influence might be at work here, rather than a vaguer source. Others argued otherwise, however; if some kind of universal super-consciousness—or *our* consciousness—was at work, there was nothing to say that an image of a face might not be thrown up amongst the other more ambiguous symbols.

But all of this was thrown into a shocking relief with the arrival of the second Chilbolton formation of 2001 five days after the face, and just a few hundred feet from it.

Another rectangular offering, but longer and thinner (90 feet by 264 feet), this also had small standing elements within it, but they did not resolve into anything as obvious as a face. Instead, it was soon realized that it contained information of even more impact.

In 1974, a direct "message" in digital binary code was first transmitted into deep space (towards star cluster M13) from the huge Arecibo dish in Puerto Rico as part of the SETI project (Search for Extra-Terrestrial Intelligences). Intended as a test transmission (devised by various astronomers, including Carl Sagan, a devout circle skeptic), it contained information about the human race, our DNA, etc., and the conditions and chemical make-up of our planet. It was hoped this could be decoded by any intelligence receiving the message (though some have argued that it would be very difficult for another race to know *how*).[36]

In a dramatic twist, the formation which appeared on August 19th, 2001 appeared to be a direct "response" to this transmission! It looked almost identical in its layout, but was subtly altered from the original; the version in the field showed an altered DNA structure from our own, added a chemical element not originally included (silicon), featured a creature with a larger head than human beings and depicted a different solar system diagram with a much higher planetary population density than ours. Among other small differences, instead of a digital rendering of the Arecibo transmitter itself (featured in the original), what we 'got back" showed a very pixilated diagram of the 2000 formation which appeared in the same field, thus creating a clear continuity with the year before. Interestingly, the symmetry of the "reply" was reversed (horizontally flipped) to what was originally beamed out, thus referencing the reversed version shown in some printed sources, and not the actual transmission.

With a clear representation of a face lying next to it, this second formation seriously shook many researchers, and awakened the attention of various fringe groups (such as ufologists and alien "contact" groups) who had cooled on crop circles of late. Suddenly they leaped on these formations as evidence that aliens were perhaps, after all, communicating with us via the grain fields.

The more dubious pointed to the fact that the message beamed into space wouldn't actually be received for another 20,000 years, due to the length of time presumed necessary for it to reach its destination, so how could this be a reply? However, it was countered that any alien intelligence worth its salt which had been putting down crop patterns for years and interacting with human beings would know very well what we had sent out in 1974 (it has reportedly been transmitted again since), or had maybe intercepted the message in space.

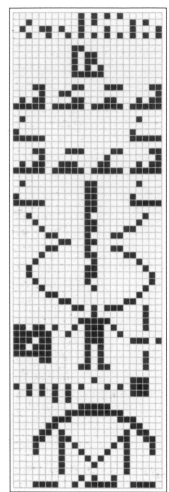

Left: The original Arecibo binary transmission of 1974, depicting information about life on our planet—see text. Diagram by Jay Goldner, from his German book *ET Hat Geantwortet* (Silberschnur 2002). Right: The Chilbolton crop formation of August 19, 2001, which appears to be a subtly but deliberately altered version of the Arecibo message. . . . Photo: Francine Blake. The transmission diagram has been reversed horizontally from the original as sent, for better comparison with the formation (shown as it appeared), which oddly was a flipped variation on the Arecibo message.

Ironically, if perhaps inevitably, the SETI project itself dismissed the Chilbolton formations as nothing more than a charming prank, and even the staff at the nearby radio telescope showed little interest, leaving the intense speculation and fevered—and sometimes hysterical—writings which followed to the websites and journals of what they would see as "fanatics."

Some circle enthusiasts found the face and the "code" formations a little too clearly pictorial for their liking—it seemed to go against the ethos shown before by the phenomenon, ie. that of ambiguous prodding, rather than direct communication. Again, some argued that the appearance of such a clearly recognizable item still was not proof that the crop circles were being made by aliens and that other sources could possibly throw up such a reference. Others said the Chilbolton events were so different to the usual design of crop circles that perhaps they had a different source altogether to the more familiar phenomenon?

There was some suspicion, too. With a Hollywood movie due the next summer, could these be simply an elaborate publicity stunt, the truth of which would be sprung at a later date? Whatever, many agreed that if ever shown to be man-made, the Chilbolton formations would certainly constitute one of the most ambitious pranks ever played.

If, on the other hand, it *was* a direct extra-terrestrial "reply" to our own communication, what did it mean? Was it really so straightforward as to simply be showing us what life was like for the originators of the message? Or was it, as some suggested, a pointer towards what our *own race* may one day become? Or were the two formations just random images plucked from our culture and thrown up by some more spontaneous and less meaningful source?

To some degree, despite renewed lobbying from the ET-theorists, the direct symbolism shown at Chilbolton in 2001 intensified the debate over the source of the crop circles rather than settled it. Certainly the stakes had been raised by these designs and expectations were suddenly high for what might follow the season after; were the face and code just a one-off aberration of the phenomenon, or the beginning of a new phase, one in which the human race was considered at last to be ready for more obvious pictorial and less cryptic information? Was this a crucial new step in an ongoing communication process, taking us to higher levels, or simply a red herring?

Only time, as ever, would tell.

Where Next?

In spite of a number of surprisingly unjudgmental circle-spreads in the tabloids here and there, in the face of all the years of evidence to the contrary some sections of the media still seem determined to denigrate the circle phenomenon. Regularly portrayed as being nothing more than the work of clever folk heroes out to brighten up the countryside with their ingenious and simply-created art, the fact is that these people have been consistently unable to demonstrate their claimed abilities in public under proper circumstances or full scrutiny when it comes to attempting anything like the more advanced beauty we have seen in the fields. And naturally, with a media forum with a rich appetite for such pretenders, ignorant of the details which might challenge their assertions, those who pose as the sole mysterious artists are eager to play along with the illusion of omnipotence, attaching themselves and their egos to works far beyond their abilities. Yet there are those willing to stand up and contest such misperceptions. It is painfully obvious to a substantial amount of open-minded observers that despite what hoaxes there may be, many of the crop circles constitute something of great value beyond such mundane explanations and every day more people are awakening to this realization despite the best efforts of those keen to block it.

This potted chronology, long as it may seem to some readers, does little more than scratch the surface of a rich and extraordinary history which may yet, scanned further, yield its wider patterns, secrets and revelations in time.

As each season passes, a little fear grows that suddenly the symbol will arrive that signifies "The End"—and the circles will be no more. After all, they haven't been with us on such a scale throughout history and may not continue forever, when their purpose is done or stimulus runs dry. But the Chilbolton events (and the few formations which trickled off elsewhere in the closing weeks of the 2001 season, including one very late entry of rings and circles near Etchilhampton on September 16th) showed no signs of being the last of their kind. Instead, they seemed to be a cryptic signing off, with a hint of even more remarkable—and perplexing—things to come. What the following season would bring was, like the phenomenon itself, a mystery. One thing for certain with the crop circles was that for the future, all that could be expected was the unexpected.

NOTES

1. This idea is explored in Dr. (George) Terence Meaden's book *The Goddess of the Stones*.

2. The full account is reproduced in the Dr. Terence Meaden-edited *Circles from the Sky* and Jim Schnabel's mischievous attack on crop circle research *Round in Circles*.

3. Michael Hesemann in his otherwise excellent book *The Cosmic Connection*, asserts there is no evidence for crop circles before 1972 (despite reporting a 1966 Australian "UFO nest"—a crop circle by any other name—as mentioned below). However, work by, among others, Terry Wilson neatly refutes this by documenting many reports of crop circles in previous years. Hesemann also claims the Mowing Devil account reports that the entire field was cut and not in circles, yet the pamphlet clearly states otherwise.

4. *Sussex Notes and Queries*, Volume 6, page 139. Previously, as reported in my book *Fields of Mystery*, the earliest account of crop circles in Sussex was at Tangmere—also close to Chichester—in 1943. In fact the very earliest Sussex formation now appears to have been in the Cissbury/Chanctonbury area, West Sussex in 1927.

5. *The Cosmic Connection*, Chapter 5, page 61, Michael Hesemann.

6. Their account is told in full in *The Cosmic Connection*.

7. *Circular Evidence*, Chapter 1, page 17, Pat Delgado and Colin Andrews.

8. Lord Healey tells the full story in his preface to *Fields of Mystery*.

9. *The Crop Circle Enigma*, Chapter 9, *Beyond the Current Paradigm*, pages 104–105, George Wingfield.

10. This appears to be what led Jim Schnabel to nonsensically insinuate in his book *Round in Circles* that the CCCS was a front for a black magic organization. Others have suggested it was actually set up by intelligence services to monitor at first-hand the activities of potential subversives!

11. Reported in full by its perpetrator Erik Beckjord in *SC*, issue 43, July 1995.

12. *The Cosmic Connection*, Chapter 5, pages 52–54, Michael Hesemann. Interesting to note that the 1996 US TV sci-fi series *Dark Skies*, which featured crop circles heavily, utilized the idea of such plates as part of its story.

13. *The Monuments of Mars; A City on the Edge of Forever*,

Chapter XVII, pages 364–365, Frog, Ltd. 1987, revised 1992, 1996 and 2001. This concept is also presented in *Two Thirds*, David P Myers and David Percy.

14. The excellent booklet *Ciphers in the Crops*, edited by Beth Davis, examines the significance of both the Mandelbrot Set and Barbury Castle in detail.

15. First reported in *SC*, issue 8, August 1992, and then in Colin Andrews' own words in *SC*, issue 11, November 1992. Also documented in *The Cosmic Connection*, Chapter 14, pages 148–150.

16. Few circle researchers really enjoy giving credit to others, it seems—my two first books on crop circles, while receiving notices in many other varied journals, were totally ignored by cerealogical publications!

17. The Sussex formations and the communication experiments are documented fully in the books *Fields of Mystery* and *Quest For Contact* respectively.

18. Including the bizarre dark objects seen by Martin Noakes, Griller Gilgannon and myself, as recorded in *Quest For Contact*, Chapter 6, page 77.

19. Judith Newman raises the issue in detail in *SC*, issue 42, June 1995.

20. When an invisible circle-making energy appears in court, it should be quite interesting.

21. Reported in full in *Fields of Mystery*, pages 60–62.

22. Again, all this is recorded in *Fields of Mystery* and *Quest For Contact*.

23. Described by one famous American channeller as the most important crop design ever to have appeared—see photo caption.

24. In which one starts with 1, adds it together with itself and then adds that total to the previous number and so on, ie. 1, 1, 2, 3, 5, 8, 13, 21, 34, 55, 89, 144, etc.

25. Reports of *exact* times vary, but this is as close as is known, as an average.

26. *SC*, issue 57, October 1996, page 12.

27. The full significance of the "Tree of Life" is discussed by Debbie Pardoe in *SC*, issue 65, June 1997, pages 4–5. There can be variations in the spelling of "Qabalah" (Kabbalah, Cabala, Kabala).

28. Described by Barry Reynolds, *SC*, issue 67, August 1997, page 12.

29. Naisha and Lili's full story is detailed in *SC*, issue 85, July/August 1999, page 19. Nikki Saville's testimony can be found at *www.swirlednews.com*, July 2001 archives.

30. In 1998, Ian Baillie produced several analyses of the geometry of human demonstrations, including the *Country File* creation, comparing them to classic formations—the stilted awkwardness of the human efforts are quite obvious when examined side by side. Some examples of his work appear on page 18, Chapter 2, of Lucy Pringle's book *Crop Circles: The Greatest Mystery of Modern Times*.

31. Jack Sullivan's work was debuted in fine detail in *SC* issues 81, 82, 84, 87 and 89 between 1998 and 2000 and has since been reproduced and referenced in other journals and websites.

32. The Antahkarana is said by Reiki author Diane Stein to be thousands of years old and is "a symbol that cannot be used in negative ways" (*Essential Reiki*, Crossing Press, 1995).

33. Michael Glickman tells the full story behind the Silbury Hill hole in his article *Silbury Hollow, SC*, issue 91, July/August 2000, page 3.

34. Jack Sullivan rips *The Mail on Sunday*'s claim apart by the simplest of analyses in *SC*, issue 92, September/October 2000, pages 15–16.

35. Nancy Talbott's sighting article, which gives much fuller details than these excerpts, officially debuted on *www.swirlednews.com*, and can be found in the October 2001 archives.

36. Of the method used in the original Arecibo message, Martin Noakes writes: *"This is a series of 1's and 0's / Yes and No's / On and Offs. The design was a rectangular shape, about three times as tall as it was wide, and when all the 1s and 0s were in place it created a crude schematic diagram. It was made up of 1679 bits of information, which was the unique sum of two prime numbers multiplied. These numbers were 23 and 73, ie. 23 x 73 = 1679. The reason for this approach was to ensure that the message could only be arranged one way."*

Martin's full report, which fully details the differences between the Arecibo message and the Chilbolton "reply" can be found in the September 2001 archives of *www.swirlednews.com*. Another excellent analysis of these events, by Paul Vigay, can be found in the archives of *www.cropcircleresearch.com*

The canvas destroyed . . . until another season. Photo: Grant Wakefield

From Genesis . . . to Revelation? Color Photo Gallery

The following twenty-eight pages chart the progression of some of the more notable and beautiful crop formations from the late 1980s to 2001 . . .

LEFT and ABOVE: The "Devil's Punchbowl," Cheesefoot Head, Hampshire, July 1987. This ringed circle was just one of many formations to grace this distinctive landscape and the surrounding fields over the years. Photos: Dr. Terence Meaden

BELOW RIGHT: Silbury Hill, Wiltshire, August 1988. Quintuplets and grapeshot nest around the famous and mysterious mound, which has been a focal point for the circle phenomenon for many years. Photo: Dr. Terence Meaden

ABOVE: Beckhampton, Wiltshire, August 3, 1988. A fine example of a classic "quintuplet." Photo: Dr. Terence Meaden

ABOVE: Hungerford, Berkshire, August 1988. A typical example of a circle with scattered grapeshot. Photo: Dr. Terence Meaden

ABOVE: Avebury Trusloe, Wiltshire, May 1989. A spring formation in low immature crop. Photo: Dr. Terence Meaden

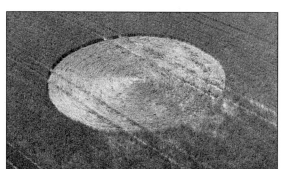

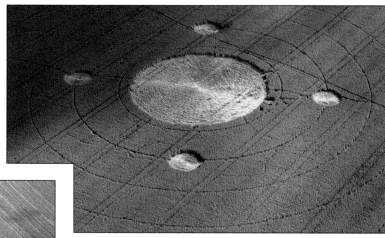

ABOVE LEFT: Fawley Down, Hampshire, May 25, 1990. Classic single circle of the kind which began it all. Photo: Michael and Christine Green

ABOVE: Upton Scudamore, Wiltshire, June 29, 1990. By now a branch of the quintuplets had developed rings (very fine in this case) to become "Celtic crosses." Photo: Dr. Terence Meaden

LEFT: Bishops Cannings, Wiltshire, May 19, 1990. The apparently random grapeshot bizarrely peppering this quadruple-ringer would become a less common sight in time (see page 20). Photo: Dr. Terence Meaden

ABOVE: Crawley Down, Hampshire, July 13, 1990. A pristine early pictogram with excellent examples of the rectangular boxes which would be a recurring motif for a while. Photo: Dr. Terence Meaden

ABOVE: Chilcomb, Hampshire, May 23, 1990. Officially the very first pictogram. One can only imagine the excitement of the researchers who experienced this initial view of the most major development ever to occur to the phenomenon (see page 36). Photo: Dr. Terence Meaden

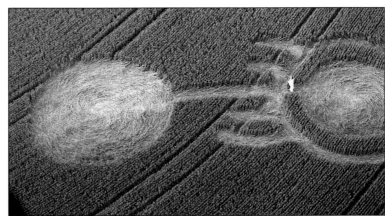

ABOVE: Cheesefoot Head, Hampshire, June 2, 1990. Many felt this tentacled pictogram had a sad, drooping quality to it. Photo: Michael and Christine Green

LEFT: Chilcomb, Hampshire, June 16, 1990. This triple-haloed symbol seems to have an ancient feel to its symbolism. Photo: Michael and Christine Green

LEFT and ABOVE: Alton Barnes, Wiltshire, July 11, 1990. The huge pictogram which shocked the world, emblazoned in newspapers and magazines, attracting thousands of visitors (see page 36). Aerial photo: Dr. Terence Meaden. Ground photo: Michael and Christine Green

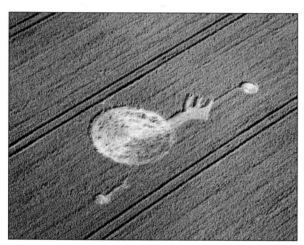

ABOVE LEFT: Stanton St Bernard, Wiltshire, July 1990, not far from the pictogram below and dubbed "the hand of God" by some. The lines to the grapeshot were added by visitors. Photo: Dr. Terence Meaden

ABOVE: East Kennett, Wiltshire, July 26, 1990. Like each of the three large pictograms depicted here, this was very similar, but not identical, to its sisters. Photo: Dr. Terence Meaden

LEFT: Stanton St Bernard, Wiltshire, July 11, 1990. This appeared the same night as the Alton Barnes motif, but received less publicity. A glowing aerial object was later videotaped nearby (see pages 131 and 132). Photo: Dr. Terence Meaden

ABOVE: Beckhampton, Wiltshire, August 1, 1991. One of three nearly identical aquatic-looking pictograms which appeared that summer in a perfect isosceles triangle (see page 27). Photo: Andrew King

BELOW: Froxfield, Wiltshire, August 19, 1991. Photo: Andrew King

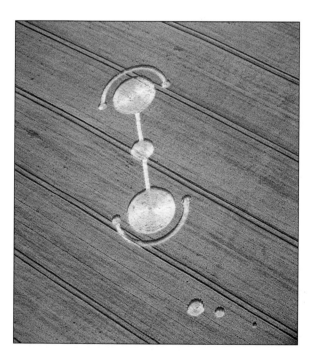

ABOVE: Hungerford, Berkshire, August 18, 1991. Photo: Richard Wintle/Calyx Photo Services

BELOW: Milk Hill, Wiltshire, August 1991. This was interpreted as ancient writing by some, but in which language? (See page 40.) Photo: Andrew King

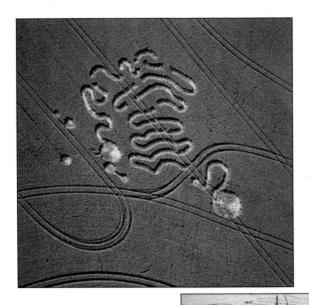

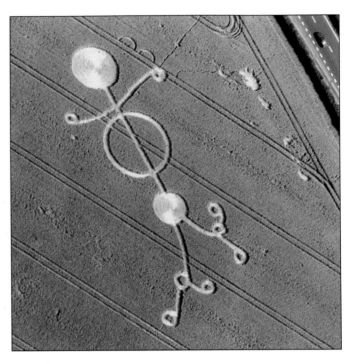

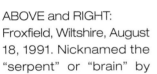

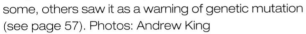

ABOVE and RIGHT: Froxfield, Wiltshire, August 18, 1991. Nicknamed the "serpent" or "brain" by some, others saw it as a warning of genetic mutation (see page 57). Photos: Andrew King

ABOVE: Micheldever, Hampshire, August 2, 1991. Roads in circle photos are good at revealing the scale of the patterns, as can be seen from the car on the A303 to the right. Photo: Andrew King

BELOW: East Kennett, Wiltshire, July 27, 1991. This beautiful shot, taken with a fish-eye lens, shows how formations leap out of the landscape when viewed aerially. Photo: David Parker/Science Photo Library

ABOVE: Barbury Castle, Wiltshire, July 17, 1991. Arguably the most impressive pictogram which had ever appeared at that time, it remains one of the finesl works of the phenomenon (see pages 40 and 41). Photo: Richard Wintle/ Calyx Photo Services

BELOW: Ickleton, Cambridgeshire, August 12, 1991. The "Mandelbrot Set," as this fractal configuration is known, was the first truly unambiguous crop symbol to appear (see page 41). Photo: David Parker / Science Photo Library

ABOVE: Alton Barnes, Wiltshire, July 9, 1992. Some ridiculed this "snail" pattern, but its symbolism may have deeper meaning (see page 44). Photo: Andrew King

BELOW: Silbury Hill, Wiltshire, August 16, 1992. The "charm bracelet" (see page 45). Photo: Andrew King

ABOVE and BELOW: Inside the "charm bracelet." Swirl photo: Andrew King. Pole shots of the ring and the strange disrupted area around the water trough: Grant Wakefield.

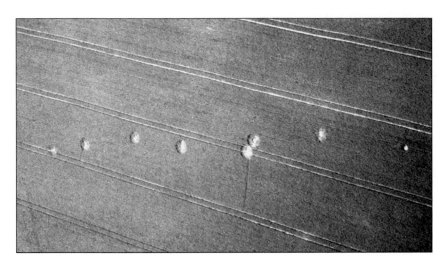

ABOVE: Bishops Cannings, Wiltshire, June 11, 1992. One of three "musical note" formations, one of which suggested the tune of a hymn (see page 44). Photo: Michael and Christine Green

ABOVE: Milk Hill, Wiltshire, July 16, 1992. Deceptively simple-looking, this has some remarkable geometric qualities (see diagram on page 24). Photo: Andrew King

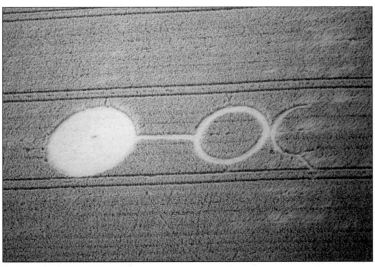

ABOVE: West Stowell, Wiltshire, August 2, 1992. Another rare unambiguous symbol, in this case the astrological sign for Mercury. Photo: Andrew King

LEFT: West Kennett, Wiltshire, July 11, 1993. This appeared just below the Avebury stone avenue. Photo: Michael Hubbard

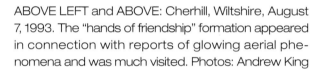

BELOW: Charley Knoll, Loughborough, Leicestershire, July 7, 1993. The East Midland's best, some likened this pictogram to the Northern Cross star constellation. Photo: Tony Caldicott

ABOVE LEFT and ABOVE: Cherhill, Wiltshire, August 7, 1993. The "hands of friendship" formation appeared in connection with reports of glowing aerial phenomena and was much visited. Photos: Andrew King

BELOW: West Overton, Wiltshire, July 11, 1993. The "666" formation, so named for obvious reasons, was host to some uncanny effects and coincidences (see page 136). Photo: Michael Hubbard

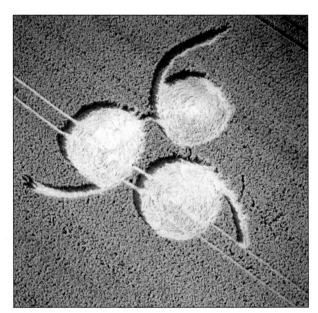

ABOVE LEFT: Bythorn, Cambridgeshire, September 4, 1993. A gorgeous new style for the phenomenon (see page 48). The crude paths around the outside were made by visitors. Photo: Michael and Christine Green

ABOVE RIGHT: West Kennett, Wiltshire, July 1994. The "Celtic barmaid" (shown upside down for effect), complete with tray of drinks! Photo: Michael Hesemann

ABOVE: West Overton, Wiltshire, July 28, 1994. A mathematical "infinity" symbol? Photo: Michael Hesemann

LEFT: Moulsford, Oxfordshire, July 17, 1994. One of several "thought bubble" designs that year (see page 49). Photo: Michael and Christine Green

ABOVE: East Dean, West Sussex, July 23, 1994. A very similar design lay just over the brow. Photo: Andy Thomas

ABOVE: Furze Knoll, Wiltshire, May 7, 1994. Some felt this to be rather sinister (see page 136). The standing tufts were precursors to the "galaxies" which would follow. Photo: Andrew King

RIGHT: Barbury Castle, Wiltshire, July 7, 1994. An insect made from planetary phase diagrams? (See page 51.) Photo: Michael Hesemann

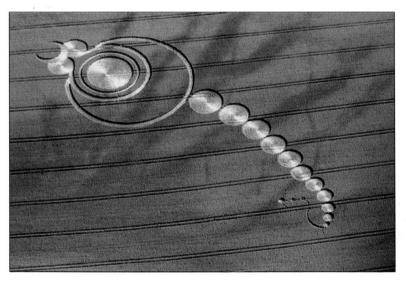

BELOW LEFT and RIGHT: Bishops Cannings, Wiltshire, July 15, 1994. The "scorpion" from the air (photo: Steve Alexander) and from the A361 road (photo: Andy Thomas). (See page 50.)

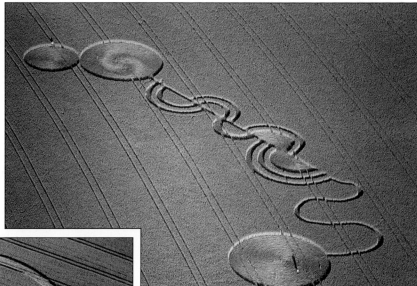

RIGHT: Barton Stacey, Hampshire, July 27, 1994. In some ways a more impressive and less bizarre cousin of the "Celtic barmaid" on page 111. Photo: Michael Hesemann

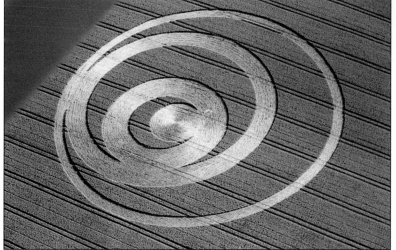

LEFT: Oliver's Castle, Wiltshire, July 27, 1994. The tips of the crescents tapered down to the width of one stem in this stunning formation. Note the tiny swirled circle to the right of the central crescent's upper tip, actually within the main lay of the crop (see pages 52 and 167). Photo: Michael Hesemann

BELOW LEFT and RIGHT: West Stowell, Wiltshire, July 23, 1994. The best of the "galaxy" designs from that summer, as seen aerially (photo: Steve Alexander) and internally, walking across the "gigantic pinball machine" (photo: Andy Thomas). This depicted a future astronomical alignment on April 6–7, 2000 (see pages 51, 52, 73 and 80).

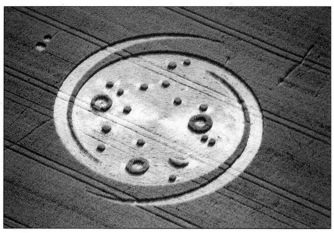

BELOW and RIGHT: Avebury, Wiltshire, August 11–12, 1994. The "web" or "dreamcatcher," one of the most striking formations of all time (see page 53). The shimmering effect is created by opposing lay directions. Photos: Andrew King

BELOW: Pole shots of the extraordinary web design. Photos: Steve Alexander

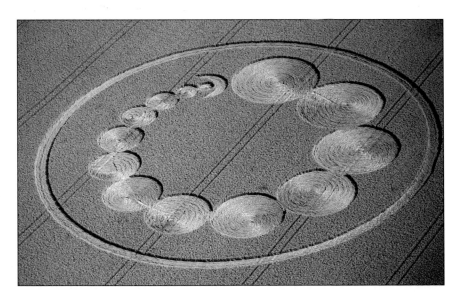

ABOVE: Avebury Trusloe, Wiltshire, August 14, 1994. The final major pattern of the year: the "scorpions" going into hibernation or more planetary phases? (See page 54.) Photo: Ron Russell

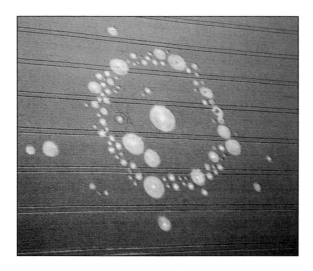

ABOVE: Bishop's Sutton, Hampshire, June 20, 1995. First of the "asteroid" designs (see pages 56 and 74). Photo: Michael Hubbard

ABOVE: Beckhampton, Wiltshire, May 29, 1995. Storm clouds gather over the "spiral" formation (see page 54). This picture won a photography award. Photo: Steve Alexander

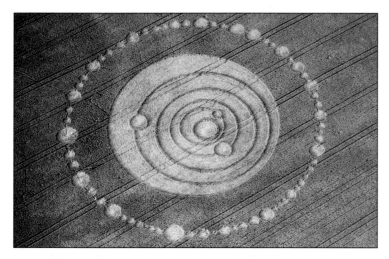

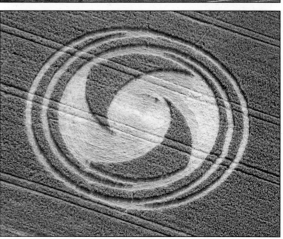

ABOVE: Longwood Warren, Hampshire, June 26, 1995. This astonishing configuration appears to show the inner planets of our solar system—minus the Earth! Much speculation followed.... (See pages 52 and 73.) The standing rings are impressive. Photo: Steve Alexander

ABOVE RIGHT: Cissbury Ring, West Sussex, July 15, 1995. As these beautiful off-center rings demonstrate, 1995 was a good year for Sussex (see page 54). Photo: Michael Hubbard

RIGHT: Wilmington, East Sussex, July 25, 1995. This torturously difficult to draw nest of crescents arrived next to the famous "Long Man" hill figure. Photo: Michael Hubbard

LEFT and BELOW LEFT: Stonehenge, Wiltshire, July 7, 1996. 151 circles made up this fractal pattern, which appeared within 45 minutes one Sunday afternoon (see page 58). Overhead photo: Steve Alexander. Landscape photo: Andrew King

BELOW: Ashbury, Oxfordshire, July 26, 1996. A "vesica pisces." Photo: Andrew King

BELOW: Girton, Cambridgeshire, June 12, 1996. One of two "sprouting bulb" designs, which began the season in that area (page 57). Photo: Steve Alexander

BELOW: Littlebury Green, Essex, July 12, 1996. The best formation ever to visit the county (see page 59). Photo: Russell Stannard

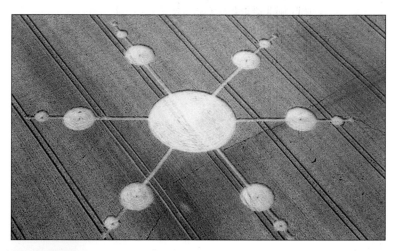

BELOW and RIGHT: Oliver's Castle, Wiltshire, August 11, 1996. Perhaps the most controversial crop circle of all, this was the first anyone claimed to have videotaped forming (see page 60). The subsequent fighting over the sequence's authenticity later threw doubt on the formation itself, but nothing was proved and the swirls inside were impressive. Aerial photo: Michael Hubbard. Swirl photos: Andy Thomas

BELOW: Liddington Castle, Wiltshire, August 2, 1996. The complexity of the floor lay in the main emblem was one of the best examples of the year. Photo: Steve Alexander

BELOW: Alton Barnes, Wiltshire, 17 June 1996. The "DNA" formation (pages 57 and 171). The way the spiralling circles grow larger and smaller, as if to give perspective, is ingenious. Photo: Steve Alexander

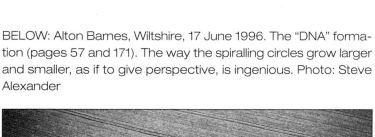

BELOW: Alton Priors, Wiltshire, July 11, 1997. This "torus knot" had a three-dimensional quality to it (see page 66). Photo: Andrew King

ABOVE: Windmill Hill, Wiltshire, July 29, 1996. Another fractal design, there were 194 circles spanning hundreds of feet. For many, the most impressive formation of all time (see page 61). Photo: Andrew King

BELOW: Stonehenge, Wiltshire, June 9, 1997. This snowflake motif sat on almost exactly the same spot as its 1996 predecessor (see page 64). Photo: Steve Alexander

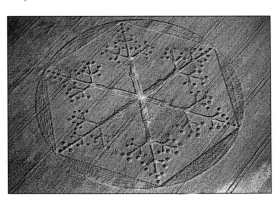

ABOVE: Barbury Castle, Wiltshire, April 20, 1997 (see page 62). This design shares the same perimeter shape as the Littlebury Green flower of 1996, shown on page 116. The yellow rape flowers had not yet fully opened when this picture was taken. Photo: Steve Alexander

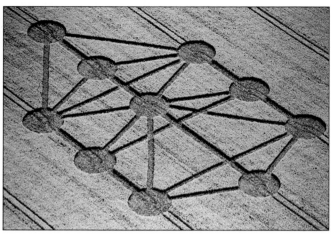

ABOVE: Winterbourne Bassett, Wiltshire, June 1, 1997. The stark sheen of the design may be due to the fact that only the center and the perimeter are laid in swirls—everything else is mostly in straight lines (see page 63). Photo: Steve Alexander

ABOVE: Burderop Down, Wiltshire, May 4, 1997. Several formations had suggested the "qabalah" before, but here it was in its entirety at last (see page 63). Photo: Steve Alexander

ABOVE: Dreischor, Holland, July 16, 1997. One of the best non-UK designs yet to have appeared—but not without controversy (see page 65). Photo: Joop van Houdt

ABOVE RIGHT and RIGHT: Bodenhausen and Burghasungen, Germany, July 4, 1997. The first time sacred labyrinths/mazes had been found as formations (see page 65). Photos: Wolfgang Schöppe

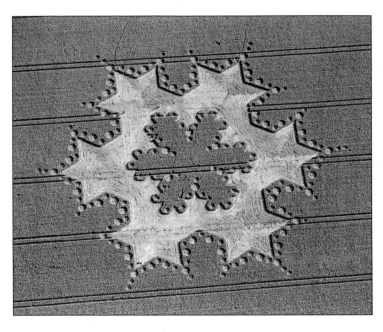

ABOVE: Milk Hill, Wiltshire, August 8, 1997. The most staggering design of the year (see page 68). Photo: Steve Alexander

BELOW: Silbury Hill, Wiltshire, July 23, 1997. A ring of meditating figures contemplate the first of the triangular fractals (see page 68). Photo: Patricia Murray

BELOW: Etchilhampton, Wiltshire, August 1, 1997. A countdown to the end of the Mayan calendar (page 67). Photo: Steve Alexander

BELOW: Hackpen Hill, Wiltshire, August 18, 1997. The last English event of 1997. Photo: Steve Alexander

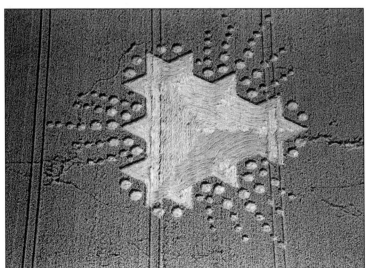

ABOVE and BELOW: Alton Barnes, Wiltshire, July 9, 1998. Above and within the seven-fold mandala, the largest single area of flattened crop in a formation to date (see page 70). Aerial photo: Werner Anderhub. Internal photo: Andy Thomas

ABOVE: West Kennett, Wiltshire, May 4, 1998. This "wheel of fire" is said to have appeared within two and a half hours (see page 69). Photo: Andrew King

BELOW: Tawsmead Copse, Alton Priors, Wiltshire, August 9, 1998. Several witnesses saw this shape appearing beneath aerial phenomena the night it formed (see page 71). Photo: Frank Laumen

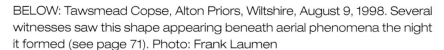

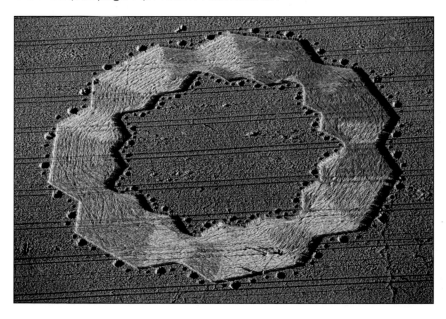

BELOW: Lockeridge, Wiltshire, August 7, 1998. Nicknamed "the Queen" or "the spaceship" (see page 72). Photo: Frank Laumen

ABOVE: Dadford, Buckinghamshire, July 4, 1998. One of several inventive pentagram variations, with companion symbols (see page 71). Photo: Steve Alexander

BELOW: Alton Barnes, Wiltshire, June 12, 1999. An unexpected compendium of early 90s symbolism! Over 1000 feet long, this arrived within a time window of an hour and a half.... (See page 75.) Photo: Frank Laumen

ABOVE: Beckhampton, Wiltshire, July 21, 1998. The "manta ray" (see page 72). Photo: Frank Laumen

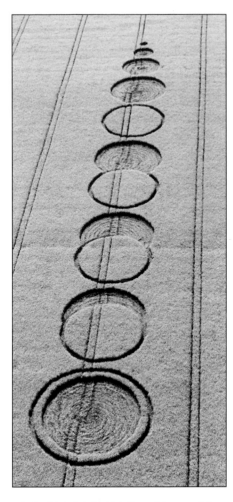

LEFT:
Hackpen Hill,
Wiltshire, July 4,
1999 (see page
78). Clever
geometry!
Photo: Frank
Laumen

ABOVE: Middle Wallop, Hampshire,
May 3, 1999. An eclipse...? (See page
74) Photo: Steve Alexander

BELOW: Cherhill, Wiltshire, July 18,
1999. An astonishing example of accuracy and neatness (see page 77).
Photo: Frank Laumen

ABOVE and LEFT: Roundway, Wiltshire,
July 31, 1999. The "splash" formation (see
page 77). Aerial photo: Frank Laumen.
Internal photo: Andy Thomas

BELOW: Barbury Castle, Wiltshire, May 31,
1999. This Hebrew "Menorah" made headlines in the Jewish press (see page 75).
Photo: Werner Anderhub

ABOVE: Beckhampton, Wiltshire, July 28, 1999. The amazing 3-D "ribbon" (see page 78). Photo: Werner Anderhub

ABOVE: Bishops Cannings, Wiltshire, August 6, 1999. The famous "basket weave" photo. This very unusual formation was cut down within hours of its appearance, making images of it a rare commodity.... (See page 78.) Photo: Ulrich Kox (THE BASKET © 1999 Ulrich Kox)

LEFT: East Kennett, Wiltshire, July 2, 2000. There are a remarkable 1,600 components making up this grid, which shift in width across the pattern (see page 82). Photo: Francine Blake

BELOW: Inside the East Kennett grid. The crop flowed around each individual element of the design. Photo: Frank Laumen

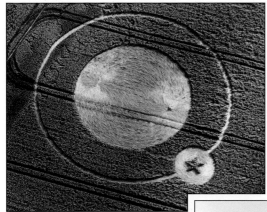

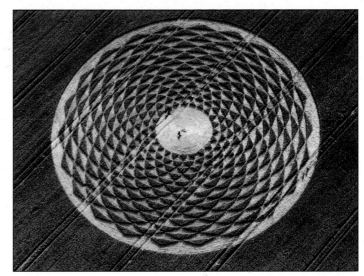

ABOVE: Picked Hill, Wiltshire, August 13, 2000. Forty-four inter-secting arcs create this sunflower-like design (see page 83). Photo: Frank Laumen

LEFT: Horton, Wiltshire, August 6, 2000. The lay had two centers, the flow sweeping radially around to form a standing clump at the opposite end! (See page 84.) Aerial photo: Frank Laumen. Internal photos: Andy Thomas

BELOW: Everleigh Ashes, Wiltshire, July 19, 2000. This has ingeniously incorporated a round barrow into its design (see page 82). Photo: Andreas Müller

BELOW: Windmill Hill, Wiltshire, June 18, 2000. The spherical-like 3-D effect is remarkable (see page 81). Photo: Francine Blake

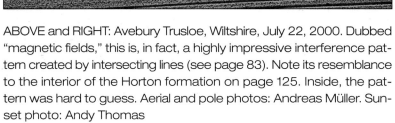

ABOVE and RIGHT: Avebury Trusloe, Wiltshire, July 22, 2000. Dubbed "magnetic fields," this is, in fact, a highly impressive interference pattern created by intersecting lines (see page 83). Note its resemblance to the interior of the Horton formation on page 125. Inside, the pattern was hard to guess. Aerial and pole photos: Andreas Müller. Sunset photo: Andy Thomas

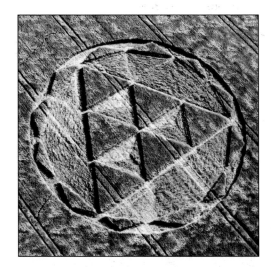

ABOVE: West Kennett, Wiltshire, June 2 and 3, 2000. This transformed itself overnight from a minor formation into a new, improved version! (See page 81.) Photo: Steve Alexander

BELOW: Uffington, Oxfordshire, July 24, 2000 (see page 83). This lay directly below the famous chalk horse carving. Photo: Werner Anderhub

ABOVE and RIGHT: Milk Hill, Wiltshire, August 12, 2001. Around 800 feet wide and with 409 circles, many with complex lays, it is the largest single diameter formation yet recorded. It made news around the world (see page 93). Aerial photo: Andrew King. Internal photos: Andy Thomas

BELOW: Chilbolton, Hampshire, August 13, 2000. A precursor to later events.... (See page 85.) Photo: Steve Alexander

ABOVE: Wakerley Woods, Barrowden, Northamptonshire, June 1, 2001. An ancient calendar? (See page 86.) Photo: Nick Nicholson

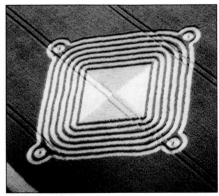

LEFT and ABOVE: Great Shelford, Cambridgeshire, July 11–13, 2001. This grew over three nights (see page 90), incorporating a ring, sacred maze and astonishing square mandala. Photos: Andrew King

RIGHT: Chilbolton, Hampshire, August 14 and 19, 2001. A "face" and "code" visit a radio telescope—a direct message at last...? (See page 95.) Photos: Francine Blake

BELOW: Great Shelford, Cambridgeshire, July 25, 2001. Christened "the angel," the straightness of the radiant lines is extraordinary (see page 90). Photo: Steve Alexander

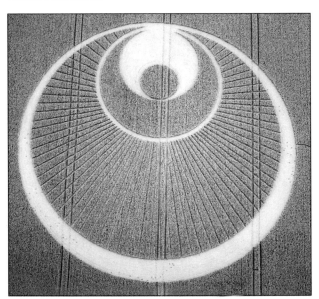

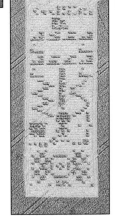

Anomalous lights are common at crop circles. The above four frames are taken from Patricia Murray's video showing the Barbury Castle formation of July 23, 1999. Shooting over a period of six minutes from the overlooking hill with a zoomed camcorder on a tripod, and unaware at the time of anything strange (probably being too distant to see the lights, as she was not looking through the viewfinder), the resultant unexpected images showed many small balls of light rising up from the flattened crop or soaring above it, as seen above. The visitors within seem unaware of the lights, possibly because they would have been mostly against the bright sky from their vantage point. Another video of a ball of light over the formation was taken by a different sightseer on the same day. Mundane explanations suggested by skeptics fail to account satisfactorily for many such sightings. (The lights have been very slightly enhanced here for clarity.)

3: STRANGE EFFECTS

It's not just the long history, scale or beauty of the crop formations that marks them out as something special. Since reports began, remarkable phenomena of light, sound and other effects have accompanied them....

Lights and Luminosities
"The Sky All of a Flame ..."

As we saw with the "Mowing Devil" account of 1678, glowing aerial phenomena have been a striking part of the crop circle mystery since reports began. Time and again strange lights are seen either coming down from the sky into fields where glyphs are subsequently found, or spotted flitting around existing ones and the areas where they form.[1] Many have seen these lights for themselves in a variety of circumstances, day and night. Of all the unusual effects which surround the circles, these are almost certainly the most documented.

This is no myth. There is enough video evidence and eye-witness testimony to show conclusively that such lights exist, whatever they may be. The luminosities tend to be a few feet or less across, amorphous and white, but variations have been witnessed, some colored and others even seeming to have some kind of material structure within their radiance.

Video Evidence

There have been several pieces of important video evidence taken over the years. One, taken by German students at Manton, Wiltshire in August 1991, shows a very small bright pin-point manoeuvring around a pictogram, sometimes above the ground, at times swooping in and out of the crop. Its brilliance fluctuates together with its size, which appears to decrease as it moves closer to the camcorder.

A year before, circle photographer Steve Alexander was lucky enough to capture footage of a bizarre tumbling object floating effortlessly on the breeze in a field at Milk Hill, Wiltshire in July 1990, not far from the large Stanton St Bernard pictogram (page 104). Again, its brightness

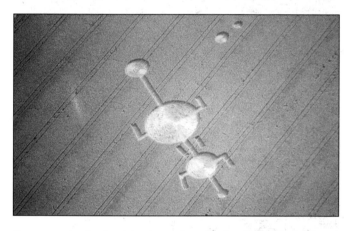

German students videotaped a glowing ball of light floating over and around this pictogram at Manton, Wiltshire, August 15, 1991. Photo: Andrew King.

seems inconsistent. After hovering around for a while, it sets off rapidly for the horizon, passing a ploughing tractor as it does. The driver later reported seeing this very object and described it as a bright disk or sphere.

Four years later, two Dutch visitors to Wiltshire were videoing the large "thought bubble" at Wilsford (page 50) from the side of the road in July 1994. As they watched, several radiant bursts of light, like arcing electricity, suddenly shot through the central ring at the top of the field.

There are several other pieces of visual evidence, including video taken by Colin Andrews in 1994 which seems to show a military helicopter pursuing a luminescent ball across fields at Alton Barnes while other helicopters swoop dangerously low over the East Field. In 1999, two separate people videoed light spheres over the same formation at Barbury Castle (see opposite and page 78). And, of course, there is the contentious footage of the Oliver's Castle snowflake appearing under swiftly circling glowing lights.

Video image from Steve Alexander's famous sequence of a glowing object hovering over fields at Stanton St Bernard, near Alton Barnes, taken from the brow of Milk Hill, July 26, 1990, 4.30 P.M.

There have, inevitably, been attempts from the skeptics to explain such videos away, ranging from accusations that the lights are nothing more than sunlit dandelion seeds (see introduction) to their being luminous seabirds (!). Even if every light recorded isn't truly anomalous, most such efforts to denigrate much of the evidence are laughably puerile and don't take into account either the circumstances at the time or the fact that other witnesses may have seen the lights for themselves with vision far better than a pixilated camera-eye.

The Camera Eye

Photographic records of balls of light are harder to verify and easier to fake or confuse with a processing anomaly. Many pictures which purport to show such effects are produced by inexperienced camera operators and are almost certainly lens flare (where the sun produces internal reflections), marks on the film emulsion, condensation on the glass or flash-illuminated moisture drops. Those who produce such pictures nine times out of ten didn't see anything at the time (just taking a normal photo in a crop circle), but vigorously defend their "proof of the paranormal" to the end.

However, there are occasionally photographs which are harder to explain in these terms, sometimes with eye-witness accounts to back them up. Researchers like Andrew Collins have also experimented with different film-stocks, speeds and unusual camera techniques and believe they have managed to capture images of energy forms not visible in the usual spectrum, but which are nevertheless present at some locations associated with crop circles and ancient sites (perhaps connected with "earth energy").[2]

What Are the Lights?

Most involved with the circles accept that the lights are very real, but few can really explain them or their role in the phenomenon. At times these luminescent globes appear to move randomly; in other circumstances they almost act with intent. They can even seem to respond to the thoughts of those observing them, which suggests that some may be psychic projections, or at least affected by human consciousness.[3] During the work carried out by members of Southern Circular Research, glowing lights seemed to form in response to the amount of activity generated towards attempted communication with the forces behind the crop circles. Carl Jung certainly believed most UFO sightings were telekinetic projections more to do with the mind than extra-terrestrials, as described in his book *Flying Saucers* (1959). But then what of those who actually claim to have witnessed structured nuts-and-bolts

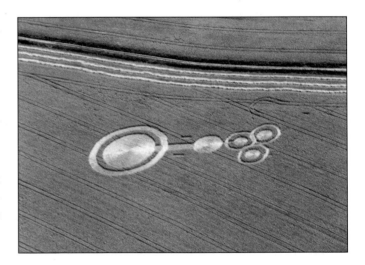

Upper Beeding, West Sussex, July 23, 1995. On the night this appeared, an eye-witness watched colored points of light moving swiftly around part of the field and up into the sky. Next morning, the pictogram was found at the very same spot. Photo: Andy Thomas

spacecraft hovering over fields making crop circles? Are these projections too? It may be there is more than one source of strange lights in the sky (and maybe even of crop formations).

Since records began, folklore has spoken of "fairy folk" who would dance through fields and woods, glowing brightly. Such luminosities have been seen without cerealogical connotations. Could there be a general cause which produces such phenomena in certain conditions? Those, like dowsers, who believe the planet is covered with a grid of energy lines produced by running water and quartz-generated piezoelectric fields (see Chapter 4) also hold that this energy can manifest visually and travel along the lines, giving the appearance of sentience. Perhaps organic life, which also produces energy fields, influences it, hence the interactive behavior observed. These effects may well be the same as "earthquake lights," luminous globes which are known to sometimes appear shortly before major movements of the Earth's crust, created by vast pressures on crystalline rock. If, as many believe, the crop circles are formed by, or channel, earth energy, the lights may be nothing more than a side product of the process involved.

On the other hand, circle lights are often seen to come *downward* from the sky, suggesting a more aerial source. Several major formations have had such associated sightings on the night of their birth. Terence Meaden believed the luminescence was produced by electrically charged plasma, spinning in an atmospheric vortex (apparently confirmed by the Tomlinson's eye-witness account, page 28) and the work of W C Levengood has confirmed many of Meaden's findings. However, some of the lights appear to be separate components rather than continuously glowing funnels. One night, an eye-witness at Upper Beeding, West Sussex in 1995 saw a number of multi-colored points moving rapidly around in amongst the standing crop of a wheat field before *ascending* upwards out of sight. Next morning a large pictogram was found at exactly the same spot.[4] In the controversial Oliver's Castle footage, the lights are seen to arc across the area where the pattern appears, without actually touching the crop. It is assumed by many that they are the agents responsible for laying the plants down in such alleged sightings, but it's possible the luminosities are simply energies produced or attracted by whatever mechanism is employed, moving in an ordered but natural spontaneous dance.

Inside the star at Bishops Cannings, Wiltshire, July 13, 1997. Even after harvesting, this seemed to hold energy of some kind, producing a discharge of light. Photo: Andy Thomas

"Ball lightning" has also been spoken of as a possible explanation, but seeing as this in itself is barely understood even by scientists and seems to appear in varied weather conditions, it may be that this simply describes one of the same processes above. Unusual "flashes," more like normal lightning, have been witnessed over circle fields, but are soundless and usually localized. One early evening in 1997, a friend and I walked what was left of the Bishops Cannings star after harvest, its pattern still clearly visible. As we deliberately traced the outline of the pentagram with our steps, there was a feeling of heat and static rising. Walking off the star, we paused for a moment and looked back. Almost instantly a streak of bright, white light shot across the top of the formation. It was as if our actions had stimulated and then discharged some energy residue in the pattern.

This recalled a similar experience I had with psychic and author Paul Bura while walking a painted maze in a meditative state, as an experiment. As one approached the center, there was a clear feeling of energy build-up and rising heat. This and similar experiments conducted by others suggests that all shapes, even two-dimensional ones, generate power of some kind which may manifest as light emissions on a larger scale.[5]

There are some who believe that the glowing points really *are* fairies, or Devas as more modernly described, nature spirits which tend to the planet's needs, giving off light as they go about their business. Some extra-terrestrial adherents are more militant about things and insist that any light in the sky must be a craft of some kind and that the balls of light are miniature "probes" sent down to create—or observe the creation of—formations. Certainly, other objects and non-luminous aerial shapes have also been observed. ("Traditional" UFOs are discussed in Chapter 4.)

Whatever the explanation, perhaps this is a literal demonstration that there's no smoke without fire and the aerial phenomena connection has convinced many observers that the crop patterns are something more than a prank. However, some alleged hoaxers have taken to claiming "their" work attracts glowing energies on the above-mentioned basis that all shapes may hold power, whatever their source. It's not just pretty lights though, that distinguish the circles' strangeness....

Sounds
Noises Off

Over the years, a number of mysterious sounds have been heard and recorded at formations. These range from electrical crackling noises to spooky "knockings," and even disembodied footsteps at the Bythorn mandala of 1993 (page 48). Sometimes such sounds are audible at the time, but on other occasions have appeared only on audio or video recordings when played back later. In extreme cases, some claim to have heard ghostly voices giving messages.

Trills and Spills

The most widely-known and controversial sound reported in connection with the circles is without doubt the infamous "trilling," first noted by Pat Delgado and Colin Andrews in the 1980s. This haunting high-pitched mechanical chattering was heard on a number of occasions, most prominently during *Operation White Crow* in 1989, where a group of crop-watchers chased this seemingly unearthly phenomena around a field in the hope of finding its source. Variations have been described: Vivien and Gary Tomlinson recall an extremely loud noise like "pan-pipes" during their experience of a circle forming around them, the effect of which apparently perforated Vivien's eardrums. The alleged Oliver's Castle 1996 cameraman claimed to have heard a distinctive tone like "crickets" just before the formation appeared (although mention of this familiar cerealogical attribute has been used as much to discredit his story as confirm it, some believing it too conveniently unlikely that he would have heard this *and* videoed a pattern forming).

It has been speculated that the trilling may be the raw product of the energy which creates the circles, an acoustic effect caused by the fast movement of air or even the "voices" of the intelligences some believe are responsible. Certainly high-frequency sound could play a role in the laying down of the crops. Experiments with "cymatics" carried out with granular particles on tight drum-skins or oil on water have shown that highly complex geometric patterns can result when different sounds are vibrated through them.[6]

For all these sophisticated possibilities though, there is a chance that many reports of such a sound may be attributable to nothing more haunting than a bird. One of the natives of southern England's meadows is the Grasshopper Warbler, so named because of the distinctive chirping it produces, day or night. Comparisons with recordings of the circle trilling and the song of the Grasshopper Warbler have allegedly shown them to be almost identical. The bird's uncanny habit of "throwing its voice" can produce disorienting effects which give the impression of an incorporeal, floating sound. Some hold that this explains all the trilling experiences in and around crop circles, but others remain unconvinced.[7]

Interestingly, as part of the experiment at Wolstonbury

Hill, West Sussex in 1995 which appeared to produce a pictogram with the power of thought (as described in *Quest For Contact*; see also page 152), notes of music were played in a chord. Recorded using synthesized "sine waves," the purest form of sound, the notes were transformed into a very high-pitched warbling tone—and bore an uncanny resemblance to the circle-trilling. Thus, while the Grasshopper Warbler may account for some reports, it doesn't have the monopoly on producing such effects.

Physical Phenomena

Energy or Psychodrama?

A significant number of people, on entering formations, experience all manner of different physical effects, not only on their own bodies but also on electronic and mechanical equipment. Most researchers agree that some kind of "energy" appears to radiate from the shapes, which can generate specific responses (see Chapter 4). Dowsers believe this is due to an earthly geophysical power grid utilized in the creation of crop patterns. Others put it down to the residue from whatever extra-terrestrial technology may be responsible. Skeptics say it's all psychosomatic claptrap, but while the auto-suggestion of being in such a mysterious space and other factors may explain some of the alleged incidents, a number suggest real forces are at work, which the presence of other anomalous phenomena supports.

Health Effects

The most basic but common experience of bodily-affected visitors is that of a mild tingling, like "pins and needles" or hot and cold waves. Mostly this is faint and not unpleasant, but occasionally some have found it severe enough to make them leave. These feelings can persist, but often recede after stepping outside the pattern, demonstrating the very localized nature of the effect. Some become energized by this, but others report feeling abnormally drained.

Other influences can be more extreme, in good and bad directions. Sharp headaches are often reported on entering circles, although simple sunstroke can be mistaken for something more unearthly. It's when such headaches vanish immediately on departing that suspicions are aroused. On the other hand, visitors *with* existing ailments who enter patterns have been known to find their symptoms gone within minutes of stepping inside. There have even

Many are tempted to rest or meditate inside circles (as here at the 1997 Bishops Cannings star), sensing radiating energies. But are these effects good or bad for people? Photo: Andy Thomas

been tales of very severe illnesses having been cured by such visits, although no proof has ever been forthcoming. Before leaping into a field to put this to the test, people should be advised that there are those who have left formations and been very ill for days afterwards.

Nausea and sore throats are common amongst the complaints recorded in circles, and sufferers have also referred to a peculiar metallic taste in their mouths. Interestingly, these effects and headaches are known to result from exposure to electrical fields in other circumstances.

Normal bodily functions can also be influenced by crop circles, it seems. Notably, a number of women who independently entered the Stonehenge and Windmill Hill fractals of 1996 found their menstrual cycles profoundly disrupted for months afterwards and more than one post-menopausal visitor experienced unexpected "periods" and sudden bleeding. Why these two formations in particular should have had this dramatic result is not known.

Specific patterns certainly seem to generate more health effects than others. Uncannily, the three tailed circles which resembled a nest of number sixes—ie. 666, the biblical "number of the beast"—at West Overton, Wiltshire in 1993 (page 110) provoked a spate of migraines and left many feeling exhausted after just a few minutes inside. Natural superstition could account for some psychological reactions, but some sufferers were unaware of its configuration when inside it. The apparent symbolism (which was only one, quite possibly incorrect, interpretation) in this case could be pure coincidence, of course. A pictogram of crescents and standing tufts at Furze Knoll, Wiltshire in 1994 (page 112) also provoked overwhelmingly bad health reactions.

Are some formations inherently positive or negative in their energy content, or do they simply accentuate the personal tendencies of visitors? Adherents to the energy grid theory (as in *Feng Shui* and geomancy) believe some energy lines can become "black" due to natural geophysical influences or deliberate psychic interference. If a pattern were to form on one of these, it might exude predominantly harmful emissions, whereas a clear line might produce a physically stimulating glyph. It has even been said that various designs may be made by different groups of extra-terrestrials, some with positive intentions and others disruptive ones in a kind of ongoing interstellar battle for the hearts and souls of humankind.... Yet some crop circles provoke good and bad reactions in different people, suggesting that sometimes, at least, they can be neutral, nudging to extremes whatever properties one takes inside in the first place.

Chemical Causes?

Before spinning off into the ether with talk of celestial energies accounting for all effects, particularly the unpleasant ones, one other cause should be considered. Unless on an organic farm, the chances are any field one ever enters is contaminated with pesticides and chemical sprays. It is

SCR member Jason Porthouse tests an electrostatic meter in search of unusual readings inside the "splash" formation (page 123) at Roundway, Wiltshire, July 31, 1999. Photo: Andy Thomas

quite possible that many of the detrimental experiences are due to contact with poisonous substances which coat the very food we eventually eat. Whether these should be utilized at all is for individuals to decide, but, like it or not, they are currently present in most crops. Gleefully, we traipse into fields, brushing the plants against our skin and clothes, breathing the dust and air around them, with barely a thought for the wisdom of this action. Reported headaches and even vomiting "caused by crop circles" may have more to do with this much neglected peril. Visiting one formation in 1995, members of Southern Circular Research discovered drums of pesticide at the field's edge and read the instructions (marked with warning symbols—and this stuff goes into the food chain!). The note strongly advised that no-one should enter the field for a full seven days after spraying.... Does it occur to farmers who give their permission to enter fields to say when they last sprayed? And do we ever think to ask?

Note of Caution

While the circles have never shown anything but benevolence, all these apparent influences on the human system, from whatever source, energy or chemical, raises the question of safety. People with delicate constitutions may be better advised to avoid entering fields, and it has been suggested that pregnant women should be cautious, especially given the effect of the 1996 fractals.

This also calls into question a new trend which involves leaving small bottles of water in circles to soak up their "essence," sold on as "health aids" in the hope that the resident energy fields will have been homeopathically recorded in the contents. Why, given the highly variable consequences noted above, is it assumed these will have healing powers? Other, more scientific tests have been conducted by burying similar bottles underneath formations to see what effects will result when later analyzed and this work needs to continue much longer before conclusions are jumped to.[8]

Animal Tragic

It's not just humans who can be oddly affected. There are many accounts of animals, particularly dogs (inevitably common as visitors' companions), exhibiting extreme behavior once inside a crop pattern. Some become cowed and nervous, others violent and uncontrollable. Whether this is a reaction to the same qualities so far discussed, or their accentuated senses can pick up things we are not attuned to, is uncertain. Some have speculated that the trilling sound associated with circles is always present, but only occasionally drops into our audible frequency. Dogs and other creatures have a far higher range of hearing than people and may respond to it more easily. On nights formations appear there are often reports of local animals reacting wildly to an unknown stimulant. It's possible they are tuning in to something we can't detect ourselves.

Dead wild animals are very rarely found inside crop patterns, where one might frequently expect to find squashed field mice and other fauna. A macabre discovery of flies, some still alive, fused to the stems in a formation at Cherhill in 1998 was a bizarre rarity.[9] Apart from occasional deceased birds, which may have been subsequently attacked by foxes as birds are very attracted to fallen crop for its easily obtainable seeds, the only noted records of directly circle-flattened victims are of two porcupines in Canada, 1992. In two separate events, both had seemingly been caught up in the swirl of the crop. One had almost disintegrated into blackened parts and the other had been squashed like a pancake....[10] (One presumes, from this unfortunate effect, that the Tomlinsons, who had a formation appear around them, were subjected to something rather less strong.) Most animals in a field, with their heightened faculties, probably sense something is about to happen and run away. Porcupines, as part of their natural defense, raise their spines and sit tight. A bad idea in the face of an imminent crop circle.

Ghost in the Machine

Other things besides organisms also seem to be adversely influenced. Mechanical and electronic hardware can be disabled, sometimes terminally, once placed inside circles. Coincidence can account for some of this, but there does seem to be an unlikely statistical tendency. Complete breakdowns of combine harvesters when crossing circles are the most dramatic examples (there have been several occurrences of this), but camera malfunctions are the most prevalent, if only because photography is the prime motivation of many visitors. Camera autowinds suddenly reel off film, or their shutters jam. Most of these effects could be attributable to unusual energies affecting the electronics, but some of the problems can be physical (manual winds failing). Worse, when cameras do work, the eventual results can be smeared with inexplicable streaks, marks or entirely black frames which appear only on the crop circle pictures, but nowhere else. Video equipment is particularly vulnerable, prone to picking up severe interference, as has been experienced by more than one TV crew.

Anything electronic seems to be at risk at circle-sites, and battery draining is a major symptom. Even fresh power packs can mysteriously die as soon as the boundary of a formation is crossed. On a few notable occasions, frustratingly, they have been known to immediately recharge when leaving again.

Magnetic compasses have also been known to behave very oddly, needles pointing in the wrong direction or spinning wildly. Sometimes this is genuinely mysterious, but it should be cautioned that this is an easy effect for someone to mistake as anomalous—the presence of any metal (ie. belt buckles, watches, etc.) can seriously divert compass dials, confusing the inexperienced.

Steve Alexander raising his camera high in the time-honored "pole shot" method of photographing crop circles, here at Southease, East Sussex, May 1995. An above-average number of unusual camera malfunctions are reported inside formations. Photo: Marcus Allen

Mobile telephones are other common victims of the circle effect. If their batteries are unharmed, they still may not work, as something appears to interfere with their transmission frequency at times. There are tales of handsets which work just a few feet outside of agriglyphs, but refuse to function a step or two within. Curiously, this signal jamming has also been noted at some stone circles. If

A TV camera crew prepare to interview researcher Karen Douglas inside a pattern at Silbury Hill, Wiltshire, June 1996. Video equipment is also prone to developing serious faults at circle sites. Photo: Andy Thomas

such monuments and crop circles are placed at similar points of earth energy as dowsers believe, maybe it's the radiating natural emissions which cause the problems, not a specific quality of the pictograms themselves.

Stories of Substance

In addition to all these effects and the physical phenomena examined by W C Levengood and others, as outlined in Chapter 1, unusual substances and markings have also been found on the laid plants themselves, ranging from unexplained red spots, carbon blackening and silver dust, to blobs of a white jelly-like substance. While some have turned out to be paint, melted sweets or natural effects, others have shown less conclusive analysis results. Such uncertainties draw sneers from skeptics, but with nothing to compare hitherto unexplored samples to, drawing firm conclusions is inevitably difficult with so little to go on, highlighting the need for further serious work in these areas.

Time Anomalies
A Glitch in Time

Incredible though it may seem, on rare occasions there have been accounts of tricks being played with chronology in and around crop formations, which seem to suggest space and time themselves are twisted by their appearance.

A few glyphs have actually seemed to wink in and out of existence — or at the very least premonitions have been received by individuals of what would soon appear, visions so strong they believed they witnessed them with their eyes. On July 28th 1992, Barry Reynolds, Martin Noakes and myself drove out to look at a new Sussex formation which had just arrived. On the way, we scanned fields in the hope of finding another — and we succeeded, spotting a new pictogram at West Blatchington. A field we also checked was one at Patcham, near Brighton, which had played host to a dumbbell the year before and was clearly visible all around. It was empty. Yet as we journeyed to and from the new pattern we had gone to see, a friend of Barry's parents Jean and Stan was trying to contact them to inform them of a new formation at Patcham … in the very field we had looked in. Jean and Stan were out for the day and uncontactable. We returned along the same road *after* this friend had made his first call and double-checked the field. There was nothing there. Later that day, Jean and Stan, by chance, also passed the field and checked it, still unaware of the friend's "discovery." It was resolutely circle-free. Next day their friend got through and reported his find. None of us could believe there was really anything there — we knew because we had all checked the field. I drove out to look, resignedly, but just in case … and there was the new pictogram exactly as he had described, in full view, *which he had seen the morning before,* even though it had not been present then.

There are other accounts of people swearing formations were present when no-one else saw them, and vice-versa. It's as if a hole in time momentarily opens up to reveal the presence of a future event — or, in some cases, a past one?

One of two anomalous photographs taken inside the 1991 "whale" at Lockeridge, Wiltshire, August 1991, appearing to show a slight but astonishing time shift. Photo: John Holman

Whale of a Time

One apparent time anomaly was actually caught on film by researcher John Holman while exploring the "whale" at Lockeridge, Wiltshire in 1991. Taking photographs on the day, John noticed nothing unusual about his visit. It was only when he received the processed film that he discovered two extraordinary frames.

The outer part of one photo is entirely normal, showing trees, sky and field, but the center, with the formation, seems, at first, to have been double-exposed, showing two slightly staggered images of three people standing inside. One of the overlapped images clearly captures the people a second or so after the positions they have in the first, as they have moved slightly. In other words, the central part of the picture shows two separate images caught at different intervals — but the photo can't be a double exposure because this effect only takes place in the middle. The outer border is without doubt one exposure only. It's as if time suddenly fractured in the localized area and leapt forward very marginally the instant the shutter clicked .

A second photo, taken a short time after the first, reverses this effect — the center of the frame is normal, but the outer part showing trees and the horizon has two staggered overlapping images showing one ghost image of each tree to the left side on the left of the picture and another ghost to the right of trees on the right. A tree at the center of the picture has ghost images on either side!

Experiments with clocks in crop patterns have produced results which suggest that time can run abnormally within them.... (Circle center, Westbury, Wiltshire, July 1987.) Photo: Dr. Terence Meaden

Both the photographs and the negatives were thoroughly checked over by laboratories at Kodak and by the president of the Photographic Society; both confirmed that this effect couldn't possibly result from double exposing or faulty processing.

Stop-Watch Crop-Watch

There have been a number of tests made comparing the behavior of extremely accurate clocks inside crop patterns with counterparts outside. A team of Russian scientists tried this in the early 1990s using electronic equipment and, fascinatingly, found that the clocks inside the circles lost about a second a day.

Enthusiast Derek Carvell and friends attempted something similar in 1995, with more dramatic results, using the Winterbourne Bassett, Wiltshire motif of rings and squares (page 56). Over three nights in July at about 1:00 A.M., a modern Avia digital stop-watch was placed inside, while an identical synchronized one was left in a car. The first night the circle stop-watch gained an astonishing thirty-one minutes, the second night it gained twenty-one and on the third it *lost* four. Derek experienced other strange occurrences while carrying out the experiments, including flashes of light. Tests showed that the stop-watches were functioning perfectly and hadn't been tampered with. Something in the crop circle had seemingly mutated time in a remarkable way.[11]

Others have had other personal brushes with apparent time anomalies, from more extreme cases like inexplicable lost intervals while visiting formations, to odd little observations like noticing that shadows around them are at completely the wrong the angle for the time of day.

What could account for all these time dilation reports, which can't all be mistake and imagination? Is it that the circles act as gateways to places where the laws of space and time differ from ours (as some believe), or that the energies radiating outward somehow bend the fabric of this dimension, taking time with it as Einsteinian theory demands it must? Or, as some have suggested, is the very force which lays the crops down no physical flattening process, but a specific warping of space which takes anything in the vicinity with it, enabling stems to curve with little obvious damage? This could also affect the local structure of time.[12]

Unifying Theories

It all sounds like science fiction. This multitude of strange effects which consistently surround and deepen the crop circle riddle remain as unexplained as the origins of the shapes themselves. Any theory to account for the phenomenon must take these challenging aspects into consideration. That many don't highlights their flaws, and never more so than with the debunkers who would have us believe it is simply a huge practical joke in the face of all this evidence, arrogantly dismissed as nonsense and lies. Until one unifying explanation comes along, the arguments and discussion as to the source of the circles will continue. However, we can explore the possibilities....

NOTES

1. Including myself, as documented in *Quest For Contact* and various *SCs*, in particular an article by Martin Noakes in issue 20, August 1993, pages 8–10.

2. The results of such experiments are recounted in Andrew Collins' books *The Circlemakers* and *Alien Energy*.

3. In *The Circlemakers*, Andrew Collins tells the story of a non-circle related skywatch at Hessdalen, Norway in which balls of light formed themselves into archetypal images for the observers, creating the shapes of Christmas trees and even Marilyn Monroe (!) on one occasion, seemingly in an interactive process.

4. *Fields of Mystery*, page 79.

5. *Quest For Contact*, Chapter 1, page 26.

6. Andrew Collins includes some examples in *The Circlemakers*, Chapter 9, page 86, and there are excellent demonstrations in Andreas Müller's German book *Kornkriese: Geometrie, Phanomene, Forschung* (A T Verlag, 2001), Chapter 8, pages 130–132.

7. This explanation was first proposed in the article *White Crow & Grasshopper Warbler*, Ken Brown, *The Cerealogist*, issue 6, Summer 1992.

8. Researcher Lucy Pringle has done the most detailed work on this aspect and keeps a comprehensive database of physical effects on people in formations. She has also experimented with monitoring brainwave reactions. Lucy's work is documented in *The Human Effect Report*, *SC*, issue 58, November 1996, pages 8–12, and heavily features in her book *Crop Circles: The Greatest Mystery of Modern Times*.

9. A good compact report on the fused flies can be found in Dr. Eltjo Haselhoff's book *The Deepening Complexity of Crop Circles*, Chapter 1, page 13.

10. *SC*, issue 20, August 1993, page 12.

11. The full story is told by Derek in *SC*, issue 46, November 1995, page 5.

12. Ronald Thomas explores this idea in *SC*, issue 31, July 1994, page 16.

Surveying a pictogram, Froxfield, Wiltshire, August 9, 1992. Photo: Grant Wakefield

4: DEFINING THE SOURCE

The question most commonly asked about crop circles is "What's making them?" Over twenty years down the line since dedicated research began, it's a puzzle that still hasn't been answered. There are, however, many theories which might account for them, though few seem to logically explain all aspects of the phenomenon. A whole book could be devoted to such speculation, but this chapter dips into the most prevalent ideas....

Cosmic Intelligences

Saucer Marks

A combination of the quintuplets and reports of lights in the sky first gave serious rise to the idea that other-worldly beings were creating the crop circles. For many, the symmetrical markings were traces of flying saucers, which had descended into the cornfields. The Australians first christened the small circular impressions they were finding in the outback "UFO nests" for the same reasons. Why a craft should want to alight in acres of awkwardly high plants instead of flat grassland has never been adequately explored, nevertheless this was a prevailing notion for a while. The resemblance of the quintuplets to the bulbous undersides of the craft allegedly witnessed by ET contactee George Adamski in the 1950s compounded this. When it was noted that the crops were actually swirled down in complex flows and not crushed, the supposition was adjusted to allow for the fact that the crops might be twisted downward by the energy fields of alien ship's drives, as opposed to physically squashed.

It's easy to be cynical here, but although the majority of strange sightings are of disembodied lights, there have been a number of reports of apparently structured craft seen hovering over fields where circles are subsequently found. In time, it began to look more likely that the crop markings were actually symbols and the belief that the circles were evidence of extra-terrestrial landings gave way to the more widely-accepted hypothesis that they were being deliberately created as overtures of cosmic communication. To begin with, flesh and blood aliens ("Greys," "Nordics," etc.) were widely assumed to be the source, but some have gone on to suspect a more ethereal other-dimensional influence from intelligences that may have no physical form as we know it.

Alphabet Soup

The basic communication theory runs that instead of extra-terrestrials turning up in huge fear-inducing *Independence Day*-type ships, a more subtle way of announcing their presence is being sought, which involves attracting the attention of humankind more gently and gradually. By creating a small number of almost insignificant ground markings, which defy mundane explanation, interest is slowly aroused in certain groups of people. As each year goes by, an increasing number are made and the circles begin to grow more complex to keep the momentum of curiosity going. When these have been accepted, they are developed into symbols which begin to transmit information on a subconscious level, like the slow introduction of an alien alphabet. Before we know it, we find ourselves caught up in a communication process and have begun to ask questions about the mystery that lead us to surmise the involvement of another intelligence. Presto! The extra-terrestrials have announced themselves without panic being generated, and in a beautiful, benevolent way have presumably prepared humanity for an eventual revelation of their full presence.

Alternatively, the crop glyphs could be warnings or symbols of something deeper than a simple communique. What they may *mean* for us is discussed more fully in the final chapter.

Grey Areas

How much evidence is there for extra-terrestrials being responsible for the circle phenomenon? One of the other great mysteries of modern times is alien abduction, where

ET-bearing flying saucers? No, in this case it's a saucepan lid, but some claim to have witnessed genuine structured craft hovering over crop circles. Photo: Danny Sotham

people claim to have made contact, usually under duress, with physical ETs, often short, grey hairless humanoids with large almond eyes, although many variations have been described. Recollection of these encounters, usually retrieved under hypnosis, can be frightening, with sinister medical "operations" being described, but other accounts have spoken of productive dialogues. A number of people recall having been shown designs which are known, or have later appeared as, crop formations. Some earlier abductees have even claimed that beings they met prophesied the coming of the pictograms decades later and showed them visions of other future events.

Some speak of having witnessed "Greys" inspecting crop circles or appearing in areas where they form. For example, in July 1994 a group of teenagers claimed to have observed a craft land opposite Silbury Hill, whereby small beings emerged and began to lay out a grid of light in the field.

To some there is no doubt at all that formations are created as messages from "conventional" ETs, whether by Greys or some other race. Michael Hesemann's book *The Cosmic Connection* puts a robust case for this. (Doug Ruby, in his book *The Gift,* takes the idea further by proposing that the symbols are actually two-dimensional blueprints for the propulsion devices used in alien craft, being offered to humanity as an overture of friendship.) The problem is that apart from very rare instances, much of the evidence is circumstantial and some events can be interpreted in a number of ways.

All manner of lights and objects have been reported in and around formations over the years, many of which have been described as "craft" in the absence of any better explanation. However, the phenomena actually videoed so far have been almost exclusively glowing spheres or amorphous radiances. With the idea of UFOs and spaceships so ingrained in our culture, some witnesses to aerial lights may simply describe them in the only frame of reference they have. As a result, the number of actual structured objects witnessed may be less than some statistics would suggest.

Those cases of "solid" sightings which remain are undeniably fascinating, and a few have been seen to emit luminous beams down into fields where crop circles are then found. A large dark object was even seen in the skies the night the 1991 Barbury Castle event occurred. But interestingly, such accounts are predominantly from overseas reports. Many are of craft seen over *existing* patterns. Why, when beheld in these circumstances, is it assumed they were responsible for creating them? If alien craft, do they have reasons of their own for loitering so obviously? Could it be they are just as curious as human visitors and are simply observing a mystery they had nothing to do with?

Work into psychic interaction with UFOs suggests that human consciousness can sometimes influence their behavior. Crop circles also respond to the stimulant of human thought (page 151). This could be taken to indicate that ETs have a certain level of telepathic awareness. However, it might also be that UFOs are not always quite as solid as they seem. Is it beyond the realms of possibility, as surmised by Andrew Collins in his books *The Circlemakers* and *Alien Energy,* that there is a raw energy which can be shaped by human expectation and that observation of UFO phenomena is a two way process in which each can affect the other? In this scenario, popular impressions in the consciousness of what a UFO should constitute may determine the nature of that which is witnessed. If this sounds extreme, it's interesting to note that something similar seems to occur at some very public apparitions of what are claimed to be the Virgin Mary or even Jesus, in which iconic Christian figures appear in a glow of light to crowds of people (most famously at Fatima, Portugal during the First World War, but visions continue around the world to this day). On occasion, those primed with a religious belief system or heightened expectation have been known to see these presences, while more agnostic observers simply report luminosities or UFO activity. The visual sightings themselves are almost certainly real on some level, but the psychic interpretation seems to be subjective.

Similarly, it has been suggested that alien abductions take place more in the realm of the mind than in physical reality, although the experience may well be "genuine." Recurring Freudian symbolism, often with sexual overtones, indicates to some that the whole scenario could be an archetypal thought-form expressing hidden traumas. In this view, any information on crop circles received from abduction recollections may still be valid, but picked up on a precognitive psychic level.

On the other hand, there are claimed eye-witnesses to people being taken up into structured craft and talk of unidentified "implants" being physically removed from abductees afterwards. "Missing time," where victims can find several hours unaccounted for during the chronology of their experiences, intensifies the puzzle. The whole abduction issue is a controversial and sensitive one which it isn't the remit of this book to explore. Likewise, the extraordinary and morbid incidences of "cattle mutilation," where animals are found dead, their major organs removed with laser-like precision and no blood trails, have been linked with UFO sightings and hence crop circles by some.[1] There have been incidences where circles have been found in the vicinity of "bovine excisions," but few can bring themselves to accept that something which can create such beauty and benevolence would also treat living beings in this way (although the same could be said of the human race!). Any links may again be circumstantial, although some have argued otherwise.

There is certainly some evidence and testimony which, on the surface, appears to support the view that structured spacecraft *are* visiting our planet. The 1947 Roswell incident (well-covered in many books), for instance, widely believed to be the retrieval of a crashed vessel and its alien occupants, together with other well-documented cases of close encounters, if true, give more credence to the view that crop formations *could* be made by ETs.

Missing Pieces

If the ET hypothesis is to be seriously considered, there are a number of missing pieces in the jigsaw that remain to be addressed.

One is the apparent dependency of formations on certain geophysical conditions in the ground, as discussed in Chapter 1. Maps of southern England's geological strata show a clear correlation with aquiferous rocks which carry water. Earth energy theorists believe these help generate the spark for circle creation. Why would beings presumably far more technologically advanced than us need to rely on the terrestrial environment to create their patterns? If, as some have proposed, the ET methods used to make them are so highly-evolved, the circle-makers could perform anywhere and on a much larger scale than they currently do. Why not place the designs in far more obvious places if they wish to attract the attention of humankind—ie. on some of the vast tracts of land in the USA, or even the White House lawn? Many have appeared in isolated, inaccessible locations. And why not make them far larger? What restricts superior forces to making their main center of activity a small European country? (Despite global events, the phenomenon is primarily European.) Why, also, do regional designs appear, occasionally of seeming symbolic relevance only to specific groups of people in certain areas? Why would ETs go to the trouble of targeting individuals and then doing so in such an indecipherable manner (unless they were training them in some obscure way)?

Geographically, it could be argued that there is something special about the landscape with Stonehenge at its center to which ETs are trying to draw our attention. Maybe they are not as advanced as we presume and rely on natural energy as their tool. Yet such a reliance effectively makes the crop formations only selectively available to the world's population on any useful scale, which does rather call the whole scenario into question.

If the glyphs are direct communications to be interpreted, as many consider, why do they remain so wilfully ambiguous? Messages written in human letters would admittedly either scare or, most likely, not be taken seriously, considering the general reception even the symbols have had (there have been letter formations—all have been branded hoaxes), but if ETs really wanted to reach out just to speak to us, they could give clearer indications than the circles provide. This, of course, assumes they understand our language (although Greys reportedly do). Perhaps our races are so different that only the universal (we presume!) language of geometry and mathematics is viable at this stage. The symbolic obscurity is also more understandable if the glyphs are placed not to speak as such, but to instead inspire questioning which makes us reach further within ourselves. They may be a test or an attempt to educate and further our evolution. But what of the plethora of simple circles which seem to have been appearing for several centuries now? In times when extraterrestrial life was barely even contemplated, would there have been a point in creating such austere markings for so long, which attracted almost no attention? Or could it be that a genuine atmospheric condition which produces natural circle-forming vortices on rare occasions has only recently been adapted for intelligent use to make predetermined symbols?

There may well be answers to these conundrums which will make more sense of the ET hypothesis, but at present they remain elusive.

Extra-Dimensionals

For those convinced the formations are the intervention of sentient intelligence, not all see it in terms of physical aliens operating structured craft, or at least not ones in the same dimension as us. Some have surmised highly-evolved superbeings existing as conscious energy fields, which have transcended material structure and have the ability to create dimensional gateways through which they enter, leaving crop circles behind them as evidence of life beyond the earthly plain. (It's possible the two-dimensional markings we see in the fields are produced by three-dimensional energy forms passing through the Earth's surface.)

Perhaps ancient minds, which may have monitored our evolutionary progress since time began, are attempting to stimulate humanity's progress at different stages in history by transmitting symbols of deep spiritual truths in the landscape, rather like the purpose of the enigmatic monoliths in the film *2001: A Space Odyssey* (the premise of which has been likened to the crop circles on several occasions).

However, even in this more esoteric scenario, many of the same questions which challenge the basic ET theory still raise their heads.

Gaia and Her Nature Spirits

It was James Lovelock who first proposed the "Gaia" principle, that the Earth is a massive self-regulating superorganism of which human activity is simply one system. Some take this principle one stage further. The fact that the crop glyphs are carved onto the surface of the planet in mostly chemically-treated organic matter has led many to see them as messages from a sentient, spiritually-evolved Earth Mother, using the manipulation of natural energy fields to call attention to her plight, threatened by pollution and mineral exploitation. Believers in nature spirits or "Devas" (the fairies of old) see these invisible servants of the planet as being inextricably involved in the process, acting as organized strata of consciousness for each thread of life on Earth.

Those who speak of "Ascension," whereby the Earth is said to be rising to a new and glorious "vibrational frequency" which will leave evil and negativity behind, see the circles as symbols calling humankind to awareness of its own part in this evolution, subliminally unlocking subconsciously contained information which will enable us to adapt to the new conditions our planet will take on after certain geophysical alterations have taken place. Much of this information has been received by psychics and channellers, some who foresee these changes in a catastrophic light and others who predict a more gentle progress.

The source of such information invites attack as New Age claptrap, and the Earth Mother fixation from some quarters has very much opened croppies up (wrongly) to be painted as head-in-the-clouds hippies, but an increasing number of people do find themselves drawn to clairvoyant methods of defining the origins of the circles. Problems arise in that conventional verification is practically impossible and faith in the absence of evidence has to play a big part (not that this has affected the development of religion).

The Gaia theory doesn't rule out the involvement of cosmic intelligences (both the Earth Spirit and various extra-terrestrial "councils" have supposedly been contacted by channellers). Accepting that the Earth itself is a thinking being suggests that every celestial body may have some semblance of consciousness, and some see the arrival of the circles as a combined effort from a general cosmological intelligence made up of stars, planets and the life which exists on them,[2] concerned with events on one of its spheres and wishing to alert its inhabitants to imminent developments. Some have described this as the awakening of the "Seed People," the circles being subliminal wake-up calls for souls who have incarnated in these times to help the Earth through a time of apocalyptic change. Whether physical ETs are involved in this process of creating the symbols in conjunction with Gaia, somehow taking orders from "above," or whether it all takes place more ethereally, differs according to varying channelled sources.

Postcards from God

The ultimate cosmic intelligence, for many, is the concept of an all-enveloping conscious force more popularly known as "God" (the cosmological composite force mentioned above may well amount to the same thing). A sensitive subject to speculate on, this being is worshiped by several organized global faiths and all have at some point or another identified certain symbols in the crops as their religious icons. Could it be the hand of God is carving glyphs into our fields?

Christians seem, at first glance, to do the best. As we have seen, the Lockeridge "whale" in 1991 was for some a representation of the Virgin Mary, and the square footage of laid crop in the Barbury Castle pictogram of the same year had significance for Christian numerology. A number of crosses have also appeared, although this shape has long been a sign of power, pre-dating Christianity by many centuries. Nevertheless, a local Christian group in Somerset claimed victory after they reportedly prayed for the appearance of a crucifix as a crop formation in 1996—a ringed cross then arrived in their county at Martock a few weeks later.

On the other hand, we have also seen iconography from other religions in the fields. Muslims can point to the many stars and crescents which have popped up since 1992 (although the crescent can also be representative of Mary) and Hindus even got treated to (a slightly mutated) "Aum" sign next to the Telegraph Hill "quintuplet of quintuplets"

Some believe the circles are heralding a religious message, a last chance from God to repent. On the other hand, a few believe they are corrupting distractions from Satan. . . . Photo: Danny Sotham (Barbury Castle 1991 photo: Richard Wintle/Calyx Photo Services)

in 1995. Pagans, though, can claim as much victory as any other religion, with the appearance of many markings from ancient pre-Christian beliefs.

Not that all believers *want* to be linked with the phenomenon. In the same way the observers of 1678 saw the Devil as being responsible for the Hertfordshire circles, to this day, for a few (largely Christians) the circles are Satan's work, signs sent to confuse and challenge the faithful by leading people into heathen ways of the occult and paranormal (oddly, apparitions are seen as perfectly acceptable). The array of "evil" Pagan symbols amongst the religious ones in crop patterns is used to support this view. There are even rumors that an order of Catholic nuns monitor crop circle and UFO activity, and it was interesting that, in an infamous secretly taped telephone conversation with alleged circle-faker Jim Schnabel, he once cited the Vatican as one of the organizations who would like to destroy the credibility of the formations (although it's unclear as to whether he was being deliberately misleading to thwart the caller).

The flipside of this is that other devoted Christians have welcomed the circles as examples of the "signs and wonders" that precede the final apocalypse and the ultimate triumph of Christ over evil, as foretold in the book of *Revelation*.

The fact is, the crop circles seem to draw on the symbolism of many cultures and belief systems, as if wanting to appeal to as many individuals as possible. Is this God trying to unite his people, coincidence and suggestion, or, in the consciousness-connection view, simply a reflection of the collective psyche of humankind, all things represented? Again, if the phenomenon *is* the work of an all-powerful creator-God, why are the locations of the glyphs so geophysically restricted and why aren't there more of them spread widely to reach as many people as possible? Et cetera.

Natural Forces

Circular Heresy

It's become almost heretical to consider natural forces as being solely responsible for the circles in the face of such suggestively intelligent complexity, but they can't be entirely ruled out. The tendencies for formations to be attracted to specific places and conditions seems more indicative of

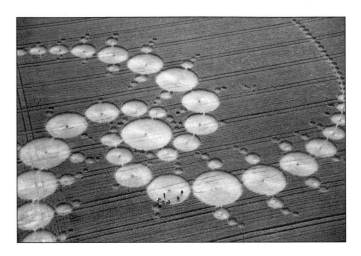

The incredible fractal pattern of 194 circles at Windmill Hill, Wiltshire, July 29, 1996. Could the fractals suggest the circles are simply nature expressing its inherent structure in the fields? Photo: Andrew King

at least an aspect of the phenomenon having a terrestrial origin.

Those who found their belief-systems too stretched by the development of the pictograms were long ago backed into the position of stating that the simple circular patterns were genuine meteorological anomalies, but anything more elaborate was the work of man. But as science discovers more about the structure of nature, particularly through fractal physics, which illustrates mathematically how incredible order can result from apparently chaotic systems, it could transpire that even some of the very intricate crop patterns may be a product of natural processes. The increasing examples of raw fractal "designs" being discovered add weight to such a view (although not all pictograms are so easily explained in this light—see below). If this possibility seems hard to swallow, it's worth remembering the astonishing splendor of snowflakes and other highly-ordered geometric patterns found in plants, minerals and even animals. Chapter 3 has already referred to how sound can vibrate small particles into very structured patterns.

Atmospheric Vortices

The most comprehensive investigation into the meteorological circle hypothesis was almost certainly the work of Dr. Terence Meaden and fellow members of TORRO (Tornado and Storm Research Organization) in the 1980s. This is excellently detailed in the books *The Circles Effect and its Mysteries* and *Circles from the Sky*. It concluded that crop circles were formed from organized electrically charged atmospheric vortices (individually called "the plasma vortex") created by certain rare weather conditions. The theory was continually fine-tuned as the circles began to develop, and could adapt to rings and symmetry, but began to stall when the pictograms arrived. Even here, attempts were made to push the idea out to accommodate keys, claws and rectangles, but by the Barbury Castle triangle of 1991, further expansion was becoming impossible without a major reappraisal of what actually *triggered* the basic laying mechanism, which certainly appeared to make some sense in Meaden's terms.

Had a little time for reflection been allowed, mediation might have been applied and the prominent body of cosmic intelligence-slanted researchers would have examined the good points of the vortex hypothesis and tried to marry these to their own views. Instead, the baby was thrown out with the bathwater, any meteorological influences were largely dismissed and Meaden withdrew from the game after being cruelly humiliated on Channel 4's *Equinox* (see Chapter 2). This is a great shame because had both sides been able to reconcile their differences and Meaden continued his work, we might be a lot closer now to understanding at least the mechanism of the crop-laying process, if not the cause. There were a few holes in the vortex view, exposed when it became clear that some formations didn't comply to the required hypothetical behavior (page 26) but these might have been ironed out given the chance. Not dissimilar work by Donald L Cyr, which proposed "whistlers," lightning-induced electromagnetic radio pulses, as the cause of circles also sank without trace about the same time. Now the more recent and continuing work of W C Levengood seems to be vindicating many of Meaden's findings, the plasma vortex, while not being seen as the whole answer to the conundrum (other factors besides meteorological forces, natural or otherwise, must surely be involved to organize the patterns so highly), is again being given more regard.

Certainly, circles and simple patterns may indeed result from such phenomena, as was suggested by laboratory experiments with electrostatic discharges leaving markings in trays of substances. This exercise, notably, also produced small balls of light. It has fallen to pioneers like croppie physicist Jim Lyons to expand on these basic ideas by noting that *all* energy forces work in a vortex, producing toroidal and circular shapes, and that accepted physics, earth energy and consciousness ultimately fall within the same parameters.

Earth Energy

From the earliest days of crop circles, the dowsing community immediately noted a relation between the phenomenon and "energy lines," the grid of natural power they believe covers the entire planet, much as meridian lines of *ch'i* flow through the body in acupuncture. Dowsing is an ancient practice, which can be used to detect not just water, as is commonly known, but any substance, lost objects, hidden information—and energy fields. It is a mysterious art which appears to tap into levels of knowledge held in some higher plain of consciousness. Using physical tools made of anything, rods, twigs or pendulums, these devices pick up on tiny involuntary movements in the dowser's muscles as they respond to hidden senses, denoting yes or no answers to questions or detecting fluctuations in earth energy.[3]

"Earth energy" may play a crucial role in circle creation, but as yet only the art of "dowsing" seems capable of detecting it. Seasoned dowser David Russell checks out one of the Celtic crosses at Sompting, West Sussex, June 1993. Photo: Andy Thomas

A combine harvester prepares to eat a pictogram over-looking the stone circle at Avebury, Wiltshire, July 1992. Crop circles have long been attracted to sites marked by ancient monuments, possibly due to an earth energy connection. Photo: Andy Thomas

Members of Southern Circular Research photograph a dumbbell that appeared next to the new stretch of the A27 by-pass (background) at Patcham, East Sussex on the very day it opened, June 24, 1992. Crop circles have been known to break out in areas where the ground has been grossly disrupted, and many formations hugged the new A27 during its construction. Photo: Andy Thomas

According to dowsers, formations are almost uniformly placed on areas where lines of this energy cross or are very strong. As they hold that ancient man could instinctively feel it and built his stone circles and burial mounds at spe-cific points accordingly to focus and increase its power, this, if correct, would explain why crop circles continually appear to proliferate around these places. Certainly, two of the most powerful lines, christened Michael and Mary in Hamish Miller and Paul Broadhurst's book *The Sun and the Serpent,* are believed to pass directly through several major circle areas, in particular Avebury, center of so much activity. The earth energy connection would make sense of the phenomenon's affinity for returning to favorite spots, and its apparent geophysical restriction in distribution patterns. As already explored, there is evidence to suggest that piezoelectric fields sparked by underground water and the pressure of quartz-based rock may well generate this energy, explaining many unusual effects, such as aerial lights. Although western science doesn't yet officially acknowledge its existence, a growing body of thinkers accept its presence as given. The culturally-accepted art of geomancy or *Feng Shui* in oriental countries, where buildings are carefully designed and aligned not to disrupt the flow of natural energetic order in the landscape, utilizes very similar notions.

Presumably, energy centers spiralling outward as invisible vortices, in Jim Lyons' terms, must also have an effect on the local meteorology, perhaps inducing the atmospheric phenomena proposed by Meaden. As above, so below. Are the circles appearing almost as natural acupuncture points on the Earth's surface, where energy builds up or becomes disrupted in some way? It's interesting to note that outbreaks of crop circles have notably occurred around new road construction sites, where energy lines must presumably be cut through. Could it be there is an entirely natural process which can produce simple patterns, but which can be stimulated or manipulated by other influences to generate more complexity on occasion? Consciousness, (human or extra-terrestrial), which to some observers is simply another energy field, may be the key. This might explain why some circles are more rough and random than others which suggest the hand of something rather more organized.

Other Energy Concepts

A variation on the earth energy theory is "orgone," an idea first proposed by Wilhelm Reich earlier this century. This holds that all living beings exude fields which collect together into a kind of semi-conscious ether, producing "bio-forms," globular clusters of orgone which can manifest as lights and other anomalous effects observed at crop circles, behaving much as the earth energy hypothesis, but with subtle differences. In this scenario, impacting bioforms drawn to key points on the Earth's surface produce the formations by leaving "ultrasonic sound signatures" according to Andrew Collins' book *The Circlemakers,* which supports the idea and takes into account the effect consciousness can have on the process.

Others, like Anne Arnold-Silk, have suggested a more down-to-earth cause for the crop glyphs—disruption of the planet's natural power fields by civilization's electronic pollution. As increasing amounts of electricity pylons and microwave transmitters are erected to accommodate our growing global communication network, complex interference patterns are set up against the Earth's background energy emanations. These could create unstable electrical vortices, leaving physical traces in the fields. It is an interesting thought that all these beautiful markings which have meant so much to so many, *could,* in this view, be nothing more than an attractive but worrying symptom of a sick planet's disrupted system, a bit like measles breaking out....

Doing What Comes Naturally?

While all these natural energy solutions are more tantalizingly likely to those unable to accept that other intelligences may play a part in the phenomenon, there are a few unsolved problems. A big minus is that, with the possible exception of Levengood and Meaden's work, proposals for actual mechanisms in these hypotheses are vague and uncertain, sometimes relying on "pseudo-science" to fill the holes. Dowsing, for instance, though a popular and growing hobby for many, which certainly *can* work, is, for all the cries to the contrary from some of its proponents, far from reliable. Different dowsers have been known to come up with entirely disparate results from the same formation when trying to ascertain either its genuineness or the shape of its energy webs. The "blind man's elephant" plea, that they are simply picking up different aspects of the same force, may be true, but doesn't help anyone with solid answers. The quality of results gained from dowsing are heavily reliant on the individual's experience and ability, and until uniform practices and yardsticks can be agreed on, the art will remain a sideline research tool. Likewise, until someone invents a machine which can detect earth

energy on a meter (although reports suggest this is being worked towards), those who doubt its existence will continue to ignore its potentially important part in the crop circle puzzle as, for good or ill, we live in a world that increasingly refuses to acknowledge anything unless science gives it the stamp of validation.

The biggest challenge to the natural debate, however, is to explain the seeming predetermination of some of the crop designs, aside from understanding where alleged sightings of structured UFOs come into it. We have seen with fractal physics that extremely complex patterns can occur in nature, and the huge fractal formations could be a manifestation of this process. But how can the phenomenon's noted interactive behavior and motifs like the Earth's inner solar system from 1995 or the insectograms, which clearly seem to depict *things* be explained? Patterns like these seem to indicate the presence of a specific trigger or intelligent impulse. *If* the circle-making process is a natural force there may be a missing component to the theory.... Consciousness, perhaps?

Humans by Non-physical Means
Consciousness Interaction

To say, as some have, that recognizable or highly particular designs are human hoaxes, but the rest are natural forces at work, doesn't tie up with the observational evidence, which shows both to be constructed in identical ways. There have been various occasions where circles have arrived seemingly in response to requests or invocations, or have produced certain designs in answer to questions put by an observer just a few days or even hours before. All this suggests that the circle-making process is something which can be affected by direct, if involuntary, stimulation.

The work undertaken by members of the SCR team, as recounted in my book *Quest For Contact,* appeared to demonstrate that the more activity generated towards attempted interaction with the circle-making forces, the more the phenomenon seemed to respond. The first important—and secret—meeting of those involved was greeted by the arrival of the first Sussex formation of 1993 in the field closest to the venue as was possible to get. Like Andrew Collins' investigations, some of the team also found themselves party to increasing sightings of the glowing lights so often associated with the circles, as the project

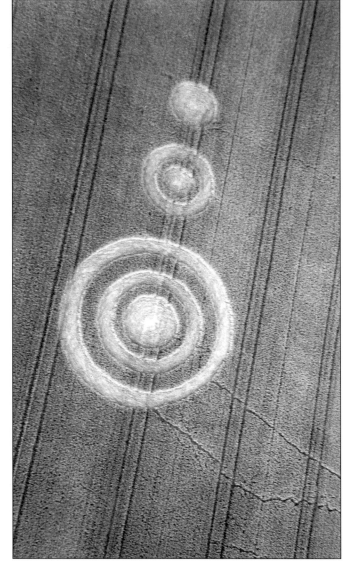

A meditation experiment carried out on top of Wolstonbury Hill, West Sussex on June 28, 1995 by members of Southern Circular Research (with medium Paul Bura in the wheelchair—the stones mark the participants' positions) seemingly produced the formation that appeared that night at Felbridge, West Sussex. Its shape was accurately predicted, suggesting once again that the circle phenomenon is in some way psychically linked with the human mind. Wolstonbury photo: Barry Reynolds. Felbridge photo: SCR

intensified. This was taken to its ultimate conclusion with an experiment involving crystals, meditation and sound, where thought energy was concentrated towards a projected site in an effort to influence the creation of a crop pattern. Although it didn't appear exactly where expected, the arrival that very night of a pictogram in exactly the shape predicted was as near to success as anyone could hope for.

If these were stand-alone experiences, they could, perhaps, be written off as coincidence (and indeed have been by critics), but the fact that other teams have tried similar successful approaches, as with CSETI in 1992 (page 44), shows clearly that human consciousness seems to be, at the very least, a link in the chain of whatever creates the circles.

The phenomenon always seems to know what is being thought or expected of it, and delights in either confounding predictions (several "scientific" pronouncements about what the circles can and can't do have been quickly contradicted) or unexpectedly fulfilling desires (in 1986 Busty Taylor once remarked, after seeing a quintuplet, how nice it would be to find one with the outer circles linked by a ring. Within twenty-four hours, the first official Celtic cross arrived). Several people have had such experiences of the circles seemingly reacting to remarks made about them, or appearing where requests have been made. One SCR member, Jason Porthouse, managed to precipitate the next-day appearance of two separate formations simply by asking for them, once at Sompting, West Sussex in 1992 (with his brother), and the following year at nearby Shoreham.[4] Though such instances are unpredictable and irregular (perhaps some people are very specifically attuned), there are certainly many other documented instances of personal interaction. Laboratory experiments with telekinesis in other circumstances have demonstrated the ability of the mind to affect the physical world—it's possible we could be seeing a wider demonstration of such abilities in the fields.

Collective Sparks

Assuming that psychic connections aren't the result of cosmic intelligences listening in and responding accordingly, could this ability of the phenomenon to be influenced by human thought be taken on a wider scale to account for its entire existence? Some hold that through some unspecified process, the accumulative power of humankind's collective subconscious has actually attained the ability to project shapes into the Earth's natural energy fields, sparking random atmospheric vortices (which may create simple or fractal patterns by themselves) and nudging them into ordered archetypal configurations.

Work with symbology has shown that many patterns have universal qualities which everyone recognizes and responds to in similar ways. Psychologists like Carl Jung believed our race held these shapes in its collective memory. Working with disturbed individuals earlier in the 20th century, Jung encouraged them to draw their state of mind as abstract designs instead of expressing it in words. Some of the results were not so very different to what has appeared in our crops in recent years. Jung once wrote: *"Symbols are clues, activated by your own unconscious energy.... Their meaning is hidden from your conscious control."*

If the planet does have energy fields spun out in a grid of lines, and they are expanding as part of some natural cycle of evolution, it follows that our personal energy fields, auras, whatever, must also be expanding and interacting. Every thought we ever think is a pulse of electricity, the movement of energy. It may not be beyond the realms of possibility that all these intermingled fields combine to form some kind of conscious unified whole, and that universal symbols held within our minds somehow move natural crop-laying forces to manifest these shapes physically. Maybe this collective unconscious has gained some kind of autonomy, acting as a kind of supermind capable of creating symbols to aid its own component parts' development. The evolution of such a force might be a combination of growing geophysical and psychic energy, and would certainly explain the gradual elaboration of the crop patterns over recent years.

The weakness of this scenario is, of course, the very absence of a known mechanism which could affect natural systems in this way, laying it open to ridicule. Yet the notion of such a process would explain more of the observed behavior of the phenomenon than some other theories of origin, and allow for the geophysical connection. If earth energy travels down connecting lines, perhaps consciousness energy is similarly drawn to places where it is strong enough to create or influence natural vortices, depending on favorable geophysical conditions to form a pattern, and conforming to the areas of circle distribution which appear to exist. The semi-randomness of this hypothesis would also explain why some of the symbols remain obscure: while a few are direct and clear, others seem to be a mish-mash of multi-cultural designs, a jumble of global archetypes. Some may be affected, however unintentionally, by the thoughts of pockets of individuals, as opposed to the collective whole, hence apparent regional designs and connections to local symbols or events.

On the other hand, why then have we not seen very widely known symbols in our fields, say, the *McDonald's* logo? (Maybe these are too historically recent to have lodged firmly in the collective mind, or maybe we have an in-built resistance to promoting free advertising....) And what of the inherent construction lines in some patterns, which at least appear to suggest intelligent premeditation? Could a semi-natural process begin by producing a skeletal structure as a framework? Like all circle theories, though the consciousness connection might explain more than others, gaps still remain. This is not to say they will never be filled.

A number of people take the consciousness idea further and assert that the phenomenon is a deliberately instigated program on the part of psychokinetic teams creating the circles for purposes of their own. Others believe the energy blueprints for the designs may have been laid down aeons ago by shamens and high priests, almost as etheric temples lying in wait until such time the energy levels were high enough to spark them off, or those with the knowledge could reactivate them to leave markings in modern crops. Psychic practitioners of this sort may have been sending a message from the past to our present, to impart a specific wisdom needed in these times.

Graveyard Shift

There have been suggestions that the circles are indeed created by human psychic projection, but from people who have passed beyond this world into whatever awaits on the other side; messages from the dead, in other words.

Using the "diatonic" ratios found in the musical scale, as extracted from crop circle dimensions and measurements using techniques pioneered by Professor Gerald Hawkins, it is possible to convert numbers to alphabetical sequences. Some of the original members of the Society for Psychical Research, like Oliver Lodge, reputedly promised they would try to contact those remaining once they died, and a few descendant members claim to have found evidence for such contact in crop formation data. Extricating letters diatonically has apparently produced an uncanny number of initials of prominent deceased SPR fellows.... For some, this is good enough evidence that Lodge and his colleagues are fulfilling their promises by projecting ciphers from the afterlife.[5]

The weakness of *this* assertion is that diatonic ratios require extremely accurate measurements in the first place, and the difficulty of gaining such figures to the nearest fraction for this kind of scrutiny, especially when surveying the larger formations, leaves such data open to concerns over fudging and auto-suggestion.

Systems in Place

There is as much going for the consciousness connection theory as any other explanation for the crop circles, in some ways more. There certainly seem to be systems in place which could allow for it if the work of people like Dr. Rupert Sheldrake has validity. This, concludes that all living things are linked by "morphic fields," which allow information to be transmitted to all members of a species without physical lines of communication. Quantum particle physics is revealing a strange, yet somehow *right,* world in which the observer can never be considered separate from the process observed. One seems to have an effect on the other and neither can exist independently. While a mechanism which allows symbols to be projected from our minds into fields of plants remains elusive, there may yet be one to discover when hard science allows the full implications of quantum theory to be fully absorbed.

Of course, if human thoughts can affect a basic natural crop-laying process, this doesn't rule out other influences playing a part on a similar level. It may well be that the final answer to the crop circle mystery is a combination of all the speculations. Everyone must make up their own minds. Whatever, there are more options than just the aliens-or-hoaxers arguments, which are all that ever seem to be allowed for by the media. It's a fair bet that whatever the solution, it isn't as simple and clear-cut as many would like to think. Few things are.

Eye in the Sky

A less metaphysical human influence on crop circles through non-physical means has also been considered. There is a prevailing belief amongst some that "the military," an unspecified conglomeration of international armed forces, is responsible for creating crop circles with secret energy weapon technology, probably beamed from satellites. It has even been suggested this ability might have been derived from crashed ET craft. Quite why they should want to test such devices so publicly has never been explained, however. Why perform so openly when there are vast tracts of restricted land available to the military?

Some propose that the circles are created as a diversion for the public, invented mysteries to distract people from political and social issues, which authorities would rather weren't challenged. Others even believe that UFOs, asso-

A military helicopter hovers over a pictogram at Alton Barnes, Wiltshire, July 1991. There have been many sightings of such craft, and some have been known to harass researchers. The military are clearly interested in the phenomenon—even if they're not responsible for it, as a few believe they are. Photo: Andy Thomas

ciated phenomena and crop circles are *all* the work of shadowy official organizations, designed to frighten the public into fears of alien invasion. By this, they then gain support for increased military control and political unification around the world, putting power into the hands of a few and keeping booming war-readiness economics buoyant in the name of protecting the masses from an unspecified threat.

The problem with the military solution is that there appear to have been stringent efforts to divert public attention *away* from the phenomenon over the years (official denial, the Bratton Castle incident, various proclamations from suspicious "hoaxers," etc.), as opposed to the other way around, which one might expect if the above scenario was true. Claims of these diversions being part of some bizarre double-bluff have to be considered, but would only really make sense if the world as a whole had been alerted to the "threat" from the circle-makers in a big way with a *small* amount of balancing debunking to make it all look convincing. As it is, a *majority* seem to have been convinced by the media and authorities that the circles are just a man-made prank—surely a bad call for a movement wanting things the other way around? And again, why not make crop circles everywhere instead of the usual haunts? (Salisbury Plain in Wiltshire is a well-known military training ground, another reason some have suggested a connection.)

The military are certainly *interested* in the glyphs. Most active researchers have at some time or another seen their helicopters hovering low over the latest Wiltshire designs, clearly scrutinizing them. (A few actually thought the circles were the results of downdrafts from helicopters to begin with—the later observed messes left in fields by such low-flying craft soon put paid to this idea.) Why expend time and energy documenting something of no more value than human landscape art? The military clearly believe something more important is occurring. This isn't to suggest they have any greater understanding than anyone else, unlike the UFO phenomenon, on which they are clearly holding back information. They're probably as flummoxed as anyone else, but would like to get their hands on a technique which can perform largely unseen so dexterously. If nothing else, the access the military have to satellite surveillance could put an end to any talk of human hoaxers at work in the fields. With camera resolution that can focus onto objects just a few feet across, a week's monitoring in Wiltshire would show beyond any doubt the truth of the matter. On this, the military remain resolutely silent. (Though frankly, if they broke this silence and declared the regular spotting of human artist activity, this in itself would be dismissed as a diversionary cover-up by many, and probably rightly, given the contrary evidence.)

Lastly, if the military *were* making the formations themselves, one can't help feeling the patterns would lack the grace they have shown, radiate less beauty, and be rather more martial and masculine.

Outside of the military, there is a possibility private inventors may have found methods of creating crop circles with some kind of high technology, yet one suspects the level of sophisticated equipment demanded would require funding and facilities way beyond the means of most individuals. In any case, whether military or civilian, would such capabilities exist back in earlier centuries and the beginning of this one, to explain the historical circle reports? Probably not, unless someone has only recently learned to harness an existing natural force for their own ends.

Humans by Physical Means
A-maze-ing Tales

Consider for a moment, that the owners of an English stately home wish to commission the creation of a new maze to be laid out and grown in their grounds. Do they hire the services of a team who will spend weeks, maybe months, of detailed planning, and then probably days or weeks marking out the required pathways at the location itself before planting? Or do they pop up the road to a bunch of local artists who say "Righto guv, don't worry about all that geometrical planning lark, we'll knock it up for you freehand in a couple of hours or so. And just to ensure the best quality, we'll do it at night without lights."

Which approach would result in the finest maze in terms of accuracy and execution? Exactly. Yet there are people who would have us believe there are several groups capable of producing just such geometrical miracles anywhere, anytime in any conditions, in the space of a few hours, unseen, unheard, undiscovered.

Aside from ETs, the most widely-held notion as to the source of the circles is without doubt the hoaxing scenario. It needs little introduction because it's been rammed down most people's throats for so long that many can think of nothing else being responsible.

Even in the earliest days of basic circles, a few voices raised the contention that they might simply be a prank, but the development of the pictograms, their increasing size, complexity and huge numbers stalled serious considerations of the notion until Doug and Dave came along, the idea asserted itself and most people's brains inexplicably stopped working. Since then it has been a struggle for the phenomenon to be taken seriously again, largely because people aren't aware of its full extent or continuing presence on such a scale.

Chapter 2 outlined the development of views on hoax-

Smiley face at Cocking, West Sussex, July 16, 1995. Many known or suspected hoaxes are of this genre. Sceptics, of course, believe the majority of formations in this book are also man-made. Photo: Michael Hubbard

ing. As the subject has already received a massively disproportionate amount of coverage elsewhere, there's little need to discuss the pros of it and every need to look at the balancing arguments. Briefly, the case runs that the formations are simply the work of people tramping down crop with planks, ropes, rollers or other physical implements. As we have seen, claims for their motivation have changed to account for the extraordinary leap in size and sophistication over the last decade; first it was all a jokey "prank," as stated by Doug and Dave, but later claimants have portrayed themselves as serious landscape artists out to enlighten and amaze with their art.

On the surface, in a world where paranormal phenomena isn't generally seen to break out so visibly and on such a scale, the man-made theorem seems the most obvious answer to the mystery for those with just the basic facts in front of them. Surely anyone can make pretty patterns in squashed crop? Indeed, one of Doug and Dave's repeated justifications for their claims' validity was that the formations were *"just flattened corn."* In truth, this was a fundamental misjudgment, which illustrated neatly the weak grasp they had on just what was really being found and what it meant to so many people. It is an underestimation which has been repeated since. By now, most who have read this book thus far should have enough of a perspective to see that there is far, far more to the crop circle phenomenon than just flattened corn.

What Is a Hoax?

So what constitutes a hoax and how does one tell the difference? The constant struggle to find a reliable litmus test has challenged researchers from the earliest days, as explored in the first two chapters, yet the very idea of a hoaxed circle implies that there must be such thing as a genuine one. Technically, a hoax is only a hoax when masquerading as something known to be the real thing, and only a very few formations have ever had their source *indisputably* proved (eye-witness accounts of circles forming out of nowhere, or those known beyond any doubt to be man-made). Therefore, in this view, have there ever been any hoaxes? Patterns made in full view of observers for experimental or demonstration purposes are *not* hoaxes as they aren't intended to deceive and should really be classified as "man-made." Those, like German researchers Joachim Koch and Hans-Jurgen Kyborg, for instance, who each year legitimately pay a farmer to allow them to make what they see as reply communications to the circlemakers, cannot really be considered hoaxers. Nevertheless, the notion of a man-made circle created in any circumstances has become generically known as a hoax and we'll use the term here for convenience.

Given the lack of *proven* hoaxes and the absence of a reliable litmus test, aside from W C Levengood's discoveries, which certainly seem the nearest thing, how should one judge between "genuine" and "hoaxed" circles? First of all, one has to ascertain that there *are* non-man-made circles in the first place. A growing number of people believe the statistical evidence and anomalous effects observed speak for themselves in this respect, and the eye-witness accounts would seem to provide the crowning evidence. Indeed, the whole thrust of this book should have provided a clear case for this and most of those who disagree will probably have shut the cover by now, so let's accept "real" circles on that basis. Telling the difference between these, then, and hoaxes becomes a combination of physical observation and looking logically at the phenomenon overall. Even with the former, agreement is hard to reach—several researchers have asserted grounds for detecting man-made activity; using "Indian tracking skills," dowsing, looking for "plank-mark" ridges in crop lay, infrared photography ... the list goes on. All *may* work, but remain contentious, subjective and therefore unreliable. Only Levengood's scientific work and as yet unreproduced-by-humans effects (see Chapter 1) seem to remain unchallenged criteria. The general picture may be what we have to judge the phenomenon's viability on, and this becomes pretty obvious when the logical cases for and against mass-hoaxing are examined, never mind the physical evidence. Removing subjectivity and employing logic may be the only clear path to an answer.

Vital Statistics

The shocking truth is that *statistically*, based on unequivocal evidence, the databases of each season's formations show that, on average, no more than 3% of any year's designs can actually be *proven* to be man-made. This is based on solid information and facts, nothing else, and is a far cry from the regular assertions of "95%" or "80%" which are plucked out of nowhere by the skeptical to justify their own views. As comedian Vic Reeves once said

"88.5% of all statistics are made up on the spot." How true. Crop circle statistical *facts* reveal something quite different from the picture so often painted.

This doesn't mean the percentage of hoaxes isn't more than 3%, but it does leave a vast majority of formations entirely unexplained. This figure doesn't include *claims* of hoaxing, but evidence from eye-witnesses to the hoax, where people were caught in the act or photographs were taken of its construction. Even all the formations which *are* claimed only make up about 10% of a season's circular product, and most alleged hoaxes are only *claims*. It's much easier to say one made something than actually expend energy having to really do it.

So, there is a little evidence for *some* hoaxing, and most researchers accept there is a proportion of man-made patterns each year. Experiments have shown it is possible to construct only modest designs in a restricted time period and more ambitious creations if highly favorable conditions and many man-hours are available. Yet almost none of these have managed to adequately replicate the unexplained stunning beauty which appears mostly in darkness in far from perfect conditions on virtually every night of high summer. Those that have tried to approach it (like the 1998 NBC TV demonstration, which used floodlights) have been constructed in unrealistic circumstances. Also absent from known man-made efforts is the complexity of lay, layering and flow generally observed. Circular swirls tend to be unimaginatively tight spirals (again, clearly visible in the NBC pattern), not the sweeping S-shapes and off-center splays often observed. Hoaxes *can* be neat, but generally lack geometrical grace. Awkward geometry and misaligned proportions which jar the eye are often the first signs of human activity, although one has to be careful of dismissing too quickly—some of the more unruly squiggles have been exquisite inside. More obviously suspect designs are largely smiley faces or rude words. Other known hoax attempts have often simply been appalling messes. For the more ostentatious efforts, it was inevitable that sooner or later people would learn to emulate a crop-flattening process that bore *superficial* resemblances to that being inexplicably found in the fields. However, it's in the fine detail that hoaxes struggle to replicate.

To repeat an overused but valuable cliché, the discovery of one or two counterfeit coins do not mean all coins are counterfeit. Humans have always been great copyists—

witness great painting frauds. Do we burn and dismiss the Mona Lisa if it turns out someone has tried to produce an imitation?

With much time to hand, the use of various equipment and certain techniques, it has been shown that some of the complex formations can be approximated—*but not created under the circumstances in which they appear, or with many of the effects observed.* If people were responsible for making the majority of crop glyphs, surely it would have been easy to prove by now? And yet, after all this time, some very basic questions still haven't been tackled convincingly....

Questions Which Remain to Be Answered by the Mass-Hoaxing Scenario:

How can such huge designs be accurately created in such short time periods?

The hoaxing competition of 1992 showed that to construct a fairly small pictogram took somewhere in the region of two to three hours for the fastest contenders. Other man-made experiments have shown a similar time scale is needed to achieve any sort of accuracy. In the summer months, there are barely five hours of darkness available to cover the activities of would-be hoaxers working in very visible fields, as most, though not all, formations appear overnight. To create some of the highly complex patterns covering several hundred feet would take far longer than a night's work (The NBC formation took six hours—the Mitsubishi car (page 72) the same year took *two days,* remember). Why don't people drive past fields early in the morning and watch hoaxers still going about their business? Most formations are discovered whole at first light when it is known the field was empty the previous evening.

On paper, just drawing some of the designs we have seen would take hours. Marking elaborately huge configurations out in dark fields would require many more, let alone then laying the crops down with the skill observed. The US surveying company contacted by Rod Bearcloud (Chapter 2) quoted a necessary window of over a *week* to accurately lay out the Windmill Hill triple Julia Set or the Milk Hill Koch Snowflake if working by night, and only a few days less for daytime operation. In full light, on the flat it is impossible to see much beyond thirty feet around

one in a formation, and the shape being visited is sometimes difficult to guess. How, then, in near-pitch blackness on moonless nights, can anyone accurately gauge such sublime geometric positioning and proportions like that, for instance, of Windmill Hill 1996, especially if *teams* of individuals, however compact, are involved, as such size and complexity would require? Co-ordinating groups to work efficiently against the clock is difficult enough, but everyone has different ways of doing things. A picture painted by a committee, however small or select, isn't likely to be very satisfactory and the same goes for crop circles. Yet most large formations show a striking uniformity of lay and design style, and geometrical errors are rare—when present they are usually glaring give-aways.

Recognizing the difficulty these aspects present, attempts have been made by skeptics to circumvent them by claiming formations are *not* made overnight in the dark, but calmly and calculatedly over a period of days at dawn light before people are up and about to catch them. This is plainly nonsensical given that the area of Wiltshire, for example, which sees the most cerealogical activity, is flown over virtually *every day of every summer,* by people out sight-seeing or circle-hunting. Obvious half or quarter-finished designs are never discovered (there is a certain completeness to the geometry of most). Tapes and stakes, which might be needed to mark out planned crop patterns are never seen. Formations *occasionally* grow or alter, but by and large are discovered fully-formed. There would never be the time to make anything substantial in the first hours of light—most farmers are active before dawn, motorways and major roads by which designs have appeared are already busy by four in the morning, and places like Alton Barnes often have people out cropwatching at all hours. Very few people are caught hoaxing—returning to the same spot every morning to continue their handiwork would be very risky and more culprits would have been apprehended by now. Given the large amounts of bulky equipment some of the teams used at the 1992 circle-making competition to gain any degree of accuracy, transporting this around would require cars and vans which would soon arouse suspicion parked up on grass verges (and provide a problem for the hoaxers having to carry their tools into dark fields without mishap or falling over).

The time-factor also has to take into account cases like the 1999 Alton Barnes pictogram (see pages 75 and 122) or the Stonehenge fractal of 1996 which arrived in full-view one Sunday afternoon within around forty-five minutes. The available window and the conditions rule out any possibility that this was hoaxed. Even here, the skeptics deny to the last, preferring to believe the formation was visible all day, but only noticed at teatime, despite the testimony of those who *know* it wasn't there before then. There have been other daylight creations. And what of the appearances of several identically-made crop glyphs, which arrive over fairly wide areas *on the same night?* The Bishops Cannings "scorpion" and the Wilsford and Ipsden "thought bubbles," spanning two counties, shared the same date of birth. The 1996 Windmill Hill fractal appeared the same night as the longest pictogram ever found, at Etchilhampton. Many widely-distributed formations over different counties have manifested simultaneously with remarkably consistent features. If making just one of these patterns would be a major push for human artists in one night, three would be impossible. The only, unlikely, answer to this is that several teams, working in tandem with identical skills and agreed methods of crop-laying would have to be active, in which case, the next question needs to be asked....

A classic "thought bubble" at Ipsden, Oxfordshire, July 15, 1994 (the strange paths may have been created by running water from springs—or a residue of the circle-making process). This appeared the same night as the Wilsford thought bubble (page 50) and the Bishops Canning scorpion (page 112) in Wiltshire, created in identical styles.... Even granting human teams the hypothetical ability to produce this kind of thing at all, where would the time be available in one night for the same people to create this vast exquisiteness over such distances? Photo: Michael and Christine Green

Who are all these hoaxers and why have they never proved their existence?

To account for even half of the crop circles each year in the circumstances under which they appear would imply the existence of several human circle-making teams (however large or small) out prowling the fields *every night of every summer,* working in tandem—there is a great uniformity to the effects seen in crop lays across the counties, and indeed the globe, even if some of the designs themselves seem to follow regional trends, implying regional teams to skeptics. Who are these people if they exist? How do they co-ordinate their skills so closely? What are their motives for spending so many nights in the damp, dark air constructing highly-complex and physically-draining pathways and circles for no money and no recognition? Don't these people have to get up for work in the morning? Even if, say, the existence of just five active hoaxing teams is surmised, two hundred and fifty or so English formations divided between them across a few summer months is still a lot of work, bearing in mind the weeks of planning involved for even one formation of which some claimants have spoken. With the number of individuals who would have to be involved, a) one might have expected someone to have convincingly blown the gaffe by now, and b) they would have to have some pretty good reason to be doing it. Those who *have* come forward to claim the circles as their own work only rarely provide any evidence of their skills and seldom give a credible motive for all this effort on such a scale.

It certainly wouldn't be a prank—two decades of high circle activity is a long time to keep a gag going when no-one's laughing. Or taking any notice at all for the most part. (That's one of the areas in which Doug and Dave's story falls down.) "Landscape art" is a better claimed motive, but why force oneself to work under such difficult conditions when one could pay off a farmer for some crop, create the design comfortably with all the time in the world *and* charge people admission to see it, thus "selling" the works like proper landscape artists (who grow patterns in flowers, etc.)? It has been stated by some claimants that part of the "art" is the thrill of the risk, the joy of performing the unexpected in unpredictable places. Art terrorism, as it were. But is it reasonable to believe that after all this time, with so many glyphs having appeared, someone wouldn't have tried to financially capitalize on it by now? Free exhibitions have even been mounted by hoax claimants who have bought pictures of what they call "their own work," taken by other photographers. Surely, if they were really serious about so many formations being their own, they would hire airplanes, photograph them themselves and sell the results instead of letting others have all the financial rewards? No-one has ever tried to copyright the designs. Some, who presumably have never looked in the eyes of a circle-enraged farmer, have suggested that hoaxers operate in cahoots with landowners and secretly get their money from the admission fees some farmers charge to see crop patterns! (What would the National Farmers' Union say to that?) This falls down when one considers how very few farmers do open their fields up to the public for cash.

If the crop circles *were* all man-made, the people responsible would have to have some pretty serious motives, probably religious or philosophical, trying to provoke exactly the reaction seen. This idea was actually mooted by Jim Schnabel, who once implied, whether truthfully or not, in the infamous secretly taped telephone conversation, that his and other open hoax-claimants' mission in hoaxing and then exposing formations was to help reveal the real individuals who might be out to corrupt the public by creating evil Pagan symbols. In turn, many believed Schnabel to be an evil agent himself, working for some sinister authority out to discredit the phenomenon at any cost, for selfish reasons of its own.

Certainly, as we have seen, there *is* evidence to suggest some want to promote the notion of hoaxing to distract from the significance of the crop glyphs. Intrigue surrounding the Doug and Dave campaign seemed to suggest a wider agenda behind them, and some even linked what turned out to be a non-existent press agency ("MBF Services"), which originally issued their story, with the British intelligence group MI5. There did appear to be links with Schnabel, another group of claimants called the "Wessex Skeptics" and other British "skeptic" (with a "k") groups with the US-based organization CSICOP (Committee for the Scientific Investigation of Claims of the Paranormal), a think tank of hard scientists who actively debunk and attack all popular paranormal beliefs and "alternative" lifestyles. A surprising number of well-known public figures and prominent thinkers are members, who regularly pop up on television (without announcing their skeptic establishment credentials, of course) to superciliously and patronizingly

sneer at anything which might have a potentially metaphysical cause. The respected astronomer Carl Sagan was one such person, and a very vocal critic of interest in the crop circles. How one so enlightened in some areas could *really* believe Doug and Dave were the most likely cause of the phenomenon is something which has puzzled many.

CSICOP has been linked with other groups who seem to feel threatened by things which challenge accepted scientific or religious paradigms, like the CIA and even the Vatican. A seminal investigation of CSICOP's connections with hoaxing was carried out by *Nexus* magazine's Marcus Allen in 1993 and 1994, the results of which were first published in *SC* and have been widely circulated since.[6] Funding and encouraging claimants and making the occasional real hoax is one way of muddying the waters of the phenomenon's credibility. But how far this deception extended and whether it is still actively continued isn't known, although it could be argued it's now hardly necessary. With the mission of convincing the general public the circles are all hoaxed apparently successful, why go to the effort of continually targeting the few remaining faithful, when they can simply be written off as cranks? Despite this, rumors that hoax claimants are persistently funded to continue their PR activities refuse to go away and some take quite seriously the notion that there is a highly orchestrated effort to debunk. Perhaps some bodies are more scared than we know.

Some researchers even claim to have been threatened or offered bribes by international intelligence agencies to stay away from or debunk the crop circles, although such remarks are often taken with a major pinch of salt by cynics who see them as little more than mystique-creation by the storytellers. The sudden skeptical about-turns or changes in certain established cerealogists' attitudes around 1992–93, however, do support such assertions to some eyes. It is fairly well-known that one or two researchers are funded by mysterious benefactors, and their motives have been called into question by the suspicious.

As far as direct evidence of hoaxers' abilities goes, as we have seen it's been thin on the ground, and the disruption that has been caused has been largely rumor-based. Doug and Dave's demonstration formations should have ended their story then and there and Schnabel's recreation of the Silbury "charm bracelet" was better, but still far from the quality of the original. Most demonstrations since have been little improved. As we have seen, designs made for com-

Jim Schnabel's demonstration formation made at a Suffolk farm, July 3, 1993. Though superficially neat, it was geometrically naive and severely lacked the grace and complexity of lay seen in some of the designs he had claimed. Most other demonstrations of "hoaxing skills" have told the same story. Photo: Grant Wakefield

mercial purposes (for use in adverts, etc.) have taken days to perfect. Others now annually perform to limited effect in front of cameras for various projects, usually in unrealistic conditions, which don't make for useful comparisons.

Most human presentations over-compensate, creating multi-element bonanzas superficially pretty to the untrained eye, but nearly always geometrically or aesthetically flawed (as with the 2001 HTV West effort—see page 89). The 1998 NBC TV demonstration remains one of the most elaborate man-made designs yet attempted (an impressive but rather crass amalgamation of several styles, an incorrect Mandelbrot at the center of a stumpy triple-armed fractal), made by the claimants of Stonehenge and Windmill Hill 1996. Arguments soon broke out over the truth of the claims of how easy it was to make. The fact that the formation was made in New Zealand, far away from active researchers, and that the field was cut down immediately after the television crew finished, raised justified suspicions. No examination of the lay at close quarters was made by any established researcher, nor were samples taken for analysis. Another opportunity lost, for those who otherwise sound so confident, to prove the true extent of their skills.

Beyond that, most alleged hoaxes aren't witnessed by anyone and the perpetrators very rarely bother to film their activities as back up. When they claim to, the evidence is mostly useless— photographs supposedly showing the

Bythorn mandala of 1993 (Chapter 2) in two stages of construction on different days, proffered as hoaxing proof from its claimant, were taken at such an oblique angle that almost no difference between the two could be discerned, beyond that which a slight change in camera positioning might produce, despite claims to the contrary. (The lighting conditions were also near-identical in each photo, taken from the same vantage point at some distance from the formation. Why not photograph it *inside* for a foolproof case?) The fact that *The Cerealogist* magazine accidentally printed the same photo twice on the same page instead of the before and after versions, says it all. (However, as seen with the Oliver's Castle video, in these days of cheaply available photo-manipulation computer programs, photographic or video evidence is no longer enough to prove a case anyway.)

Apart from these contentious efforts, most such "evidence" of hoaxing is little more than third-hand pub gossip and paranoia, spread yet further with the advent of Internet home pages and web sites, which have been both a blessing and a curse to the spread of fast circle information. Most claimants don't try to make any effort to back up their stories and, as with one of the supposed perpetrators of the 1996 fractal formations, who was challenged on camera for ITV's *Cyber Cafe* (though, typically, this was selectively edited out of the final TV program), have mostly publicly refused to reproduce their skills in front of lenses or witnesses.[7] They imply that such an act would compromise their role as artists or that to force them to reproduce an identical pattern twice would be unfair—but given the strict geometrical rules followed in most designs why shouldn't this be possible? Talk of artistic integrity seems to drop pretty quickly when money is waved, however, and this is when most alleged hoaxers begin to brush up on skills for the cameras. It's as if they can't decide whether to be artists, secret agents or con men.

How do the hoaxers create unreproducable and anomalous effects?

The whole book has explored this issue, but it's worth restating—if most of the formations are man-made, how do the perpetrators manage to create the weaving and layering which has been observed many times and never yet recreated in any demonstration pattern? Experiments with rollers, planks and feet have failed to reproduce this effect and, while sometimes tidy, lack the graceful flow usually seen. How are so many examples of curved but unbroken stems and non-phototropic bent and swollen plant nodes accounted for (pages 22 and 23) when this is impossible to achieve by hand? What of the discoveries of W C Levengood and the biological changes found at microscopic levels, never yet duplicated by mechanically-flattened tests? The only way skeptics have dealt with this is by attacking Levengood's methodology and abilities or making ludicrous suggestions of hoaxers spraying chemicals unknown to science to create these abnormalities.

How are the many occasions of witnessed anomalies to be accounted for, of glowing lights and all the other strange effects discussed in Chapter 3? Apart from attempts to deny their existence, those skeptics and hoax claimants aware of this conundrum have more recently begun to play up supposed connections with higher forces, either geophysical or celestial, asserting that any shape in organic matter will attract such phenomena. This might be true and could be due to natural earth mysteries, but claims are now sometimes going several steps further by implying that hoaxers may be "guided" by unseen intelligent forces to create their work, thus becoming tools in a much wider process, explaining the extraordinary expertise they appear to have. A few find this a good crossover theory, but most see it as a last desperate grasp for credibility.

And what of the eye-witness accounts of formations appearing? Are all these people liars or hallucinating delusionals? And are hoaxers really so diligent that they check out geological charts before performing their art, to make sure it's placed correctly on aquiferous strata?

These people, "circlemakers" as they like to be called, actively encourage the view that they are in contact with the guiding hand of an unexplained force, almost as if this is the only way they can be seen to admit they do actually believe in a real phenomenon of some kind. Privately, a few know full well there are genuinely mysterious elements at work making patterns in the fields, and even their occasional man-made handiwork has been known to have extra bits added on afterwards in strange circumstances.

Why don't hoaxers leave more trace marks?

With all the required bodies allegedly trudging their way around fields at night, surprisingly few traces of their activity are found. There is also a notable absence of "human" mistakes, such as marks where people have stumbled into the standing crop while co-ordinating themselves in the darkness.

Although most formations appear in fields with tractor tramlines, this is not universally the case, especially in America where this farming method isn't used. On occasions where circles have appeared in a lineless canvas or between tractor marks, no entry marks have been visible; walking through crops *without* leaving paths is very difficult. Doug and Dave's pole-vaulting yarns, their claimed method of avoiding trails (two pensioners, mind), have become comedy legend.

The detection of footprints is an uncertain and controversial art in dry, late-season crops, but in young wheat or barley formations, the stems are green and retain a white powdery film. Footprints are instantly detectable on such a sensitive floor, but are generally absent in very new circles. Prints in wet mud and the resultant mess on the stems can be another give-away, yet many designs which have appeared on nights of pouring rain have been pristine and unmarked when first entered (it has been countered that dirt washes off the floor lay in continued rain—but why choose to go out circlemaking in such unsavory conditions?). Those who claim to find footprints and mud in every other formation sometimes forget the very obvious fact that they may not have been the first in (and this is difficult to verify, even on the first day—some enthusiasts are early birds). This has led to many heated debates with cocksure researchers, certain that only *they* can detect the tell-tale signs, but unwilling to concede that others may have beaten them to it. Sometimes footprint pronouncements are made after observing a floor lay *several days* after appearance, a laughable and meaningless effort when several hundred people may have visited by then.

It has been alleged by some that planks and rollers leave signature "spokes" and grooves in the flattened crop, pointing to such visible features in some formations. These have been earmarked as physical evidence of hoaxing, yet *known* man-made circles actually created with such techniques don't uniformly display these scars, which rather demolishes this assumption. Given that the flattening forces generally seem to work in an outward spiralling motion of thin paths (perhaps created by the "mini-whirlwinds" seen by the Tomlinsons, page 28), as recorded in some eye-witness accounts and observable in the crop lay itself, these marks are as likely to be artifacts of circle-making vortices.

One problem with the practicalities of the hoax theory, much overlooked, is the claim that arcs and circular patterns are co-ordinated by placing ropes on stakes hammered into the ground (alternatively, somebody stands and holds the rope). This method may work with smaller patterns, but to operate on the scale seen in some would be impossible due to the incredible force of tension placed on anything stretched out much beyond thirty feet. Experience of surveying patterns with even light tape measures demonstrates the extreme difficulty of keeping such a length taut without its falling into and damaging the standing crop. Yet areas of semi-downed plants are rarely features of large, complex designs with arcs of a hundred feet or more. No human grasp, or stake, however well-driven, would be able to withstand such a pull, illustrating the nonsense of hoaxing stories in which camera tripods and the suchlike are supposedly utilized as anchors. A huge arced path connecting two circles at Liddington Castle, Wiltshire in 1997 was a perfect example that the rope method couldn't have been used, yet there is no way a human could have walked such a finely defined curve "freehand" without erring. Formations are only occasionally found with holes at the centers of the circles, which one might expect to be a regular feature such would be the depth of the hole required to secure a stake, but even this is not a sure sign of hoaxing activity. Some research groups, including SCR, actually drive stakes into existing circle centers to aid tape measure surveys. Other, more mischievous visitors, have even been known to deliberately *dig* such holes in new lays to cast doubt on their origins. Hole-finding is certainly no litmus test.

The lack of physical traces of hoaxers has led some desperate speculators to insist that the patterns are laid down months before in newly-sown fields by the spraying of chemicals, which later weaken the stems, allowing them to fall into shape in light winds. Never minding that spraying in such a manner would probably require even *more* accuracy from the perpetrators than physically knocking down that which they can *see* in conventional hoaxing terms, a simple glance at the complexity of the lays, swirls and layering in formations kills this theory. Collapsing crop is one thing, woven beauty is quite another.

Who created the historical crop circles?

That Doug and Dave's hoaxing claims only went back as far as 1978 should immediately have raised concerns, but

Liddington Castle, Wiltshire, August 7, 1997. To create an arc such as the path linking these circles, a center point would be needed for a rope to be suspended, like a compass needle on a page. The sweep of this arc would require the distance to the center to be so great that no stake or person would be able to support the incredibly strong tension it would produce—yet it would be impossible to walk "freehand." Photo: Andrew King

Measuring tape on a stake at the center of the Cissbury Ring formation, West Sussex, July 15, 1995—such stakes are the source of some holes found in circles and are not evidence of hoaxing. Just keeping light tapes such as this above the heads of the crop is a strain much beyond thirty feet. Photo: Andy Thomas

when their story broke only a few were aware of just how long the phenomenon had been occurring. We now know, as seen in Chapter 2, from the trawling of many archives, that it dates back several centuries and may even have been with us since time began. As Terry Wilson's research has shown, they weren't always just simple circles either.

It beggars belief that crop circle making should be a human art which has been secretly handed down over the ages. Clearly, another cause has been at work throughout history, whether natural, intelligently directed or whatever. The vast increase in numbers and sophistication cannot simply be explained by the sudden arrival of copycat pranksters, especially when the same laying techniques observed when simple circles were first seriously examined are still being found in modern, complex patterns.

Mystery of the Myth

Chapter 2 has already explored some of the reasons mass-hoaxing has received such disproportionate media coverage over the years, in the absence of any real evidence to support its existence. So many years down the line from Doug and Dave, how is it the concept has been allowed to thrive instead of shrivelling up and dying in the face of the astonishing patterns which have graced the fields since?

Some human circlemakers may by now actually believe they and their kin really are responsible for the entire phenomenon. So used to spinning legends and fictions around themselves, they may have convinced each other that the few designs they might have made are augmented by unknown others out there filling in for their own lack of real activity. But a number of claimants acknowledge there is a wider picture of which they are just a part, and admit they can't explain everything.

On a basic level, society has adopted the very convenient notion of "Occam's Razor" as its measure for assessing the integrity of any mystery: the most obvious solution is the one most likely to be true. In reality this theorem states that "the fewest possible assumptions should be made in explaining a thing" according to the *Oxford Reference Dictionary*, which is quite different. But the common woolly interpretation has been used to justify many a deception and misconception, and assumes that everything is black and white, never grey. Yet the quickest of glances at history shows that most areas are grey, or "overdetermined," meaning there are many causes behind one effect.

On the face of it, a few circles in fields here and there, never personally witnessed, only heard about through the standard channels of misinformation, could easily be thought of as just the work of a few ambitious japesters. But it's the grey areas that make the difference; the scope, the scale, the longevity of the phenomenon, the many anomalous effects; all these and more mark the crop circles out as something less easily explained. The popular use of Occam's

Razor ignores too much of what's really going on.

Watch jaws drop and eyes widen when open-minded people are finally faced with the real evidence of what's been occurring. The images speak for themselves, but the stories behind them go even further. If the wave of a wand could instantly enlighten the world's population to the whole story behind the circles, total skepticism would be harder to sustain, as most of it is born of ignorance.

Skeptical Motivation

What is it that motivates debunkers, either individual or institutional (like CSICOP) to continually attack and criticize something which presents no immediate threat to anyone—harmless artistic doodles in their eyes, surely? Why go to such lengths to smash the credibility of the crop circles if they are of such little importance?

Despite serious attempts to open people's eyes to something which should long ago have demanded the attention of certain sections of society, still some dig their heels in and refuse to be informed. To paraphrase, don't bother them with the facts, their minds are made up. Most of the scientific community, for instance, remains defiantly opposed to even considering another side to the phenomenon, as if scared to broaden its horizons, lest the door to some new dark age of superstition be opened. But if science were to explore these extraordinary patterns properly, as its few daring messengers such as W C Levengood have attempted to do, it might actually *lessen* the chances of this happening by finding at least the beginnings of some rational explanation that fits the facts. Until science can accept that a *lack* of empirical evidence is not proof that something *doesn't* exist or has no validity, any "paranormal" subject will remain sidelined as a "crank" interest.

Fear seems to be a big factor in those who actively resist further scrutiny of the circles by generating hostility toward them, not only from science, but from the media and people in general. It is a fear of the unknown, a fear of finding evidence for a reality they would rather not exist because it challenges too much which has already been neatly accepted and pigeonholed—even though these things might just be *wrong,* or at least only partly understood. Nobody wants to rewrite the textbooks if they can avoid it. To accept the circles as genuine requires further thought to assess the implications and that's just *too* much effort for some.

General skepticism, it seems, is set to prevail even in places one might expect it not to, as we have seen with a few in the research community itself. Battling egos, hurt pride and opinion masquerading as fact have led some in the croppie world into a climate of paranoia. Hunted and taunted by hoax claimants and debunkers, they have become afraid to speak up for what they really believe in for fear of their reputations being challenged, preferring to err on the skeptical side for safety. The habit has tipped certain individuals permanently into negativity, but instead of bowing out gracefully, they have been loathe to give up their platforms and have stayed around to infect novices and many channels of information with destructive views, still taken as gospel by some who rely on others for their background facts and don't know the other side of the story.

Understandably, some can't see the logic of these individuals being leaders of a movement they don't appear to believe in, and are setting up investigations of their own. A fresh turnover of thinkers who have the benefit of hindsight and can see the pitfalls their predecessors fell into continually arrive to re-take the high ground, seeing the phenomenon in a much wider context and a purer light. It is so obvious to these discerning observers that human activity simply cannot explain a large part of what's going on, that the hoaxes there are no longer worry them; indeed they simply add to the general mystique.

What motivates the hoax claimants themselves and their activities in self-promotion has been much debated; maybe it's the ego trip of a lifetime to attach their names to great works of art they would like to have created, in a way which is difficult for the uninformed majority to contest. Perhaps this is the only route by which some can feel close to something they find beautiful—by making it their own in a curious manner. The apparently universal public ownership of the patterns provides the ultimate arena for anyone to play the game. The thrill of mischief-making, playing the role of shadowy jokers no-one can pin down but everybody talks about, is probably enough to stimulate others, the buzz from the espionage of it all a heady addiction. They may be kept in the fray by financial back-handers from sinister authorities if there's anything to the anti-circle conspiracy theory. On a more psychological level, those who do produce the odd formation here and there may just be trying to convince themselves there is no threatening paranormal phenomenon by acting out their own theoretical possibilities in reality. For a few, perhaps art and the need to create really does play a role in their motivation—but the messages they give out in their often dark behavior suggests less integrity. Too many opportunities have been missed to demonstrate either their commitment to inspiring beauty or the exact abilities with which to pursue it.

The facts are there to see for those with the ability to step back and assess them; here is an enigma that has clearly had a certain amount of human involvement in its production, but which remains largely unexplained, as mystifying as it was when first it began to make its mark on our society. And what a mark; lives have been changed and universal outlooks turned upside down by the presence of these glyphs, testament to their enduring power in a climate of indifference and attack from those who actually validate the circles' importance by the force of their venom. And perhaps this aspect, the effect these patterns have had on individuals, is the most significant of all....

NOTES

1. The most prominent study of the cattle mutilation phenomenon is *Alien Harvest* (Littleton/Co. 1989) by Linda Moulton Howe. Her linking of it with the circles has upset some who challenge such a connection. As for UFO books, take your pick—there are literally hundreds of titles to choose from.

2. Described as "Archon" and defined by Michael Green in *Crop Circles: Harbingers of World Change*, Chapter 8, pages 138–140.

3. The book *Dowsing The Crop Circles* looks in detail at the application of this art to the phenomenon.

4. Fields of Mystery, page 45 and 57. See also *Quest For Contact*, Chapter 1.

5. This work is outlined more fully in *SC*, issue 20, August 1993, page 11.

6. *Behind The Hoaxers, SC*, issue 33, September 1994, pages 5–8.

7. Note that I studiously avoid giving the names of most hoax claimants, with a few notable exceptions, throughout this book. These people thrive on the oxygen of publicity. Why give them more?

A nest of crescents graces the landscape below Oliver's Castle, Wiltshire, July 27, 1994, inspiring some remarkable conversations among the picnickers looking down on it. . . . Photo: Andy Thomas

5. VITAL SIGNS

Regardless of their real source or intention, the crop circles have had a massive impact on many people's lives by compelling them to rethink their understanding of the universe around them. The continuing mystery has forced speculation about what the phenomenon means and opened hearts up to deeper levels, changing the world in its own subtle way. Are the questions raised by the circles more important than the answers, and will the answers ever be forthcoming...?

Oliver's Army

High up on the embankments of the Iron Age hill-fort Oliver's Castle, near Devizes in Wiltshire, one can gaze out across acres of fields, trees and houses stretching to the horizon. It's a ideal place for picnics, and in summer people lie on its grassy slopes, children play and youths fly kites and model airplanes.

When crop circles appear below, they can't be missed, staring up at visitors, their definition changing as the sun moves and shadows lengthen, but always present, somehow sentient. In the hot months of 1994, long before the name Oliver's Castle became inextricably caught up with controversies over videos, a field on its lower slopes was visited by a quite magnificent emblem of nested crescents. Breathtakingly beautiful, they asserted their presence peace-

Photographers take pole shots inside the 1994 Oliver's Castle crescents. Inside some formations, it's almost impossible to grasp the exact configuration until seen from above. Photo: Andy Thomas

fully but assuredly, instantly drawing the eye of anyone looking out across the vista.

As a small group of us sat, contemplating the object of our interest on a warm, hazy afternoon, we became aware of the buzz of fascination from other visitors who weren't there for the same reasons. As they came and went, the picnickers and kite-flyers, even the children, were all being drawn like moths to the curve of the hill, which directly overlooked the motif. Nearly every conversation drifting on the breeze could be heard to have turned to speculation about the enigma below. People were talking, some on basic levels, others more complex, about ETs, the possibility of life elsewhere, their place in the Universe, even God. Why was that pattern there and what had made it? What did it mean? Even the more cynical observers sounded impressed despite themselves, admiring the perfect execution of the shapes before them.

We were struck then with the realization that what we were witnessing was a microcosm of the overall effect crop circles have had on those across the globe lucky enough to come into contact with them. As the people on the hill were discovering, the presence of these patterns raises initial questions about their nature, which in turn lead to far more incisive questions about ... well, everything. As our enquiries pass the many filter systems of our minds, what can and can't be accepted by our logic begins to lead to unusual avenues of thought. Many, faced with the reality of the circles for the first time, are left with no choice but to dismiss the concept of their all being a joke, forced to consider other possibilities. But these possibilities then require reassessment of other precepts and conditions they may have grown up with, impressed on them by society. Before long, the inquirers begin to question everything they ever believed in and find themselves no longer able to function within normal parameters. Once the doors are opened, there's no going back. People from all walks of life, sometimes with no previous interest in anything remotely "paranormal," find their lives change, their needs, their friends. There is no archetypal croppie. What previously fulfilled them or covered holes in their existence suddenly seems hollow. After the crop circles, trivia becomes a happy distraction, but no longer enough to live for. Deeper waters have to be stirred.

All this from a few shapes of "flattened corn"? Yes. There are enough living examples who will testify to the truth of this, myself included. Whether this is what the phenomenon is supposed to achieve is irrelevant. It may be there is no purpose to it at all, or the effect intended is something quite different. *But this is the effect the circles are having,* whatever their real source. They are, in their own way, changing the world. The way to global transition isn't sweeping political decisions or enforced belief systems. Only alterations in individual hearts can make a real difference. The domino effect does the rest. Friends and relatives of those involved in the circles and other transformational phenomena cannot help but be touched in some way by the new insights of the first domino. Short of walking away, there's no way they can't in some way be influenced, even if unaware the circles are the cause.

Domino Dancing

On a more basic level, the news of the crop circles and their real story is also being carried by the chain. Where the media has failed, word of mouth is doing the rest, although debunkers are trying their hardest to counteract this by tipping their own dominoes. Nevertheless, there is something about these glyphs that speak to people regardless of what they hear from detractors. For some, the source is irrelevant. A number of those who, despite all the contrary evidence, insist they must have a mundane explanation, still admit to finding the formations beautiful and enlightening, no less valid than the spiritual lift given by the work of the Michelangelos and Da Vincis of this world. This is something often missed by the most intense skeptics—no matter how much they insist the circles are all man-made, the significance of the symbolism doesn't go away. Why are these patterns being chosen? What do they have to say about these times that people are being compelled (in this

frame of reference) to pull these shapes from their psyches and carve them into the fields? To damn the phenomenon as human landscape art doesn't for everyone destroy the extraordinary inspiration people are drawing from it.

Meanwhile, those for whom the circles cannot be explained by hoaxers are finding themselves compelled into other areas of investigation. ET believers are speculating on the significance of life on other worlds or realms and the impact of contact with them on our culture, campaigning to release information they believe governments are restricting. Others are getting involved in psychic areas and exploring their own telekinetic capabilities (which science insists they're not supposed to have), realizing that humans have hidden gifts. Many have been drawn to far deeper spiritual levels, contemplation of the soul and its connection to the infinite, God, whatever. All from flattened corn. Strange, unlikely, ridiculous maybe, but that's how it is for many whose lives have been touched by the crop circles.

Joy and Sorrow

Is this a uniform effect? The research community has illustrated that the phenomenon seems to bring out the best and worst in people. Whatever an individual's inherent tendencies, they get exaggerated to extremes by the emotions the patterns raise. Overall, most have found their lives enhanced and invigorated, forging productive relationships with other thinkers, and finding kinship and camaraderie. Some have gone on to take the lessons into other areas of their lives, aspiring to new horizons. Sometimes they even leave the circles behind them, rather like nursery toys one will always be fond of but no longer need.

A few have gone the other way, still unable to grasp the real issues, confused and disappointed by the lack of answers, but unable to leave the phenomenon alone, using it as the only prop they have in life, but never really coming to terms with it. These are the ones who tend to slide into skepticism, preferring to destroy that which has failed them personally, yet always remaining prisoners to it, bitter and resentful of those who still find the joy they once felt themselves, embroiling themselves in croppie politics, mean-spirited criticism and petty bickering as some kind of substitute.

Mostly, though, irrational but intoxicating delight is the overriding gift from the circles. To walk into a new for-

The enclosures created by shapes in the field draw people like moths to gather inside and commune, as here at Bishops Cannings, Wiltshire, July 13, 1997. Researcher Michael Glickman lies in the foreground. Photo: Andy Thomas

mation remains a constant thrill. Huge grins often break onto the faces of visitors, somehow aware and thankful of the fact that the maze they explore like children challenges everything they were ever taught. There *is* something child-like about the crop glyphs. A paragraph above referred to nursery toys. Michael Glickman has spoken of the circles being toys thrown on the mat for us to play with so that guardians can observe our behavior. It's a nice analogy, even if it does presume intelligent manipulation, for which there is conflicting evidence. If human consciousness is involved, perhaps the joy we feel is that of seeing our own children, the toys *we* have created. Some have suggested the circles may not be aimed at, or connected with, humanity in any way. The strong reaction to them implies that while this is a possibility, many nevertheless feel a deep and intangible affinity with them, forging a bond which *makes* them our business.

Yet there does seem to be a specifically inviting quality about the patterns. They sometimes entice people into them by their positioning within the field, providing "gateways" in the designs themselves, bits which just *feel* right to enter from. No-one quite knows what to make of the fact they appear to be created on a human scale, large and complex enough to adequately challenge most hoax claims, but not so overwhelming as to be impossible to traverse (although a few, like the Milk Hill event of 2001, come close). Walking a formation is just as important an experience as see-

ing it from the air. Sacred labyrinths were once used to concentrate the mind in the same way, and perhaps the pictograms also serve this purpose. Once in, it takes great discipline to actually perform proper research, which, for good or ill, less and less people adhere to. Rather, the urge is simply to throw all measuring tools and rucksacks aside and *play,* run around, lie in the crop, just revel in an area of lowered stems, which has become a *place* in an otherwise featureless sea of plants. Some feel the urge to meditate, instinctively drawn to a specific spot. Some sit and contemplate, sunbathe or sleep. Others, in secluded fields, even make love. Part of the compulsion for all this recreation is induced by the beauty of the countryside, the heady air, the birdsong, the scenery, all added joys of being a croppie. But there is something special about the presence of the shape itself, and many would never find themselves in a summer meadow otherwise. The circle is the lure.

Taking the Bait

Taking the bait is an experience worth recounting. A network of enthusiasts, eyes and ears open to many sources or out looking themselves, now ensure news of circles spreads fast. One learns to drive while looking anywhere but the road. When a new pattern is spotted, the telephone rings, or the web page uncovers the latest offerings, there's always a simultaneous jolt of thrill and anxiety. Excitement at the significance of the fresh visitation is usually followed by confusion. Telephone descriptions are notoriously difficult (comparing dictated drawings to eventual images of the real thing can be quite fun), but stumbling across a new design in the countryside and trying to see its shape can be equally challenging unless there is enough elevation to take in its entirety (even inside, one is often unaware of the exact configuration, and it sometimes takes aerial photographs to fully comprehend). The anxiety follows with the usual mind-spinning the implications of the discovery provokes, and at the prospect of identifying the exact location if not known, contacting the farmer to obtain permission to enter the field and arranging rendezvous details with friends or colleagues. With these chores done and the object of fascination finally before you, usually some walking distance away, the anticipation begins. A false start often entails when you realize you've taken the wrong set of tramlines, by-passing the actual formation. Not wanting to damage the field by short cuts, sensible people then try again. Successful this time, unless the shape is close to the edge of the field, it always feels like aeons to reach, but suddenly it's there, taking you by surprise. One stands just outside for a moment and surveys what can be seen, waiting almost as a sign of respect. Some get a feeling like having been kicked in the pit of their stomach, of being faced with the utterly inexplicable. A kind of logic seizure sets in, which thrills and confuses in equal measure. Then one enters and, for those who still retain the naked joy of the phenomenon, the big grin starts unless what you see, on inspection, is very obviously awful, in which case a wry grin can be allowed.

Deciphering the Indecipherable?

But is this talk of joy and enlightened questioning the correct response to the circles or some kind of nervous laugh to something very profound and of potentially grave significance?

An enduring conundrum of the crop circle mystery is that for all the attempted litmus tests and physical examinations, no-one has actually cracked the code of what they are telling us, despite many efforts and conflicting conclusions. Many correlations have been sought, which might reveal a hidden but direct message, everything from exam-

ining the dates of appearance and comparing astrological charts, to taking into account phases of the moon and mathematical dimensions. Some have likened the glyphs to sacred ground markings like the vast Nazca lines in Peru or other known symbols from ancient and modern cultures, but exact matches are rare.

If the pictograms are a language or communication of some kind, we seem to be a little slow on the uptake, unless over a decade of pictograms isn't very long in which to learn something so intense. Maybe initial confusion is accepted by the creators as part of the communicative process, yet one can't help the nagging feeling that the spontaneous and almost random multi-cultural symbolism of some of the patterns isn't indicative of something wishing to transmit a coherent message. No application of any known human language or hieroglyph has yet produced a fail-safe and consistent key, although there have occasionally been similarities which have produced potential interpretations. Work by people like Wolfgang Schindler in ordering all the known pictograms into visual sequences have produced interesting results and clearly show recurring features in some groups. Yet the shapes have developed considerably since 1990, and some of the later patterns, especially the fractals, are hard to tie in with their

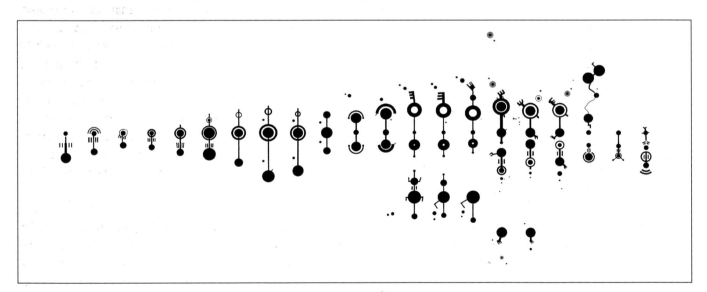

Many have wondered whether placing the crop circle designs into specific sequences reveals a wider agenda. These pictograms from 1990, 1991 and 1992 have been arranged into apparent stages of evolution by Wolfgang Schindler simply from visual assessment, not date of appearance. They seem to suggest some kind of meaningful progression, but definitive conclusions remain frustratingly elusive. Sequences based on other criteria have been tried, but with less result. Diagram: Wolfgang Schindler

more chunky ancestors. One would still expect, for instance, "keys and claws" to feature regularly if they were intended to be consistent with a decipherable communication, yet these components have become scarce in recent years.

Maybe the designs are not meant to be taken in this way, and are to be viewed more literally, simply pictures to be interpreted. Yet even here, no-one can agree on what they mean and we are left with having to guess or dispensing with the view that they can be understood at all. This confusion and apparent illogicality could, of course, be the very point if this is another intelligence's efforts to jump-start human evolution by making us reach further inside ourselves for solutions. Giving us clarification would rather spoil such a test. Certainly, the formations pose more questions than they give answers.

The End Is Nigh?

It seems no coincidence that the crop circles should suddenly develop at a time when apocalyptic predictions are rife. Unsurprisingly, many have interpreted the patterns in these terms. The "asteroid belt" and "galaxy" formations, for instance, were cited by a few as celestial maps warning of destruction from the sky in the form of approaching comets and meteors. The "DNA" pictogram, in another twist, for some denoted an imminent genetic leap or mutation. The circles themselves could even be a deliberate attempt to alter our genes they said—what better place for an intervening intelligence to start than by dropping something into the food chain, bearing in mind that much of the crop in formations is still picked up by the blades of the combines? The work of W C Levengood and others has shown that circle-crop can be profoundly affected internally. Homeopathic remedies rely on very tiny amounts of mixture to permeate huge batches of water. Maybe only a few radiating crop circles would be needed to affect entire continents' food supplies. (If this hypothesis *is* true, we had better hope the intentions of the circle-makers are benevolent, because it's far too late to do anything about it now.... There's a thought for you when you sit down to eat your cornflakes tomorrow morning.) Otherwise, the DNA glyph, if that is what it represents, might be a warning about the drastic consequences genetic modification of food could have, a process which, now started, can never be reversed, as we foolishly dabble with the very stuff of life and threaten the balance of the eco-system through potentially devastating side-effects.

The phenomenon has been interpreted by some as a massive portent of doom akin to a giant "*The End is Nigh!*" sign emblazoned on a sandwich-board. The symbols might well speak of this if they are the fears of our own race manifesting in the fields through the influence of the collective subconscious—it's likely in this context that the shapes would indeed reflect our deepest concerns, even if it didn't connect with the eventual reality. Yet total doom-mongering doesn't quite make sense in the cosmic intelligence view—if something is trying to warn us of an impending catastrophe, the glyphs *must* bring with them some kind of redemptive quality to prevent it or help us through. Otherwise, we seem to have superior beings giving the finger to humankind, mockingly telling us we're all going to die. Why bother?

While the circles may warn of a coming crisis of some kind, they're unlikely to signify the complete extinction of our race. Nevertheless, there does seem to be a whiff of biblical fear about them, for all the joy they bring. But maybe their purpose is to lift spirits in dark times, signs of hope when war, social breakdown and environmental destruction always seem to be lurking in the wings.

On the other hand, that the designs have been seen as warnings of self-inflicted eco-disaster may say more about humankind's hidden conscience than anything else. Is this just a reflex response on our part, rather like a guilty child who jumps when a parent, not knowing anything is up, innocently enters the room? There's been nothing unquestionably specific in the symbolism to speak of ecological destruction, besides perhaps the insectogram/pesticides connection, yet it's been a recurring theme in many speculations, and a number of groups have seen the circles as a cry from the Earth, Gaia alerting us to the perils of our polluting technological path.

Many seem to treat the symbols as signs of "end times," not necessarily the end of the world, but the closing of a major era, beginning a new stage of evolution marked by a traumatic rebirth. The buzz surrounding the 2012 prophecies and the end of the Mayan calendar, enhances this view. Many are lying in wait for an "end" of some kind. Hopi Native Americans, when shown pictures of the formations a few years back, intimated they had been awaiting the "return" of these symbols for many years and that they signified a huge shift in our history. Part of the Christian world appears to think Judgement Day and the Second Coming are imminent and that the circles could constitute some of the promised "signs and wonders" which herald them. Alternative astronomers warn of the dangers of increased solar activity or unusual alignments and the gravitational intervention of drifting celestial bodies causing orbital upsets. "Ascensionists" await a devastating tilt in the Earth's axis, guided by channelled messages that promise rescue onto spacecraft for the chosen, and assorted doomsday cults and fringe religions look forward to variations on similar themes. UFO believers are ready for grand announcements and major visitations from ETs. Scientists warn of melting ice caps and climate change. Study of ancient monuments, astronomical arrangements and 12,000 year cycles by people like Graham Hancock seems to predict catastrophic effects for our times, and some see a connection with the agriglyphs as returning signs of old wisdoms from Egypt, Atlantis and beyond. Students of Edgar Cayce and other gurus and visionaries all seem to feel the horsemen of apocalypse breathing down on them, and crop circles have been mentioned in their literature.

Does this have a *direct* link with the circles though? If there's anything to the consciousness interaction theory, they may well be a symptom, as much as a cause, of all these outpourings and expectation, operating in a feedback loop. And there is a danger in this scenario—*if* crop glyphs can be manifested from the human psyche, what else can result? If enough people expect catastrophe and destruction, is there not a danger they may precipitate it themselves? Those awaiting the "end" should consider their responsibilities carefully. They may help bring about the very thing they fear—or want—most in a self-fulfilling prophecy. Few seem to consider that global change could be brought about peacefully and without disaster if, as many students of metaphysics have observed, we do indeed create our own reality. All this doom-awaiting energy could be better spent projecting positive change.

Of course, our race has lived through times of heavy apocalyptic prediction before, and survived. Nevertheless, planetary and collective consciousness energy may be more powerful and responsive now—who knows what may be possible?

The answer to the circles mystery could be disappointingly mundane; mischievous aliens writing nothing more than cheap graffiti, some mad professor testing a new device from his shed, whatever. Perhaps the timing is simply coincidence. Alternatively, the glyphs may contain incredibly complex subliminal esoteric information coming from deep sources beyond all comprehension, which this book hasn't even touched on. As already observed, whichever the case, it's the *reaction* to the circles that seems to matter, and the overwhelming response has been that they are highly significant.

Critical Mass

It's been pointed out on occasion that if the crop circles are here to make a big difference to the world, there's not nearly enough of them to work. Why are they not more

Crop circles inspire different people in a number of ways. Here at West Kennett, Wiltshire, July 11, 1993, someone has been moved to create a little altar of stones. Photo: Andy Thomas

widespread and bigger, covering several fields to attract *real* attention? With most centered on England and the remainder scattered unevenly around the world, how can they really affect enough people to achieve a purpose? If they are the result of a natural process, the question is redundant. If, however, they *are* premeditated acts of some cosmic intelligence, logic seems to be lacking unless, as previously speculated, it is trying to draw our attention to very specific places or utilizing the natural energy grid itself. If intentionally transformational, there seems to be an unfair advantage for those who have the luck to come into contact with the circles and have their lives changed for the positive. There may be masked opportunities for others, however. The subsequent soul-searching which has changed the lives of so many observers is still an absolute minority effect, but, importantly, these people are starting chains of dominoes which, added to those touched by other transfiguring phenomena, may have a far-reaching effect.

It may be that only a relative few need to be affected by consciousness-raising catalysts to tilt the whole of humanity into a less self-destructive and more sane, spiritual mode of thinking. As proponents of the "new physics" have observed, in a process which has become known as the "Hundredth Monkey," it only takes a finite amount of individuals in one species to acquire an attribute for the collective whole to suddenly adopt it with no apparent means of physical transmission. When "critical mass" is reached, psychic fields seem to carry signals which transform all.

The circles may be just one tip of a very large iceberg, which is producing other things rising to prominence right now like UFO activity, the alien abduction conundrum, psychic phenomena, religious apparitions, reports of stigmata and weeping and bleeding iconic statues from all cultures (even effigies of Elvis Presley have been reported to weep). All seem to have a profound and not dissimilar effect on those who witness them, even seemingly negative experiences like abductions, provoking questioning and new perspectives on the surrounding world, even if the conclusions people reach may be over-simplistic or even misguided. None of these may be quite what they seem, but can't all be lies. They bear strong parallels in the reactions they instigate.

Is it any accident that very religious countries seem to be those which receive the apparitions and weeping stat-ues (but less circles), while more secular or mixed-belief system cultures like modern England receive stark, secular symbols in the fields (and only very few apparitions)? Is this the same intelligence trying to make contact in whatever frame of reference most appropriate to those in certain cultures, or are all these strange marvels the psychokinetic, but very real, product of our own minds? Either way, where will all this culminate? Food for thought.

Elusive to the End

Will there ever be an answer to the crop circle mystery? Each year some await a grand revelation without really knowing what form it might take. Huge descending spacecraft over the cities of the world, their occupants claiming responsibility? A huge formation covering many miles and several fields which explains all in obvious symbolism? A sudden mass psychic revelation?

Or could it be that one day, maybe soon, maybe later, the crop circles will wind down back to rare appearances or cease to appear altogether, their impetus exhausted or task complete, the times they heralded having been reached? Assuming our continued survival, will our descendants look back at the agriglyphs in a century's time as an almost-forgotten curiosity of apocalyptic fever, never really explained, yet vaguely written off as some kind of long-running prank which gradually ran out of steam? There are strange phenomena of past centuries which have been as quickly forgotten despite much fuss at the time.

Ovingdean, East Sussex, July 27, 1996. Civilization goes about its business, while circles peacefully manifest all around it, almost unnoticed at times. Photo: Andy Thomas

Would an end without an answer frustrate or preserve the beauty of the mystery? If the glyphs are some intelligence test from other beings, giving us answers on a plate would clearly be pointless. Alternatively, these friends from above may be honor-bound to follow some kind of *Star Trek*-like "prime directive," which forbids them to intervene directly in the affairs of lesser races, stimulation-by-glyph the only contact allowed. If the source is natural or consciousness-sparked we'll probably never know for sure unless many more stringent attempts to create circles with the power of thought are carried out or specific atmospheric conditions can be nudged into the necessary behavior.

Perhaps not knowing is the best compromise between all the different factions and theories. No-one will ever know if they were right or wrong. No fingers can be pointed or I-told-you-so's claimed. Certainly, the phenomenon is showing no signs of giving itself away just yet. Neither esoteric nor skeptic speculation has explained it.

Be prepared for the mystery to remain.

Vital Signs for Crucial Moments

As our society finds itself afflicted by social disillusionment and despair, despite all its scientific achievements, it's beginning to realize that somewhere along the way it lost its soul. There's concern for a future which isn't clear; cultural breakdown, economic hardship, war, pollution, famine, climatic disruption and genetic and political manipulation threaten many parts of the globe. Some seek extremism and fundamentalism as the only answers, or sink into trivial distractions, computer games, narcotic hazes or soap opera addiction. Others have simply given up and settled down to await apocalypse, abdicating their responsibilities to effect change themselves as if nothing but destruction can make a difference.

Of course, there are always happy exceptions to all this and beacons of light continually fight against the gloom. There does seem to be an inherent *rightness* to the fact that as society slides into confusion, little glimmers of hope spring up. Amongst these, as if to balance the darkness, patterns of grace and beauty are peacefully manifesting out of nowhere in some of our most sacred landscapes and beyond, radiating warmth, charm and who knows what else to those drawn to them. While a very small minority fear a black agenda, the circles have never displayed any-

thing but benevolence. For most, they seem to hold promise for new realities and fresh insights for a civilization whose progress has run up against a brick wall, technologically brilliant, but unable to go beyond the physical. The ability to do so may be the necessary step in solving our problems.

These perplexing shapes may be just one small jigsaw piece in a far wider picture of which we know almost nothing. But the crop circles, in their own modest way, have already made a difference to our lives by opening minds and stirring complacent hives. Vital signs for what may be a crucial moment in history.

Whatever the circles' real nature, they are *here*, are beautiful and are among us *now*. They may not endure forever. Let's enjoy the formations while we have them and validate their significance simply by the fact they are gorgeous to look at, have made many very happy and left us carved a little deeper and a little wiser by the questions and issues they have raised.

Visually, if nothing else, the circles have brightened up the world with their splendor. For one thing everyone agrees on, even the most committed skeptics, is that wherever they come from, the glyphs are art of the highest order. Art is often the first step in opening the doors to the spirit, be it through paintings, music or prose. It is an outward expression of that contained within, and reaches to the heart. It is that made real which cannot be held within material bounds, providing a gateway to the soul, to transformation.

If grace and beauty are *all* the crop circles have brought into our world, we have reason enough to be thankful.

Tawsmead Copse, Wiltshire, August 9, 1992. Photo: Grant Wakefield

Appendix A: Guide for the Armchair Cerealogist

There are many sources of crop circle information, and this appendix gives some useful pointers as to where to find out more about the phenomenon. In particular, over the years there have been a significant number of books, some general, others covering specific aspects. Many of them are now rather dated, given the phenomenon's continual leaps in development, but still remain valuable reading as records of specific periods, pools of raw data or speculative material. Those wishing to plunge deeper into unravelling the mystery may wish to seek out some of the English language tomes listed below in alphabetical order of authors' or editors' names (there are a number of good overseas volumes in various languages not included here). Most are now out of print, but can often be picked up from specialist dealers, collector's fairs and circle conferences. The era covered by the books sometimes goes up to the year of publication date, but more often to the year before.

At the end follows a less comprehensive but handy guide to some notable crop circle videos, journals, websites, general merchandise and live events.

Books

Crop Circle Year Books
by Steve Alexander and Karen Douglas, Temporary Temple Press, 1999 onwards, 28pp
It's amazing that no-one had thought of a crop circle annual before 1999, but the concept was worth the wait. Each edition, though short, is large format and very colorful, being a compact guide to the cerealogical season of its year, with Steve Alexander's renowned photographs and partner Karen Douglas's thoughtful text and captions. Karen was the first to describe crop circles as "*temporary temples for the modern age,*" a now oft-quoted phrase. Focused largely on the Wiltshire area, with a smattering of Hampshire thrown in, each book neatly negates the need to buy those stacks of individual circle postcards every summer, packing all the best images of the most important formations into one source. The photographic quality (taken on detail-capturing large-format negatives) and

attention to print reproduction is second to none. See Appendix C for more.

The Secret of Crop Circles
by Werner Anderhub and Hans Peter Roth, Lark Books, 2002, 144pp
This new English translation of a German language book first published in 2000 is a useful addition to any croppie's library, with circular history, theories and the various attempts at interpreting the symbols explored. Werner Anderhub has been one of the most active European researchers, and an extensive gallery of color and black and white images, largely from his own portfolio, makes the book an attractive package.

Crop Circles—Harbingers of World Change
edited by Alick Bartholomew, Gateway, 1991, 192pp
Essentially a sequel to *The Crop Circle Enigma* (qv), this was the first book to concentrate more on the message of the circles rather than the mechanism, updating events to 1991, a year excellently illustrated with color photographs. Like its predecessor, several leading enthusiasts of the time contribute their own personal perspective, this time reaching much deeper into speculation and soul-searching. A bit New Agey for some, to own *Enigma* without also having this is nevertheless unthinkable. Sadly, it did rather less well than it might have, having the ill-fortune to be published around the same time the Doug and Dave hoax scam broke.

Crop Circles, Gods and Their Secrets
by Robert J Boerman, The Ptah Foundation, 2000, 162pp
A dense, mystical book which asserts that a cabbalistic code runs through several crop formations, tying the phenomenon in with the work of Zecharia Sitchin and his belief that the lost planet "Nibiru" (and its inhabitants) is about to return from a large elliptical orbit back into our region of space. A bit esoteric for some tastes, and with some curious English here and there (the author is Dutch), the book nevertheless makes some fascinating claims which, if true,

demand further investigation, such as Boerman's belief that many crop glyphs embody the mathematics of the Equinoxal Precession cycle. Illustrated with a few black and white photos and several diagrams, this is a worthwhile read for the more advanced croppie student.

Crop Circle Wisdom

by Denni Clarke, SpiritPassage, 2001, 107pp
Denni has long been a familiar figure in the Wiltshire fields each summer, and this attractively packaged book, subtitled *Simple Teachings from the Circlemakers*, draws together her spiritual musings on how the crop formations inspire people, and what we have learned through them. Each color photo of a particular crop pattern faces a page of suitable meditative text on internal issues of the sort the phenomenon seems to stir up. Not for those of the hardened scientific approach, admittedly, but others of a more soulful bent will find the book much to their liking.

The Circlemakers

by Andrew Collins, ABC Books, 1992, 351pp
The garishly dramatic cover suggests a science fiction novel, but the reality is a sober and somewhat undervalued application of Wilhelm Reich's orgone energy theories to the circle phenomenon. Using his explorations with a group of psychics in the 1991 crop circles as a starting point, Collins was one of the first researchers to really explore the connection between human consciousness and the behavior of formations and UFOs, coming to conclusions considered heretical in the nuts-and-bolts ufology world. Mainly text with a few black and white photos, this can be heavy going (pagewise, the longest circle book ever written), but it did provide a different angle on cerealogical studies for its time and, if the hypothesis is valid, has consequences for other paranormal phenomena.

Crop Circle Secrets

edited by Donald L Cyr, Stonehenge Viewpoint, 1991, 80pp
Several highly technical dissertations from six writers, based around the "whistler" hypothesis, lightning-induced pulses the authors believe to be responsible for the crop circles, although at this point only the early pictograms had appeared. Unusually, for such a scientific view, the theory takes into account ley-lines, earth energies and the connection with ancient sites. Lots of diagrams, but only

a few black and white photographs. Followed by a near-identical sequel *America's First Crop Circle—Crop Circle Secrets II*.

Ciphers in the Crops

edited by Beth Davis, Gateway, 1992, 88pp
A series of thoughtful essays by different contributors, which could almost have been included in *Harbingers of World Change* (qv), looking at the significance, evidential and symbolic, of just three important formations from 1991, Barbury Castle, the Mandelbrot and the Froxfield "serpent" or "brain." Eight pages of color photos help make this a valuable tribute to what were then the most spectacular designs to have appeared, the book all the stronger for keeping to a narrow agenda.

Circular Evidence

by Pat Delgado and Colin Andrews, Bloomsbury, 1989, 190pp
The book that launched the phenomenon into the public eye, documenting the authors' discoveries in the circles of the pre-pictogram 80s, complete with compelling anecdotes of associated strange happenings. Viciously attacked as paranormal claptrap by some who were seeking scientifically credible solutions to the mystery, this is nevertheless what caught people's imaginations and inspired the creation of circle research groups around the world. In retrospect, its speculation is actually remarkably restrained, but brief talk of UFOs drops tiny hints at the investigative paths the authors would soon take, well-balanced with straight observational data and copious color photos. An essential guide to simpler times, written long before Andrews became more skeptical about many of the later formations.

Crop Circles: The Latest Evidence

by Pat Delgado and Colin Andrews, Bloomsbury, 1990, 80pp
By now the media circus was in full swing and the front cover reflects this with its telling blurb "*Could* it be aliens?" next to an array of the elaborate pictograms which shocked the world in 1990. Little more than a diary of the latest events, as the title suggests, it documents the new developments which had dated the authors' previous tome almost overnight and was clearly a necessary publication; as such the book delivers, although its limelight was rather eclipsed by the launch of *The Crop Circle Enigma* (qv) the

same year. Attractive photos and economic text make this an undemanding but useful read.

Conclusive Evidence?
by Pat Delgado, Bloomsbury, 1992, 159pp
This was published in the immediate wake of the Doug and Dave hoax shenanigans, and it shows—the question mark, which renders the title meaningless, is telling. Not a bad book, Delgado's musings are, however, rather more lightweight and non-committal than before, as if anxious to avoid controversy, although he does briefly put the record straight on misquotes and disinformation at the height of the pensioners' scam. Essentially a well-illustrated color record of the 1991 season, the author (now solo) also includes some overseas formations and a few miscellaneous anecdotes and observations. Delgado retired from active research soon after.

The Tao of the Circles
by Carl Garant, Humanics, 2000, 180pp
This simple book of black and white shadow diagrams takes some famous and not-so-famous crop patterns from over the years (up to 1998) and allows intuitive responses from the author to well up in response to them using the techniques of Lao Tzu's *Tao Te Ching*. Thus, accompanying each of the 81 glyphs are short passages of deep and thoughtful insights which, as always with such a genre, will either resonate with the reader or not. Intellectually dense, the graphic reproduction is rather less solid, but this may interest people who believe the thoughts the glyphs inspire are more important than the unending search to identify the mechanisms or minds behind them.

Crop Circles: An Introduction (Crop Circles of Wessex)
by Kent Goodman, Wessex Books, 1996/2000, 30pp
A brief souvenir guide seemingly aimed at the Wiltshire tourist market, this was first published in 1996 as *Crop Circles of Wessex* and later much improved in an updated and retitled edition. Attractively packaged with color and black and white photographs, diagrams and maps, it adequately performs its function as an introduction to the phenomenon for the absolute beginner. Reg Presley (UK pop singer/circle enthusiast) and Pat Delgado contribute endorsements.

Corn Circles/Crop Circles
by Michael Glickman, Wooden Books, 1996/2000, 51pp/58pp
One in a series of little books by different authors examining sacred art in the English landscape in a pleasingly plain, simple format. Crop circles, or *corn* circles as the original title insists, are prime examples of modern sacred art, and the author, a trained architect and very well-known researcher, exalts the poetic and geometric virtues of the designs. There is an almost exclusive focus on the development of the patterns themselves, and the phenomenon's other aspects aren't on the agenda. This works as a strength rather than a weakness, allowing the sheer genius of the anonymous draughtsmanship to speak for itself in simple silhouette drawings. Substantially updated in 2000 and re-issued under its new title of *Crop Circles*.

The Deepening Complexity of Crop Circles
by Dr. Eltjo Haselhoff, Frog Ltd., 2001, 157pp
Subtitled *Scientific Research and Urban Legends*, the author uses his scientific background and credentials (as one of only two people to have had a contribution on crop circles published in a peer-review science journal) to produce a highly credible case for a mysterious cause behind the phenomenon by balancing impressive biological analysis with the other more "paranormal" aspects of the mystery without compromising either; deeper speculation isn't shied away from. However, the science side of cerealogy has been woefully underrepresented in print, and this very readable book goes a long way to providing an excellent encapsulation of the more important discoveries made by plant sample examination and other lines of diagnostic investigation. Color photos and attractively presented diagrams throughout help keep things accessible at all times.

The Cosmic Connection
by Michael Hesemann, Gateway, 1996, 168pp
This assertive tome, translated from German, makes no bones about its intentions, which is to convince the reader that crop formations are made by ETs, half its pages devoted to the circles and the remainder to UFO-related material. As such, it makes its case efficiently and enthusiastically, but doesn't address some unanswered questions thrown up by the hypothesis. An excellent and detailed round up of modern circular history to 1994 (despite clear evidence

to the contrary, Hesemann doesn't believe in pre-war circle reports, though), attractive color photos and a good thrashing to total skeptics more than justify its acquisition.

Mysterious Lights and Crop Circles

by Linda Moulton Howe, Paper Chase Press, 2000, 342pp
Essentially written as a journalistic travelogue, this book is a valuable document of, and investigation into, the many luminosities, balls of light and other aerial phenomena seen in and around crop circles. The large number of testimonies from different people the author interviews in her travels through Wiltshire attests to the reality of this aspect of the circle mystery, and long-talked about incidents, photos and videos are properly recorded in one printed source at last. A color section augments the many black and white photographs included, and most will be in no doubt by the end of the book that something very odd indeed is going on in the fields.

1991—Scientific Evidence for the Crop Circle Phenomenon

by Montague Keen, Elvery Dowers Publications/CCCS, 1992, 47pp
A brief booklet produced for CCCS outlining the tentative inroads made by the title date in discovering a scientific "litmus test" for crop circles. Dudley and Chorost's uncertain search for radioactive particles and W C Levengood's early work on biological changes in circle-affected stems is outlined in layman's terms as far as possible in a simple format illustrated by a few murky black and white photos and diagrams. A useful examination of the physical evidence found in formations thus far, it inevitably frustrates due to its inconclusive nature, which the author, then CCCS "scientific officer," openly acknowledges here. (Keen would later grow more cautious and challenge Levengood's initial methodology.)

Crop Circle Apocalypse

by John Macnish, Circlevision, 1993, 249pp
The subtitle *Crop Circles Case Closed* tells you everything you need to know about this volume, which promotes hoaxing as the answer to the mystery, with particular emphasis on Doug and Dave. Having made one of the best videos on the phenomenon, *Crop Circle Communique*, it's still astonishing that its creator should have gone on to produce this very one-sided and subjective critique, plagued with typos and sparingly illustrated with black and white photos.

Crop Circles: A Beginners Guide

by Hugh Manistre, Hodder and Stoughton, 1999, 91pp
It might be fairer not to comment too much on this book, suffice to say that if a beginner started with this, their interest would probably end here too. One in a series of little guidebooks to various metaphysical subjects, the overly-skeptical and under-informed tone of an extended essay, seemingly based largely on very limited source material from the early 90s (despite its more recent publication date), is of little help to either novice or seasoned croppie. For such a visual phenomenon, a few photographs to go with the diagrams in a tome which purports to be a guidebook would have helped enormously. Instead, incredibly, there are none at all.

Crop Circle Geometry

by John Martineau, Wooden Books, 1992 onwards, varied pages
There have been several editions and updates of this seminal work (originally titled *The Sophistication of Agriglyph Geometry*) in different formats, so page counts may differ. Martineau was one of the first to recognize the sublime geometrical qualities and explicit mathematics in the early pictograms, and his findings are presented in clear, precise silhouette diagrams traversed by lines showing the inherent construction alignments and proportional harmonies. Even allowing for possible margins of error in the original survey measurements, the ingenious accuracy and breathtaking verve of the designs is indisputable, illustrated attractively with some comparative astronomical and archaeological data thrown in for good measure. His work on crop circles would later inspire the author to investigate the entire geometry of the solar system in *A Book of Coincidence* (John Martineau, Wooden Books 1995, 132pp, later re-issued in 2001 as *A Little Book of Coincidence* in an edited format), the full impact of which deserves wider attention, being an astonishing dissection of the geometry of the solar system. Crop circles, which inspired the work, feature in the original appendix, but are omitted from the edited edition.

The Circles Effect and its Mysteries

by George Terence Meaden, Artetech, 1989, 116pp
The first major outing for the plasma vortex theory is in marked contrast to the dramatic, populist style of *Circular Evidence* (qv), which just pipped this to the post as the first ever crop circle book. Scornful of unscientific paranormal posturings, the tone is calm and regimented in a clear and largely successful desire to present itself as a serious hypothesis, published just before the pictograms set the cat among the pigeons. This book's greatest asset is the data, reports and valuable observations recorded within it, but underestimation of the circles' visual attraction has resulted in only scatterings of black and white photographs. For all the theory's difficulties in dealing with the later formations, much of the work is still valid and Meaden should stand congratulated as the first person to attempt a straight scientific investigation of the phenomenon; this book is testament to that effort.

Circles from the Sky

edited by George Terence Meaden, Souvenir, 1991, 208pp
Unattractive presentation (again only a few black and white photos) hides a collection of sometimes dry but fascinating essays on meteorological explanations for the phenomenon, compiled from reports by members of weather-investigation groups CERES and TORRO and mostly based around the plasma vortex idea. The last outing for the hypothesis before the patterns appearing could no longer be simply explained by it in its basic form, this dated very quickly, but contains some highly valuable information including eye-witness accounts and the full text of the "Mowing Devil" pamphlet from 1678. The more recent findings of W C Levengood call for a reappraisal of some of the observations included here.

Dowsing the Crop Circles

edited by John Michell, Gothic Image, 1991, 48pp
A slim but pleasing volume which collects together some of the best dowsing-related articles from the first few issues of *The Cerealogist* journal, nicely presented with attractive diagrams and a few black and white photographs. Anyone with an interest in this aspect of investigation should start here (although some dowsing skeptics have cited the differing techniques and findings outlined as being fruitlessly contrary).

Crop Circles Revealed

by Judith Moore and Barbara Lamb, Light Technology Publishing, 2001, 265pp
An open celebration of the metaphysical view of crop circles, channelled and intuitive interpretations of pictogram symbols balanced with many pages of straight information, general discussion of the phenomenon and a celebration of the culture of enthusiasts who surround it. Given the size of the book, number of pages and density of print, this is possibly the longest crop circle book yet published, a great slab of a tome to keep dippers happy for many hours. An opening color gallery gives way to black and white photos thereon. In its mission to take into account all the differing belief systems, there may be just a little too much generosity shown towards hoaxers for some tastes, and the dense ruminations may be daunting for casual readers, but as reference material for dedicated cerealogists, particularly those drawn to more psychic leanings, it is indispensable.

Crop Circles

by Carolyn North, Ronin Publishing, 2001, 91pp
Unambitious postcard-sized book which acts as a pleasantly simple all-round guide in a compact size, and gives the novice reader enough of an idea of the phenomenon to see that something amazing is going on. As such, it achieves its well-intentioned aim, let down only by a large number of upside-down photos and disappointing reproduction.

The Crop Circle Enigma

edited by Ralph Noyes, Gateway, 1990, 192pp
Still one of the very best circle books despite being inevitably dated by subsequent events, this is a collection of sober, thoughtful pieces by the cream of researchers at the time (minus Delgado and Andrews) when they were all still talking to each other. Each contributor examines a different aspect of the mystery, recording its history, proposing mechanisms and speculating on potential sources. Excellently illustrated by a comprehensive color roundup of circles from then recent years, photographic emphasis is on the 1990 pictograms, which had just shocked the world. Thought-provoking, yet level-headed, this presented a very credible case for a phenomenon worthy of serious investigation, cruelly dashed in the public eye just a year later by events which were to blight the success of its more ambitious sequel *Harbingers of World Change* (qv).

Crop Circle Classification

by Pat Palgrave-Moore, Elvery Dowers, 1991, 47pp

A brave but ultimately futile technical booklet, which attempted to pin down all the component shapes making up the early pictograms so that crop designs could be concisely documented and described with code numbers. A dumbbell, for instance, is classified as a "1B1," while a more elaborate one might be an "NaBg 50A." Had the phenomenon ceased developing this might have worked, but its evolution already challenges the book's usefulness by the end, with complex formations like Barbury Castle 1991 forcing the system to be ditched and simply being labeled No.132. Though, perhaps unsurprisingly, the idea didn't catch on, this little book is worth owning for the most comprehensive record of crop symbols (in silhouette drawings) published to that date.

Crop Circles: The Greatest Mystery of Modern Times

by Lucy Pringle, Thorsons, 1999, 144pp

The culmination of years of personal research, on the surface this is an all-round guide to the phenomenon, but puts particular emphasis on physiological and psychological effects on people entering crop formations, and other strange anomalies, as extracted from circulated survey forms or one-to-one interviews. Well-illustrated, mainly with Lucy's own photographs (the later edition corrects some upside-down entries in the original), this is a valuable record of a sometimes neglected area of cerealogical investigation, documented by a well-known figure of the crop circle world.

Crop Circles: A Mystery Solved

by Jenny Randles and Paul Fuller, Robert Hale, 1990, 250pp

If you can bite your tongue at the rather over-confident title, there is a lot of useful information, reports and valid observations in this, yet another, promotion of the plasma vortex hypothesis. Randles has written a plethora of UFO-related books over the years, but seems to imply here that a large amount of sightings are due to meteorological atmospheric phenomena. When the pictograms started to appear, she and Fuller would go on to be openly skeptical about the complex formations, but even here there is already a fair amount of hoax speculation alongside the vortex theorizing. Illustrated with a short section of unspectacular black and white photos and a few diagrams.

The Gift

by Doug Ruby, Blue Note Books, 1995, 174pp

An American publication which proposes the idea that the early pictogram shapes are two-dimensional diagrams of three-dimensional devices, which, when built, will give us the "gift" of anti-gravity propulsion as supposedly used in ET craft. Ruby actually constructs and spins scale models to make his point, illustrated here with color and black and white photos. The results are undeniably fascinating, although some may draw their own conclusions about what it all means. The steps that lead to each experiment are sensibly described with a pervading sense of boyish wonder from the author. That Ruby is clearly a newcomer to the phenomenon (he had never set foot in a formation at the time of writing and there are one or two factual errors) shows clearly, but enhances, rather than detracts from, the pleasant innocence of the book. Well presented, but no circle photos, only diagrams.

Round in Circles

by Jim Schnabel, Penguin, 1993, 295pp

The book that sent the cerealogical world into a tizzy for five minutes until everyone realized it was quite funny really, forgot it and carried on. With the exception, that is, of a few who will smart forever, and with good reason. Schnabel, a one-time alleged "hoaxer," tells the story of crop circle research from the inside, all names named and sacred cows slain, illustrated with a few black and white photos. The phenomenon itself is a secondary target to the foreground tales of bickering, egotism and self-delusion which have plagued the "community" from the beginning. Everything is exaggerated for effect, of course, but at times it's a justified critique. Its mischief is to be found in what the book *doesn't* tell you. Presented resolutely from the author's one-sided viewpoint, its factual reliability is challenged, but no-one bothered with any subsequent litigation. Skepticism toward the circles is well to the fore, but largely by implication; little actual evidence for mass-hoaxing is presented. If this were badly written it might be offensive. That it's competent, entertaining and amusing is only spoiled by the fact that it's at other people's expense.

Crop Circles of 1991

by Busty Taylor, Beckhampton Books, 1992, 48pp

Busty Taylor was one of the first to pioneer the art of overhead circle photography, either by flying or precariously raising his camera on a 30-foot pole to look down on formations. This small full color-booklet simply documents the season of the title with full-page photographs and brief captions, showing some of the many diverse designs from the air or the ground. A good souvenir of the year that produced the Barbury Castle triangle, the "whales" and the insectograms.

Fields of Mystery

by Andy Thomas, S B Publications, 1996, 100pp

This was my first book, and still stands as the most thorough documentation of crop circle activity in one area of the world yet published, collecting together many of the findings of SCR. Two major, yet relatively unsung, sites for the crop circle phenomenon are the counties of East and West Sussex on the south-east coast of England, which have seen several decades of glyphs. This book gives the full story of the crop patterns of Sussex and a potted history of the mystery world-wide, with many collected anecdotes and insights, illustrated with color and black and white photographs and diagrams.

Quest for Contact

by Andy Thomas and Paul Bura, S B Publications, 1997, 144pp

An account of SCR's four-year voyage of discovery in a quest to video a crop circle being formed by non-human forces, a mission not fulfilled, but circumvented by other extraordinary happenings. Co-written with psychic Paul Bura, we recount a saga of remarkable encounters with the circles, Sussex sacred sites, interactions with aerial phenomena, psychic entities and cosmic "coincidences," climaxing with the extraordinary experiment in which a crop formation was seemingly created with the power of thought (as referred to on page 152). To learn of both the pitfalls and the successes we encountered, any group wanting to attempt similar communication experiments might like to read this first! Thought-provoking, dramatic, humorous and (in retrospect) heart-warming in its honesty, I'm still proud of *Quest*, which is fully illustrated with photographs taken during our exploits.

The Answer

by Margot Williams and Carolyn Morgan, Grosvenor Press, 1991, 48pp

The story of the authors' attempts to interpret the 1990 Alton Barnes pictogram, and other crop circles at their home on the Isle of Wight, using psychic channeling. Their experiences in the formations are recounted in a series of heartfelt vignettes, together with accounts of claimed brushes with ETs. Not illustrated.

The Secret History of Crop Circles

by Terry Wilson, CCCS, 1998, 155pp

A documentation of the many pre-1980 crop circle reports, dating back perhaps as far as 1590. This is an important, if modestly presented, book which has filled a major hole in the research data, clearly demonstrating an enduring and genuine phenomenon, which has been developing for many years. Its style is succinct and level-headed. Diagrams and a few black and white photographs which accompany some of the reports are included, and a potted later history updates events to 1997. An essential read for research completists and a nudge in the ribs for doubters.

Other Books of Interest

Besides a few very small-scale productions not mentioned here (photocopied manuscripts, etc.) there are also many books which feature crop circles as part of a wider agenda. *Two Thirds* (David P Myers and David S Percy, Aulis Publishers 1993, revised 1999, 811pp—!!!) is a cryptic and controversial novelized history of the galaxy as celestial soap opera, apparently based on channelings. An explanation for crop circles is given in this context and they feature prominently in the illustrated appendix. The circles also feature in another Percy co-authored book, *Dark Moon* (Mary Bennett and David S Percy, Aulis Publishers 1999, 568pp), which robustly asserts that NASA faked the evidence for its moon missions. Likewise, formations appear in a similar context in Richard Hoagland's book *The Monuments of Mars* (Frog Ltd. 1987, 526pp, revised several times since), which famously explores the evidence for an artificially constructed "face" and "city" on the red planet.

Many channelled works have referred to the circles, in particular *The Only Planet of Choice* (Phyllis Schlemmer/Palden Jenkins, Gateway 1993, 398pp, revised by Mary Bennett 1994). *Alien Energy* (Andrew Collins, ABC Books 1994, 248pp—only published in a very limited print run), although more skeptical towards the phenomenon, follows up some of the ideas of *The Circlemakers* and describes orgone and psychic experiments in the Alton Barnes area, amongst other projects. *The Goddess of the Stones* and *The Stonehenge Solution* (George Terence Meaden, Souvenir Press 1991, 228pp / Souvenir Press 1992, 224pp), though primarily concerned with Neolithic monuments, propose the hypothesis that plasma vortex-created crop circles inspired their construction.

Lots of other tomes include crop circles for all sorts of reasons and purposes. Ones to avoid, though, are cheap chain-store compendiums about UFOs and the paranormal (you know the sort), usually thrown together by people with only a very basic, and flawed, knowledge of crop circles. However, beware even some glossier encyclopedias of the unexplained, which, while quite willing to accept the dodgiest of UFO photos, often seem entirely unable to be open-minded about the circles, quoting skeptical received wisdoms and the usual hoax myths as fact.

Videos

There have been all sorts of circular videos produced over the years, some professionally, others by well-intentioned amateurs who issue their best shots of the year on video. A few stand out, however, though many are inevitably very dated now:

John Macnish's *Crop Circle Communique* (1991) is still one of the best all-round looks at the phenomenon, spoilt only by the knowledge that its sequel *Revelations* (and the accompanying book *Crop Circle Apocalypse*) turned to totally one-sided skepticism.

Undeniable Evidence (1990) is essentially a pleasant conversation with researcher Colin Andrews (before he himself turned rather more skeptical), with accompanying circles footage.

Michael Hesemann's long *The Mystery of the Crop Circles* (1990) contains interviews with many early researchers, together with much film of the first pictograms and, as such, is a valuable snapshot of the pre-Doug and Dave days.

Phenomenon (1992) is a very effective wordless meditation by Grant Wakefield, with time-lapse photography, still shots and 8mm film of the circles in black and white and color,

set against atmospheric music, letting the visuals speak for themselves. Wakefield takes quite a different approach in his 1998 film *Croppies,* an irreverent, if humorously revealing, skeptical blast at the research community, "believers" and hoax claimants interviewed in "talking head" mode.

My own *Circular Sussex* (1995) is an atmospheric record of my home county's formations and the work of the SCR surveying team over two seasons.

A very good overall look at the phenomenon is Bert Janssen and Janet Ossebaard's *Crop Circles: What on Earth is Going On?* (1996) and its sequel *Crop Circles—The Research* (1999), which together make an excellent assessment of the mystery, the possible theories and the research efforts, with good circle footage. The former includes the highly controversial Oliver's Castle sequence purporting to show a formation appearing. A third entry, *Contact* (2001), documents many of the aerial phenomena videos taken in and around circles over the years, and is a valuable compendium of some extraordinary sequences. (Their other available title, *The Silbury Hole Enigma* (2001), doesn't cover crop circles, but controversially documents the events surrounding the appearance of the hole in the top of the monument in 2000, as mentioned on page 81.)

Crop Circle Update (1999), by Chris Everard, is a perhaps overlong but comprehensive series of interviews with various circle researchers and contains a detailed analysis of the Oliver's Castle video.

Frank Laumen's *Crop Circle Connections* (2000) is an impressionistic, surreal trip through several seasons of excellent circle and general sacred landscape footage set to music.

Peter Sorensen also has a large back catalogue of videos (the *Humanity's Wake-Up Call* series) documenting each season in turn from the past ten years or so, in his very own personal travelogue style.

Michael Glickman has a series of videos available under the umbrella title *The Crop Circle Lectures,* recording some of his more prominent presentations over the years (some with the help of colleague Patricia Murray), with a particular emphasis on geometry and form, and a liberal dose of skeptic-bashing.

Many more circle videos and even cinema documentaries were being put together in the run-up to the release of the movie *Signs* in 2002. There have also been a number of TV documentaries of varying quality and integrity which pop up mostly on cable and satellite stations from time to time. A few are good, but most are hack journalism which simply scratch the surface of something that takes longer than a couple of days to research and half an hour of air time to fairly assess. Beware: with one or two notable exceptions, outright skepticism is often well to the fore or the conclusions are simplistic to say the least.

Journals and Organizations

There have been a number of crop circle journals over the years, many of which have passed away *(The Crop Watcher, The Circle Hunter,* my own *SC)*. Websites are gradually replacing the printed word as the most useful way to get up-to-date crop circle information, but several publications still survive, many fronting enthusiast organizations.

The Cerealogist (now spelled *Cereologist*) was the first of its kind, and continues on; published three times a year, this A4 magazine, started in 1990, was originally intended as the Center for Crop Circle Studies in-house journal, before quickly striking out on its own. Its quality has varied greatly through changes of editorial personnel, virtually becoming a forum for skeptics at one stage, but recent years have seen a much more balanced approach and the first few John Michell-edited issues are still indispensable reading. After losing *The Cerealogist,* the CCCS produced a replacement in *The Circular,* a quarterly A4 production. Like its predecessor, its calibre has fluctuated wildly through the appointments of several different helmspeople, but its generally non-confrontational stance and straightforward reporting strikes the appropriate tone for its parent organization.

The Circular Review , now an A5 quarterly (and the only regular color publication), is grass-roots on-the-spot reporting from its East Midlands-based team, sometimes raw in its opinion, but always honest and entertaining. *The Spiral,* meanwhile, is the A5 monthly newsletter (the only monthly publication available) for the Wiltshire Crop Circle Study Group, unashamedly New Age in its stance and a staunch bastion against all skeptics. The *Medway Crop Circular* is an A4 newsletter from the lively Kent-based Medway Crop Circle group, focused largely on local events, but with observations on wider cerealogical matters. Another A4 newsletter, *Crop Circles Commentary,* comes twice-yearly from the USA, with frank, insightful views and articles on events both abroad and in the US.

Contact addresses follow alphabetically, correct as of 2002:

THE CEREOLOGIST: *Global Circles Research, 17 Spindle Road, Norwich, Norfolk, NR6 6JR, UK*

THE CIRCULAR: *Center for Crop Circle Studies, Kemberley, Victoria Gardens, Biggin Hill, Kent, UK*

THE CIRCULAR REVIEW: *39 Richmond Avenue, Ilkeston, Derbyshire, DE7 8QY, UK*

CROP CIRCLES COMMENTARY: *CCCS USA Network, 20075 SW Imperial Street, Aloha, Oregon 97006, USA*

MEDWAY CROP CIRCULAR: *Medway Crop Circle, 87 Hurstwood, Chatham, Kent, ME5 0XH, UK*

THE SPIRAL: *Wiltshire Crop Circle Study Group, PO Box 2079, Devizes, Wiltshire, SN10 1US, UK*

Websites

The Internet is now without a doubt the information source of choice for circle enthusiasts, because it is able to report new formations while there is still time to see them, and can continually update news on current events, providing a mouthpiece not provided by the media at large. There simply isn't room to list them all here, but browsing the Links sections of these four leading sites should lead you to all the others soon enough:

SWIRLED NEWS
See Appendix B for more, but essentially, the main site to access for news on events in the cerealogical world. *http://www.swirlednews.com*

CROP CIRCLE CONNECTOR
Premier site for the very latest crop circle reports and photographs.
http://www.cropcircleconnector.com

CROP CIRCLE RESEARCH
Well-informed general circle information site.
http://www.cropcircleresearch.com

INVISIBLE CIRCLE
New crop circle reports, with particular emphasis on German and mainland European formations.
http://invisiblecircle.de/uk

Merchandise

There are people who find the idea of crop circle "product" distasteful, a cheap cash-in on something of huge potential importance, but, like it or not, recent years have seen a boom in crop circle merchandise of all kinds. Each must decide for themselves on the integrity of what's at hand or avert their eyes when it comes their way. One of the better developments is the availability of good color postcards and posters of new formations, which go a long way to spreading the news of an astonishing phenomenon further out to the world by the visual message alone. Circle calendars are also an expanding business—at least three alternatives are usually produced for each season. Several small businesses now produce T-shirts and sweatshirts of circle designs from all seasons in all colors, some simply assorted silhouette shapes against a plain background, others interpretations of specific glyphs in swirling psychedelic hues. Other wares are more to individual tastes, but if you want crop circle mugs, pencils, greetings cards, tarot packs, jewellery, 3-D sculpture and beyond, it all seems to be out there. These can usually be picked up at circle conferences or through adverts in journals. Otherwise, visitors to Wiltshire would be well-advised to make their way to *The Henge Shop* in Avebury which usually carries an assorted selection of the latest products, or go one county along to Glastonbury in Somerset, where various retailers sometimes stock circular goods, particularly the shop *Growing Needs*.

Conferences

Each year, a number of crop circle events are held by various organizations, increasingly across the globe, but especially in the provinces of England. Specific events are nationally advertised in appropriate places (crop circle websites and journals obviously, but also UFO and New Age magazines, etc.) and are often well worth attending. Most conferences feature speakers from the world of cerealogy and associated interests, and they provide a good opportunity to tap into where things are at in the fields and gauge the mindset of those monitoring them. In years past, these could sometimes be rather stuffy, highbrow events, but recently a slant towards more entertaining (but equally informative) gatherings has developed, catering for all approaches to the phenomenon. (Beware though, debunking psuedo-cerealogists at more UFO-orientated events, for whom the circles are a secondary interest, presentations largely based on fourth-hand information.)

The Wiltshire Crop Circle Study Group has its annual *Crop Circle Weekend* at Devizes usually in mid-July; the Center for Crop Circle Studies holds a summer conference at Andover, Hampshire; researcher David Kingston usually holds a one day event at Dorchester in April which covers crop circles; likewise the *Mysteries of the World* group includes crop circles in their gatherings. Independent events are sometimes set up by organizations or individuals at random.

The longest-running (held since 1990) and largest gathering is the annual *Glastonbury Symposium: Investigating Crop Circles and Signs of our Times,* usually held in late July or early August at the Town Hall in the heart of this mystic capital. Attenders from around the world regularly flock to this three-day weekend to hear speakers of the highest calibre discussing not just crop circles, but many other related subjects. The atmosphere of the event spills out into the cafes, pubs and sacred landscape of Glastonbury as people relax in-between. Bias aside (I'm now one of the organizers), this comes highly recommended by many people.

For details, write to: 27 St Francis Road, Gosport, Hants, PO12 2UG, UK.

Those with Internet access should go to:
http://www.glastonburysymposium.co.uk

Appendix B: Swirled News and Southern Circular Research

WWW.SWIRLEDNEWS.COM

Swirled News is THE web site to access for informed up-to-date news and reviews on the latest happenings and discoveries in the world of crop circles, supported by incisive and frank commentary, analysis, opinion and humour.

The most recent cerealogical discoveries, pronouncements, media stories, intrigues and enlightenments … all are reported here, as *Swirled News* provides a vital information service, fighting skeptic propaganda with reason and passion. *Swirled News* is provided by the Southern Circular Research (SCR) organization, founded in 1991, which for nine years produced the influential journal *SC*. It is widely considered one of the top websites for the phenomenon. Edited by the author of this book, Andy Thomas, other regular contributors include the renowned commentator and geometer Michael Glickman, photographer Steve Alexander and researcher Karen Douglas, amongst many other names at the frontline of circle investigation. *Swirled News* is an open window into the world of current crop circle research … and it's a free service! Find us at:

http://www.swirlednews.com

SOUTHERN CIRCULAR RESEARCH
PUBLIC MEETINGS

Each month, SCR gathers at Burgess Hill, West Sussex, UK, to hear the latest crop circle news and views with slides, videos and guest speakers in a lively and friendly atmosphere. All meetings are open to the public.

Summer meetings between June and September are entertaining updates of all the latest crop circle events with slides, videos and animated discussion! Spring and autumn dates are a mix of the latest news and a special guest speaker. After each meeting, we move to *The Potter's* pub for drinks and chat.

Burgess Hill is easy to get to by road or rail, and is only 40 minutes train journey from London Victoria or London Bridge. We meet at:

THE SCOUT CENTER, STATION ROAD, BURGESS HILL, WEST SUSSEX.

Entrance is just opposite *The Potter's* pub. Meetings held in the upstairs room at 8:00 P.M. sharp. There is a modest admission charge.

Road Directions: Burgess Hill can be most easily reached by taking the A2300 from the A23 heading south from London, or by taking the A273 turn-off from the A23 shortly after leaving Brighton when heading north.

The entrance to Station Road can be approached from three ways: 1) First left at the traffic lights after the turning to Queen Elizabeth Avenue when heading south on the A273 London Road. 2) Second right at the traffic lights (with an Indian restaurant on the corner) after the big roundabout crossed shortly after entering Burgess Hill heading north on the A273. 3) Opposite *Waitrose* car park from Civic Way (near *McDonald's*).

The Scout Center driveway entrance is just opposite *The Potter's* pub and the Center has its own car park. If full, there is easy parking in Station Road.

By Rail: There are regular services to Burgess Hill from London Victoria or London Bridge, or from Brighton or Worthing.

The Scout Center is only five minutes walk from Burgess Hill railway station. Turn left as you leave the station and keep walking until you see the entrance to Station Road opposite *Waitrose* from Civic Way. Once in Station Road, *The Potter's* will be on your left after about two minutes, with the Scout Center driveway opposite. Walk up the drive, into the building, and up the staircase on the right. Simple!

For details of *Swirled News*, SCR meeting dates or other information, contact us at:

info@swirlednews.com

Or write to:

SCR, 13 Downsview Cottages, Cooksbridge, East Sussex, BN8 4TA, UK

Appendix C: Crop Circle Year Books and Photographs

Year Books

For those seeking an annual round-up of each year's crop circle season, the *Crop Circle Year Book* series is a collection of photographic books by award-winning photographer Steve Alexander and writer Karen Douglas, portraying the beautiful and mysterious crop circle phenomenon in the UK.

This popular series of full color, fine-art-reproduction books records the passing beauty of the crop circles each summer, charting their beginnings in early spring through to their finale before the harvest. Particular emphasis is placed on the visual impact of these art forms on the English countryside and the authors' view of the circles as contemporary sacred spaces in this celebrated and mythical landscape. The books combine breathtaking aerial imagery with thought-provoking commentary to create a collection of unique publications, which capture the ambience and atmosphere of this radiant phenomenon.

The *Crop Circle Year Books* 1999, 2000, 2001 and (from November 2002) 2002 are priced at £12.50. Prices include postage and packing within the UK. For European orders, £3.00 postage and packing should be added, and for USA or the rest of the world, £4.00 should be added, which includes airmail costs.

USA customers can send checks in dollars (2000 book $25.00 / 2001 book $26.00); all other orders must be accompanied by checks payable in Pounds Sterling, drawn on a bank with a British branch. All checks should be made payable to **"Steve Alexander."** Alternatively, orders can be made online with credit cards at *http://www.temporarytemples.co.uk/shop.html*

New editions to the series become available in November each year.

The Crop Circle Year Book series 1999/2000/2001 by Steve Alexander and Karen Douglas: ISBN 0-9537446-0-4 / ISBN 0-9537446-1-2 / ISBN 0-9537446-2-0

Photographs

Steve Alexander has one of the most professional and wide-ranging collections of crop circle images currently available. A supplier of many images to the media and publishers world-wide in a variety of formats, his online image library can be found at the web address below. Enquiries or requests should be sent to the address or website below.

For Year Books or photographs, contact:

Temporary Temple Press / Steve Alexander Photography
27 St Francis Road
Gosport
Hants, PO12 2UG, UK
Tel/Fax: +44 (0) 23 92 352867
Website: *www.temporarytemples.co.uk*

Index

Index does not cover notes or appendices.

The Author

Andy Thomas was born and bred in the south-east of England at Lewes, East Sussex, an area where he still lives today with his wife and son.

A founder member of the Southern Circular Research team (SCR), which carries out much active cerealogical work and has been holding regular public meetings since 1991, Andy is now editor of the popular website *www.swirlednews.com*, renowned for its outspoken and insightful reporting. He previously produced *SC*, the globally-read bimonthly crop circle journal.

Andy has written three books exploring aspects of the crop circle enigma. *Fields of Mystery: The Crop Circle Phenomenon in Sussex* was the first in 1996, followed by *Quest For Contact: A True Story of Crop Circles, Psychics and UFOs* in 1997 (with Paul Bura), which recounted some of the extraordinary experiences of the SCR team in their attempts to interact with the phenomenon. His best-known and much-praised book *Vital Signs: A Complete Guide to the Crop Circle Mystery and why it is NOT a Hoax* (1998, revised 2002) has been described by many as the definitive guide to the subject.

Andy has provided forewords and contributions for several books and written articles for many publications, including *Nexus Magazine*. He is also author of two books about his historical hometown of Lewes, *Streets of Fire* (1999), and *The Lewes Flood* (2001), and plans to expand his writing subjects further with future projects.

A prolific lecturer, Andy is famed for his lively and sometimes theatrical presentations on crop circles and other inspirational topics. He has spoken extensively in England, and more recently in Europe and America. He is currently one of the organizers and presenters of the world's largest international annual crop circle conference, The Glastonbury Symposium, a three-day event held each summer in Somerset, England.

Andy has made numerous international radio and TV appearances, including television spots on The Learning Channel, The History Channel and NBC's *Today* show. He has been featured in many programs in his home country, the UK, as well as in overseas productions in places as diverse as Italy, Denmark, Japan and Germany, and has appeared in various crop circle documentary videos.

Also a professional keyboard player, Andy has composed and recorded for various projects in years past, and gigs around south-east England with guitarist Phil Light.

Andy Thomas can be contacted through Swirled News/SCR (see Appendix B, page 186).